SALVIFIC
MANHOOD

EXPANDING FRONTIERS: INTERDISCIPLINARY APPROACHES
TO STUDIES OF WOMEN, GENDER, AND SEXUALITY

Series Editors: Karen J. Leong
                  Andrea Smith

SALVIFIC MANHOOD

James Baldwin's
Novelization of Male Intimacy

ERNEST L. GIBSON III

UNIVERSITY OF NEBRASKA PRESS | LINCOLN

Portions of the conclusion were first published
as "'Digging Through the Ruins': *Just Above My
Head* and the Memory of James Arthur Baldwin"
in *James Baldwin: Challenging Authors*, ed.
A. Scott Henderson and P. L. Thomas, 207–20
(Rotterdam NL: Sense Publishers, 2014).

Library of Congress
Cataloging-in-Publication Data
Names: Gibson, Ernest L., III, author.
Title: Salvific manhood: James Baldwin's novel-
ization of male intimacy / Ernest L. Gibson III.
Description: Lincoln: University of Nebraska Press,
[2019] | Series: Expanding Frontiers: Interdisciplinary
Approaches to Studies of Women, Gender, and Sexual-
ity | Extensive and substantial revision of author's the-
sis (doctoral)—University of Massachusetts Amherst,
2012, titled In search of the fraternal: salvific manhood
and male intimacy in the novels of James Baldwin. |
Includes bibliographical references and index. | Sum-
mary: "Salvific Manhood reimagines the complexities
of human brotherhood and masculinity by examining
distinct iterations of male intimacy within all of James
Baldwin's novels"—Provided by publisher.
Identifiers: LCCN 2019008138
ISBN 9781496217097 (cloth: alk. paper)
ISBN 9781496229053 (paperback)
ISBN 9781496217912 (epub)
ISBN 9781496217929 (mobi)
ISBN 9781496217936 (pdf)
Subjects: LCSH: Baldwin, James,
1924–1987—Criticism and interpretation. |
Men in literature. | Masculinity in literature. |
Brotherliness in literature. | Intimacy
(Psychology) in literature.
Classification: LCC PS3552.A45 Z659 2019
DDC 813/.54—dc23 LC record available at
https://lccn.loc.gov/2019008138

Set in Minion Pro by Mikala R. Kolander.
Designed by L. Auten.

In memoriam Rudolph P. Byrd (d. 2011), Mark Behr (d. 2015)

CONTENTS

ACKNOWLEDGMENTS

This book is being published before it is truly ready for the world. For nearly a decade, I have spoken and wrestled with James Baldwin over the constantly evolving thought holding these pages close to each other. If I were to be honest, I was not quite ready to share this thought. Nevertheless, it is here, and it is born out of a labor of love. By labor of love, I mean not to solely imply how the love of a subject motivates one's willingness to labor but also to suggest that love literally labors, and it has undoubtedly labored here. Beneath the theory and the analysis, *Salvific Manhood* concerns itself mostly with love—how we love and how we are loved. Throughout my writing, I have been pushed and fed by the love of many folks and various institutions, and, for them, I am grateful.

I am forever indebted to my professor Linda T. Wynn, who saw something in me at Fisk University I could not see within myself and who planted the thought for me to consider becoming a PhD. I cannot imagine myself here without her foresight, vision, and care. I am thankful for my beloved Fisk University, which both shaped me and equipped me to be vigilant in my academic pursuit and steadfast in who I am. Thanks to the Ronald E. McNair Scholars Program and the Andrew W. Mellon Foundation for the support offered through institutional workshops and continuing fellowship programs. Becoming a Mellon Mays Undergraduate Fellow set me upon the journey to aid in "transforming the face of the academy." Many of my strongest supporters were found within this network.

I owe a significant amount of gratitude to my doctoral studies home—

the W. E. B. Du Bois Department of Afro-American Studies at the University of Massachusetts–Amherst. The faculty there, many of whom were close friends of Jimmy Baldwin, along with the frequent visits from Sonia Sanchez and the late Amiri Baraka, shaped me into the interdisciplinary scholar I am today. While I entered the program fully expecting to write a dissertation on the distinguished Du Bois, the Baldwin class with Esther Terry left us both in tears and led me to the realization that Jimmy had been calling my name for longer than I knew. Through her teaching, she uncovered my love for Baldwin and my need to devote my doctoral study to his life, literature, and legacy. I am also deeply appreciative of my individual study with Ekwueme Michael Thelwell, who affirmed my petition to write on James Baldwin and encouraged me to not sacrifice the poetic to the academic, to find a way to meld the aesthetic and theoretical if I truly desired to honor Baldwin through academic study. I am thankful for my dissertation chair, James Smethurst, who was patient with and sharpening of me as I worked to make sense of this theory of mine. Thanks to Steven Tracy and Margo Crawford, who served beyond their capacities to help me bring forth a project worthy of discussion and distinction. And thanks to A. Yemisi Jimoh for the quiet exampling of intellectuality and precision from which I benefited in ways she cannot imagine.

I am thankful for my graduate studies experience in African and African American studies at Dartmouth College, which provided me with the Thurgood Marshall Doctoral Fellowship. Under the mentorship of Antonio Tillis, and with my intellectual community—Reena Goldthree, Adrienne Clay, and Russell Rickford—I was able to further develop the conceptual and theoretical frames of *Salvific Manhood*. Thanks goes to Markeysha Davis, a.k.a. "Point Five," for bearing witness and trudging along with me throughout our graduate school experience. I thank Julia Charles, Joseph Anthony Guillory, and Kelli Morgan for the friendship and community offered during our times in and beyond the Pioneer Valley, as each of them in some unique way has affirmed the fundamental ideas embedded within this work.

My extrainstitutional academic networks factor heavily in this accomplishment. I am thankful for the Institute for the Recruitment of Teachers for its continual shaping of me as a young scholar. In particular, I owe gratitude to Kelly Wise for reminding me of my ability and passion—"The heart has its reasons, which reason does not know." Thanks to Alexandra Cornelius, Asabe Poloma, Clemente White, Chera Reid, Besenia Rodriguez, and Karina Fernandez for making Phillips Academy a space of intellectual growth and safety. I also thank those amazing friends and mentors whom I found as a Mellon Fellow: Irvin Hunt (who has been a rock for me in moments he does not know about), Uri McMillan (who has executed a most masterful performance of interdisciplinary excellence), Frederick Staidum, Julius Fleming, Takkara Brunson, Jessica Marie Johnson, Courtney Thompson, Elda Maria Roman, Erica Edwards, Soyica Colbert, and Dennis Tyler. Additionally, I thank Lydia English and Cynthia Neal Spence for their fearless directorship and mentorship within the Mellon Mays Undergraduate Fellowship program (MMUF). Special thanks to the late Rudolph P. Byrd, whose presence in MMUF confirmed the possibility of my future and inspired me to move unapologetically as a Black intellectual. And thanks to those friends who fueled me before and during the writing of the book: Juanita Crider, Heidi Renée Freeman, Gilmer Cook, Jeffrey Lanier Jones, Francis Tobienne, Beau Gaitors, Heather Moore Roberson; and I am thankful for the example set by Venetria Patton.

I thank the Department of English at, and many of my colleagues from, Rhodes College, particularly Meredith Davis (for our amazing sessions within the archive room), Charles McKinney, Caki Wilkinson, Anita Davis, Luther Ivory, Russell Wigginton, Ira Lawson, Charles Hughes, and Evie Perry. I am especially thankful for my late colleague, Mark Behr, for his reminder of how beautiful humanity can be, for the warmth he offered so selflessly, and for his encouragement for me to write despite the many struggles. His unexpected death almost meant the absence of this book, and so a heartfelt thank-you goes to Zandria Robinson for urging me out of an academic paralysis by demanding I share my work with the world.

Deep appreciation is extended to my editor Alicia Christensen for believing in this work, for assuring me of its fit by speaking the language of interdisciplinarity, and for the wonderful efforts and energies shared by the entire editorial and production team at the University of Nebraska Press.

Thank you to the anonymous readers for their insightful feedback and for deeming my book worthy of such rich thought and care. Special thanks to the beautiful Baldwinites—Dwight McBride (for reaffirming my faith in mentorship), Magdalena Zaborowska, D. Quentin Miller, Douglas Field, and Rich Blint—for helping me along the way and inviting me into the special community composed of those who truly love and study Jimmy Baldwin.

I owe everything to my mother, Deborah Jones, and my two sisters, Nicole Gibson and Shawn Hemphill, who loved me, and the queerness we never knew how to name, without question or hesitation. Such love has shaped my manhood and has informed this project. Thanks to my coach, David Rachel, for holding me when I was not strong enough to hold myself, for seeing me in the world where I felt so invisible. And thanks to those friends who have always allowed me to live in a Baldwinian space of love: Raishaun Henderson, Niya Bealin, Angela Toon, Oscar Spivey-Dodd, Tyanna Clayton-Mallett (my soul-friend), Kyla Harris, and Kenneth Gilkes II. Thanks to my brothers: Leslie Fernandez, Dereck and Cory Barr-Pulliam, Kavara and Marlong Dixon-Faulkner, Lawrence Robinson, Alvin Johnson and Gerardo Guerra, Vearnon Woods, Brian Davis, Kevin Spragling, Kenyata Andrews, and Jared Moses. A thank-you goes to Terrance Martin Sweeney for teaching me along this journey. And a special thanks to Marcus Buckner Mayo for the strength of his friendship and the unwavering of his fraternity.

Finally, I thank my late grandmother, Valena Miller, for teaching me the power of salvation. I thank Sean McMillan for holding my hand and for freeing my spirit when he "reached out that quarter of an inch between us." And I thank the man who holds my heart, Ezell Wesley Allen, for the many ways his love and companionship save me each day, for embodying the beautiful salvific manhood Baldwin has promised within his pages, and for loving me as I labor to love and to love myself. *And thank you, Jimmy, thank you.*

SALVIFIC
MANHOOD

Introduction

In Search of the Fraternal

My most immediate memories of my grandmother involve the church, the Black church, to be particular. When my siblings and I were young, she forced us to attend service multiple times a week. What I felt as an imposition on my childhood was more of an introduction to God, a strategic placing of Black children in religious space, a teaching, "This is where you go for sanctum." We went because our grandmother went; because someone in our family before her went; because someone close had been ushered or pulled or called into the space, and so they went. While my grandmother would guide us in our studies of Christian doctrine, though she would tend to and cultivate our blooming faith, she never mentioned how deeply cultural this practice was, how churchgoing was a part of a larger Black tradition. She never told us the quiet parts of this ritual; the dark that engendered its necessity; how we went for our spirits and for ourselves, for our safety, and for our peace.

The last time I would see my grandmother, and the last time we would intimately share a space, was in a church. It was, quite unfortunately, her funeral. I stood in the pulpit, before family and friends, and shared some words about her, about her life, about the southern Louisiana parish that bore her into the woman I came to know and am still coming to know. I participated in the ritual of the celebration of life I had learned so well, thanked God for "His" blessings, and encouraged family to find peace. When I think about my grandmother, I almost always think of the church. What I did not know in youth, I know now as an adult man. She knew, like so many Black folks before her, that this world held certain promises for Black people. That among these will be suffering, struggle, and tragedy. She offered me one of the best things she inherited from our folk—religion. If I am to be honest, I learned the power of God long before I learned a need for it; I learned to place myself within the hands of religion long before I understood I would someday need to be held. And this is the beauty that makes the paradox of Black religious folks so crucial—religion offered itself as an entrance to God's favor, a refuge from "man's" hell. Hell had not introduced itself to me completely in the early days of my youth, or I did not know how to identify its presence, so I did not understand the complete function of religion beyond the pronounced ritual. However, soon enough, I learned why I needed the church, why religion was so central to the lives of Black people, how God's power offered itself. I learned how people found themselves called to that institution, how they went looking to be saved. While my grandmother was my first introduction to an idea of salvation, it was the literature of James Baldwin that would help me better understand how it tied humankind to a notion of God and men to each other.

There is a now classic photo of a 1963 James Baldwin standing in a church pulpit at a podium draped with the phrase "God Is Love." The idea captured by this photo mirrors Baldwin's radical philosophy of love, a philosophy born out of the Black church and a Christian ethos. The statement is both an identification of God's warmth and gentle embrace of humankind, of the principles by which we are to live, as well as an ontological claim that speaks to the heart or essence of a western conception of God. When I first saw the photo, I thought of my grandmother, of those earliest teachings of God, of Baldwin's earliest teachings. If God is love, and God is also salvation, what does that say about the relationship between the power to love and the power to save? Does it not beg for us to consider how love functions or operates in the inevitable calling for us to be saved? Does it not encourage us to rethink or reconsider the ontology of religion? Baldwin's "God is Love" photo, in the context of his writings, invites us to refigure and expand on how we have come to *know* God and exactly what we mean by religion.

I am interested in the ways in which a journeying into the worlds of novelistic Baldwin encourages a reconfiguration of religion or its sovereignty over the conception of God as love and salvation. That is, What happens when we reimagine the objects of religion as shareable, when we admit how they can be located within different institutions with the same potency? If religion's relationship to salvation is understood through how it opens itself spatially to those in need of saving, then intimacy, in its most abstracted sense, maintains the same *power*. Here, I am arguing that human intimacy, in its ability to serve as a space for refuge and a sanctum, mirrors, if not supplants—parallels, if not folds itself into—a sort of religious space. I am suggesting that, akin to how we are encouraged to read God as Love, we ought to configure intimacy as religion. After all, if institutions are defined by the artifacts they offer, then those who bear the same objects also bear a similarity in essence or in function.

In *Salvific Manhood: James Baldwin's Novelization of Male Intimacy*, I want to pursue a Baldwinian theology where "God Is Love." I want to imagine the transformative power in metaphors of the body as church and of intimacy as religion. I am asking a question of performance. How do intimacy and the body, as space and institution, perform acts of salvation? What happens when we explore physical intimacy from a metaphysical vantage? Can intimacy, as a doctrine of the body, offer deliverance or redemption? Even more, *Salvific Manhood* asks us to theorize the nature of salvation, to identify the essence of that which grants it.

Though *Salvific Manhood* is interested in salvation as an object of manhood, as a possibility born of its presence, it is also invested in examining salvation as a quality. This theorization positions people as agents of intimacy that can, by extension, save. It is a theory concerned with how these agents might be defined as salvific, as entities or institutions endowed with the power to offer salvation. This book advances "salvific manhood" as a theory positing the quality of salvation within the space of manhood. Salvation becomes the object of manhood, maleness, and masculinity; it becomes one of its defining characteristics. In this project, I am pointing toward "intimacy" as religion, as the vehicle carrying the object that is salvation. And here, I am also understanding "intimacy" as a site of exchange, a site that performs itself within another space. For instance, just as we might imagine religion as an intangible space, we must also understand intimacy this way. Just as we might admit how religion performs itself, in some ways and in some moments, within the space of the church, we might admit how intimacy performs itself, at times, within the space of the body. In these ways, *Salvific Manhood* grounds itself frequently within a theory of space: it is concerned with how the space of salvation is formed, who occupies that space, and, unfortunately, who is denied it.

The question of a denied access to salvation takes us back to the church. While I was there learning about salvation, and as Baldwin was there learning of the saving power of God, we both bore witness to how the need to locate salvation within a place or idea meant that its absence might also be endured and experienced. The lack of salvation, or the state of being unsaved, evokes a religious crisis, one in which a body is left outside the gates of deliverance and protection. The unsaved are, fundamentally, defined by two states of being. They are either those who are in need of salvation and thus in the process of seeking it out, or they are those rejected from it after the expression of need, those who are unable to occupy salvific space. In *Salvific Manhood*, this denial announces itself most regularly in spaces of exchange at the sites of the body and intimacy but can also be traced to traditional physical and institutional space. As this work is largely concerned with the *queering* of salvation—the act of moving the idea beyond the scope of religious thought and into the space where gender, as sex and sexuality, plays with and undoes itself—the idea of crisis factors prominently into the discussion.

In a way, our religious compulsions toward God, in a Judeo-Christian sense, might be understood through the rhetoric of longing and need. We might imagine a desire to be in God's favor, to come to a better conception of ourselves through a proximity mediated by doctrine. But we might also understand that longing as a manifestation of need, a need to be protected, refined, or saved. Whether we prefer the language of longing or need, the space outlining separation is best understood as crisis. Distance, despite being forced or self-intended, often announces itself through or as crisis. A faithful person's separation from God, for instance, signals incompletion, a lack of fulfillment, a wayward spirit plagued by personal or spiritual ills. Moving outside of the religious realm proper, distance also lends itself to these readings. The space distance opens up ought to be understood as rupture, as a symbolic space-in-between, and, more specifically, as a crisis. *Salvific Manhood*, with an interest in examining the distance existing between men, understands this rupture as *fraternal crisis*.

With this understanding of the theoretical aim of *Salvific Manhood* I want to reimagine the parameters of what we mean by "fraternal" or how we come to make it mean. Within this work, I push the fraternal to its etymological edges, begging for the simultaneous evoking of its literal and cultural meanings. Beginning with its Latin derivation from *frater*, meaning "brother," and reaching beyond its contemporary articulation through "fraternity," or a society of men, I am thinking of the ways in which the natural intimacy born of blood or legal kinship in the former allows the actualization of itself in the latter. That is, How does a society of men, connected outside the bonds of blood or legality, express the same type of intimacy historically and culturally reserved for those rendered kin by tradition? This work also fashions its use of the fraternal from the religious framing of the concept. Specifically, it considers the complexity of the Christian notion of brotherhood. On one hand, it understands brotherhood to be a reflection of a structured collective or organization of people corralled by common beliefs or interests. On the other, it specifies brotherhood as the intimate relationship, both ethical and moral, formed between distinct members of the group—for example, those practicing Christianity as belonging to and being within the brotherhood of Christ. It is here that my conception of the fraternal is directly informed by James Baldwin's upbringing within the church. *Salvific Manhood* sees Baldwin's exploration of the intimacy between men as beginning with his witnessing of a religious fraternal culture.

While in both the case of Rome, as explored by Cynthia Bannon in *The Brothers Romulus: Fraternal Pietas in Roman Law, Literature, and Society*, and the case of the larger Judeo-Christian practice of religious brotherhood, the notion of fraternity can be extended to include members of all sexes, *Salvific Manhood* is interested in it as a direct reflection of societies of men.[1] I am concerned with how men or male-identified persons, both the heteronormative and the queer, develop fraternity with one another and what happens when distance emerges within those relationships. This work thus argues how distance, rupture, and the symbolic space-in-between men signal what I call fraternal crisis. And it is the crisis, the expression and identification of some type of disconnect, that points to the absence of, and the desire or need for, intimacy. It is here where we venture into the true power of the salvific potential of manhood. It is here where we come to know how intimacy might be understood as religion, how the male body is something akin to the church, and how men—across bloodline, fictive kinship, friendship, and romantic love—often go in search of each other, often go in need of each other, often go in search of the fraternal with the hope of being saved. *Salvific Manhood* is, above anything else, arguing for a reading of Baldwin as a novelist invested in the continued exploration of how men save each other or, tragically, how they refuse or fail to do so.

Although they can be traced to the church, and though they evolved from that particular space into a broader philosophy of love, the earliest and most telling iterations of Baldwin's conception of the fraternal are seen in his short story "Sonny's Blues" (1957). Within this short story, Baldwin was able to marry the etymological and the cultural, locating a profound male intimacy within the space of blood kinship. Though published after he made his novelistic debut, "Sonny's Blues" provides an excellent introductory frame to the work *Salvific Manhood* dedicates itself to. The theoretical pursuits of this book, and the way it positions them as a connecting thread throughout Baldwin's novel, find themselves amplified in the relationship between the narrator and the central character. In spite of its publication history, "Sonny's Blues" is the perfect preface to Baldwin's novels, as it makes the reader contemplate brotherhood, love, intimacy, and the need to be saved.

Harkening back to my earliest introductions to Baldwin, I am reminded of how "Sonny's Blues" functioned as both a site of ingression and a meditation on the power and struggles of brotherly love. What grabbed me about the short story and resonates within the larger literary discourse is how Baldwin was able to identify what I read as a fraternal crisis—a breakdown in or challenge to "brotherhood" characterized by the absence, removal, and refusal of male intimacy and proximity. Baldwin was also able to eloquently capture its remedy, a salvation of sorts woven into same-sex love and interaction. While identifiable in Baldwin's earlier works, the idea of salvific manhood (the gendered and endowed ability to save) first came to me through "Sonny's Blues." Despite not then having the language or even the motivation to pursue it, as I write and reflect now I know with unquestionable certainty that what I strove to articulate in those trembling moments in my undergraduate literature course was that which is outlined in the pages to follow. What I did not know was how the short story was symptomatic of the author's larger novelistic collection, the extent to which it would frame my readings of Baldwin's work.

Nearly four years after the publication of his first novel, *Go Tell It on the Mountain*, the *Partisan Review* published Baldwin's short story "Sonny's Blues" in 1957. Employing one of Baldwin's most popular settings—Harlem—the story is, on the surface, a commentary on the decay of a major metropolitan space plagued by poverty, drugs and drug addiction, the pressures and depressions of politicized and racialized spaces, the absurdity emerging in the aftermath of World War II, and how a distinct population of people grappled with and within its urban cesspools. However, beneath these easily accessible existential titillations, or within "the wreckage and rumble" of the story, lies a more penetrating narrative that swivels on notions of the fraternal, salvific manhood, and the relationship between the two. Focusing on the relationship between two brothers caught in the whirlwind of fraternal negotiations, "Sonny's Blues" magnifies the search precipitated by fraternal crises and the reconciliation one hopes will follow.

"Sonny's Blues" chronicles the lives of two brothers coming to terms with both their larger social realities and their smaller, more intimate familial histories in mid-twentieth-century New York. Told through the narration of the unnamed brother, it foregrounds Sonny's, the titular brother's, struggle with heroin and prison. The death of the narrator's daughter, Grace, engenders a series of reconnections first witnessed through letters, after periods of silent communication while Sonny is imprisoned. Eventually, Sonny's release comes with a reunion between him and his brother and a delving into the difficulties men face in knowing, loving, and saving one another. "Sonny's Blues" uses flashbacks to reveal the named brother's relationship to music, his fight to survive, and his desire to be heard. Within these episodes, the story iterates the brothers' central tension and most pressing fissures, ultimately culminating in a biblically infused experience of brotherly love and redemption. Inasmuch as "Sonny's Blues" is about music, sound, voice, and noise, it is equally, if not more, about silence. Silence as portent of fraternal crisis, as signifier of that symbolic space-in-between, as the collapse or absence of a necessary intimacy.

Baldwin's famed short story opens with the unnamed narrator's confession of disbelief after having read of his brother's drug-related arrest in the papers. The disbelief is doubly functional, as it at once alludes to the "natural" shock one might imagine in such a situation as well as the more symbolic distance captured by his unpacking. In the narrator's own admission, "I couldn't believe it: but what I mean by that is that I couldn't find any room for it anywhere inside me. I had kept it outside me for a long time. I hadn't wanted to know."[2] While there are many elements established through Baldwin's chosen opening scene, there are a few that beg exploration for the purposes of framing this project. The first, relayed through the opening line itself—"I read about it in the paper, in the subway, on my way to work. I read it, and I couldn't believe it, and I read it again"—highlights how familial distance mediates the story of two brothers and their effort to reconcile themselves to each other, as well as the degree of unfamiliarity held by the narrator of his brother.[3] Additionally, the narrator's transparency with how he was both unable and unwilling to "find any room for it anywhere inside [himself]" reveals the degree to which the state of unknowing becomes characterized by expressions of privileged agency. He was not the passive unknowing "victim" of his brother's suffering; rather, he chose his awareness and thus perhaps became more complicit. Here, with the realization of possible and probable complicity, "Sonny's Blues" demands interrogations of male kinship—its intimacies and distances, its relationship to states of knowing and unknowing, and its crises and salvations.

Despite the distance between Sonny and his brother, the latter understands Sonny's suffering. Musing on the possible shared destinies of the young men he teaches, he knows the textures of their struggles, understands just how "these boys, now, were living as [Sonny and his brother had] been living then, they were growing up with a rush and their heads bumped abruptly against the low ceiling of their actual possibilities."[4] In reflecting on his students, our unnamed narrator also describes the existential plight of his brother—how Sonny, like many Black boys striving for manhood in midcentury America, was bound to face and be plagued by a racial absurdity tucked within "the silence, the darkness coming, and the darkness in the faces [frightening] the child obscurely."[5] Baldwin's play with the motif of light versus dark illumines the condition precipitating a need for fraternal intimacy. The crisis addressed within this work, however, does not reflect the suffering enacted by an absurd world; rather, it addresses the distance between brothers or the willful state of unknowing the extent of another man's suffering in a desire to protect your own privilege of perceived safety. Fraternal crisis is never happenstance; instead, it emerges through an intentional blindness or the act of keeping your brother's suffering outside of yourself.

For Baldwin, several things can be revealed by a fraternal crisis—distance, rupture, and space-in-between. The crisis, in its delineation of distance, highlights a disconnect between two men and encourages the witness to discern what is at play. It also magnifies a state of either unknowing or negligence. In the case of the former, a privilege of unknowing might be said to protect the "brother" from complete blame, though it is a function of kinship to know one's brother as one's self. For the latter, the willful blindness or inaction indicates a failure of kinship, points to the rupture as reconcilable, salvageable, or healable. For this situation, intentional neglect reflects another part of the fraternal crisis, encourages the witness toward suspicion and indictment. Both of these instances are present in Baldwin's work, and Sonny's blues become the sound by which we read his brother's ignorance and negligence.

The story makes clear Sonny's struggle and the reasons behind his suffering, while also gesturing toward something distinctly Baldwinian—the queering of salvation. Using the conversation between mother and unnamed narrator, Baldwin moves the brother's ability to save Sonny into the realm of subtext. Upon the mother's insistence, "You got to hold on to your brother . . . and don't let him fall, no matter what it looks like is happening to him and no matter how evil you gets with him," the brother responds, saying, "I won't forget . . . Don't you worry, I won't forget. I won't let nothing happen to Sonny."[6] Inevitably, we learn when and how he forgets—to the point where he must read about it in the paper, to the point where he must witness it through street revival—and his own visceral reaction. But we also learn how forgetting need not be permanent and how salvation can sometimes stretch or defy time. And at the precise moment when Sonny's suffering truly becomes legible, our narrator comes to his own necessary understanding: "I realized, with this mocking look, that there stood between us, forever, beyond the power of time or forgiveness, the fact that I had held silence—so long!—when he had needed human speech to help him."[7] The holding of silence instead of the state of being in silence further reveals the narrator's complicity in Sonny's struggle, further implicates him in the fraternal crisis. Nevertheless, this tender scene of painful understanding also signals the point at which one man can either remain inactive/silent or deliberate eradicating the distance between him and his brother. When the brother places silence as standing forever between them, he at once acknowledges distance and the cause of it—silence—and expresses the concern of its permanence. While the end of the short story revises it, in the moment this sentiment attests to the chasmic depth of denied intimacy, the failure or collapse of brotherhood, the crisis. However, as we come to see, distance needs not be permanent, and there are paths toward redemption for both brothers in Baldwin's world.

The site at which the unnamed narrator transforms from silent and complicit brother into an agent of salvation is staged by his ability and willingness to listen. His agreeing to witness his brother's performance shows support and how he, endowed with powers of salvation, must also agree to the calling. He goes from a man who does not fully know his brother's turmoil to a man who registers the true import of their music. For Baldwin, salvific manhood loses its abstraction through his narrator's insightful reading of the relationship between "the musician and his instrument" and how "he has to fill it with the breath of life, his own."[8] More specifically, it's through the act of listening to and hearing his brother that our unnamed narrator grounds himself in his salvific manhood: "[Sonny] and his boys up there were keeping it new, at the risk of ruin, destruction, madness, and death, in order to find new ways to make us listen. For while the tale of how we suffer, and how we are delighted, and how we may triumph is never new, it always must be heard. There isn't any other tale to tell, it's the only light we've got in all this darkness."[9] Admittedly, the language of saving and salvation might read heavy for a project of literary criticism. However, as "Sonny's Blues" teaches us—or points to, at least—one of Baldwin's preoccupations lies in how men are able to assist each other in their battles within and against darkness, silence, or absurdity. Or, put more literarily, Baldwin wrote at times with the hidden (and perhaps "sublime" is more accurate here) hope that his readers would come to believe what the brother in the story did: "I seemed to hear with what burning he had made it his, with what burning we had yet to make it ours, how we could cease lamenting. Freedom lurked around us and I understood, at last, that he could help us to be free if we would listen, that he would never be free until we did."[10] In the end, this story perfectly captures my pursuit of Baldwin, as he wrestled with unpronounced notions of salvific manhood and male intimacy within his novels.

If one listens to Baldwin, if one reads him, it is a remarkable experience. I say this because I have learned that some writers remind us that writing is more gift than skill, that the art of penning a script for this world takes more than a mastery of language, takes more than a mastery of form; indeed, it takes an understanding of the human spirit. Baldwin knew this well. And thus, a critical reader of his work will find a textuality capable of touch, where the words, almost literally, hold and hug tightly like struggling sons to the memories of absent fathers, like lonely expatriates to the memories of their homelands. A book becomes an experience at the moment when a tear touches the page, when the lines that separate author from audience, writer from reader, are blurred by human emotion. Baldwin seemed to write as if he dipped his pen into his heart and poured all of his pain, his longing, and his joy into every word of his work. And if one reads him closely, if one listens attentively, in the end, one does more than understand the plot of his narrative, more than glean the message of his text—one feels. This sentiment, perhaps what many might consider a poetic homage to Baldwin, is meant to direct us to how Baldwin's personal investment in his subject matter shapes how we are to read his characters. The author, the African American author in particular, must not be rendered "dead" here, cannot afford such a critical abstraction. The quiet parts of *Salvific Manhood* argue for this reality, demand us to keep Baldwin alive in our analysis. This does not mean it is concerned with the personal or biographical; rather, it insists on locating the novelistic connections in the personal striving of Baldwin. He, as a man grappling with his own series of fraternal crises, used his fiction to explore them and to push us in the direction of healing.

Yet, despite his power to move, despite the way he captures the reader with his language and lyricism, James Baldwin enjoys a very peculiar neglect in the study of American letters. The public knows him for his critique of Richard Wright; it knows him for his unrelenting essay collections *The Fire Next Time, Notes of a Native Son, Nobody Knows My Name*, et cetera. But the moment we mention him as novelist, there is a deafening silence. So why is it that we know Baldwin as an essayist at the expense of knowing him as a novelist? Why is it that we talk about the beautiful prose of *The Fire Next Time* but say nothing of the gripping prose of *Another Country*? There are many reasons, but I think the most obvious stems from the prevailing belief that Baldwin is a better essayist than he is a novelist. It comes from the idea that he handles the form of the essay with a dexterity that is lacking in his management of the novel. And perhaps this has something to do with the idea that in a discussion of forms, the essay grants the writer a greater freedom. Maybe it has something to do with the fact that the novel, as a genre, has certain prescriptions that one dares not evade. I also think it has a lot to do with the fact that in a Jamesian sense, the novelist must enjoy a peculiar detachment from the world in which he or she is writing. To take it further, from an Ellisonian perspective, African American writers, if they are to be taken seriously and to truly cultivate their craft, must detach themselves from the political landscape of a racially hostile America. If you know Baldwin, you know that he conceded to neither of these artistic mores. His novels were never the objective capturing of the world as he saw it; he was never a passive creative spectator whose purpose was to record and document. No, his novels were deeply personal—that peculiar imbrication of autobiography and fiction. And his political self was always present in his writing—he, in a sense, maintained his position as Socratic gadfly no matter which genre he assumed. This, I think, has garnered him an unfair critique and guaranteed an underwhelming treatment of his novels. There are other reasons, however, some more delicate than others.

Baldwin's first novel, *Go Tell It on the Mountain*, was published in 1953, before the historic *Brown v. Board of Education* and in the anticipation of a budding Civil Rights Movement. When one looks at this novel, it is decidedly African American. It takes place in Harlem but, more important, within two very specific spaces—a Black household and a Black church. Quite naturally, when it was published, though reviews vacillated, it placed Baldwin in the tradition of other African American writers, where themes of Black religiosity and the structure of Black families, coupled with a gentle allusion to the white racism of the South, painted it a Black novel. A year later, Baldwin echoed his exploration of the centrality of the Black church and how African Americans endure racial hostility with his play *The Amen Corner*. By this time, Baldwin was beginning to establish himself as someone with a very clear and distinct racial consciousness, and that solidified in 1955 when he published his first collection of essays, *Notes of a Native Son*. Ranging from critiques of Harriet Beecher Stowe's hypersentimental portrayal of enslaved Blacks and Richard Wright's limited portrayal of Black agency in his famed *Native Son*, the collection also explores ideas of race and place as he surveys the racial and economic realities of Black people in Harlem and of foreigners (American, African, and Black) in the European space. By this time, there was no question that Baldwin was, as many would later identify him, a "race man." His writings up to this point, both fiction and nonfiction, had showcased a preoccupation with race. However, in 1956, Baldwin published a book that would challenge how the world understood him as a writer, as a Negro writer; that book is *Giovanni's Room*.

Baldwin's second novel was seemingly very different from the first in its conspicuous absence of Black characters and its foregrounding of sexual "deviance," most notably male bisexuality and homosexuality. It was a risky endeavor, but one that was later successful because of the superficial distancing of homosexuality from blackness and, more importantly, from Americanness. Using Paris as the setting allowed Baldwin to explore taboo issues of male intimate relationships in ways that American literature was not particularly ready to confront. With the publication of this novel, however, Baldwin "outed" himself to the public and placed himself in a very interesting position within the African American community. Baldwin, never one to allow others' perceptions of him to disturb or disconcert him, handled the criticism and questioning of *Giovanni's Room* with an elegant stride. Half a decade later, he resumed his campaign as race man with the publication of another collection of essays in 1961, entitled *Nobody Knows My Name: More Notes of a Native Son.* Then, in 1962, he published his third novel, *Another Country*, which would eventually become his bestselling novel. However, more so than the novel preceding it, *Another Country* proved very controversial. It was either loved or hated, and Baldwin, who had shown himself to be resilient in the face of America's criticism, revealed his vulnerability as he was clearly hurt by some critics' castigation of this work and his work as a novelist. *Another Country* factors heavily in an epistemology of James Baldwin, for the criticism came from all areas of Baldwin's life and challenged his position as both a prominent spokesman for Black America and a critic of American practices.

A year later, Baldwin's powerful essay collection *The Fire Next Time* was published; he was featured on the cover of *Time* magazine and in the story "Nation: The Root of the Negro Problem." I need not remind the reader of the tumultuous race relations of the 1960s, a decade holding both the height of the Civil Rights Movement and the birth of the Black Power Movement. Nevertheless, I think the historical moment is very important for understanding how we understand James Baldwin as a writer. Having already established himself as a racially conscious man, and having been deemed by *Time* magazine as the spokesman of Black America or Black people in America, Baldwin became a witness to the struggle of African Americans in this country in a way that other Black writers have not. I think the cultural moment of the 1960s, with the field of Black studies being born out of the Black Arts and Black Power Movement, has largely shaped how we understand James Baldwin as a novelist. That particular era saw a redefinition of identity politics with a prioritization of Black racial consciousness. Viewed in this light, it is easy to understand why Baldwin is exalted for his essays and ignored for most of his novels—at least in the field of African American Studies. The new field of study was so deeply grounded in Black political discourse and the rhetoric of its genesis that it proved, and continues to prove in some regards, resistant to conversations provoked by Baldwin's novels. The field, while responsible for centering the Black marginalized experience, selectively reshaped how we are to understand Black history and the prominent figures within it.

If one understands that the birth of Black studies as an academic discipline is largely responsible for how the world has come to restudy African American history, literature, and culture, then one must not wonder why our epistemology of James Baldwin appears as it does. In 2001, Dwight McBride published *James Baldwin Now*, and his introduction notes how the 1990s saw a renewed interest in James Baldwin. In that same introduction, framed within a conversation between Marlon Ross's and Sharon Patricia Holland's essays, he addresses how African American literary scholarship has not successfully carved a space for the Black to speak to the queer.[11] This, I argue, is the problem with our dominant epistemology of James Baldwin—his identity has historically been and continues to be bifurcated into "warring" racial and sexual identities. Admittedly, there has been significant progress within the field, but there remains little serious treatment exploring the intersections of race, gender, and sexuality in Baldwin's fiction. More notable is the limited number of single-author full-length studies dedicated to nuancing the connections within his fictional work.

Salvific Manhood: James Baldwin's Novelization of Male Intimacy is a theoretical pursuit of constructions of manhood within the novels of James Baldwin, which explores the author's epistemological mining of men and masculinity as scripted identities and how those gendered subjectivities are inadvertently plagued by loneliness and a denied space of vulnerability. Through a reimagining of the fraternal—a complex expansion of the concept of brotherhood—it examines distinct iterations of male intimacy and how men, predominantly African American men, come to be scripted by the need and desire to be *saved*. Beginning with his earliest work, *Go Tell It on the Mountain*, and ending with his last, *Just Above My Head*, it highlights the subtle omnipresence of male loneliness, follows the male characters' pursuit of resolution through intimacy, and dissects the consequences of those strivings. Stretching literary analysis into the realm of cultural studies, it constructs a theory of "salvific manhood" that complicates predominant readings that understand male same-sex relationships in Baldwin's novels as solely homoerotic by uncovering the complex ways in which the author writes male same-sex intimacy through an identifiable need to be saved. My work, in essence, pushes the reader to reach beyond the popular while demanding a bold reappropriation of the "perverse." It argues that same-sex male sexualities, sexual encounters, and moments of intimacy are always already symbolic in Baldwin's work, that their functions are to advance the subtextual theme emerging from the writer's own preoccupation with and conceptualization of what he has called "the state of being alone." Thus, over the course of six chapters, my monograph explores how Baldwin evolves the complex phenomenon of male loneliness, longing, vulnerability, and need into a doctrine of salvation. In this regard, the project promises to be a new discursive intervention within the fields of literary studies, men and masculinity studies, queer studies, and Africana studies.

My study begins, quite naturally, with Baldwin's *Go Tell It on the Mountain*, published in 1953, in an effort to stay true to the autobiographical chronology that is marked by each novel. Baldwin's first novel is a very important starting point because, as I argue later, it is probably the most clearly autobiographical of Baldwin's novels—paralleling Baldwin's relationship with his stepfather David. Even more, however, it is important for the literary chronology because we witness the youngest of his protagonists in this novel and really see, to use his language, the "germ of the dilemma." Chapter 1, "Wrestling for Salvation: Denial, Longing, and the Beauty of Brotherhood in *Go Tell It on the Mountain*," examines two relationships—John Grimes's relationship with his stepfather, Gabriel, and John's relationship with his brother in the Christian faith, Elisha. Focusing on John's relationship with his father, I argue that the loneliness that John feels is precipitated by a fraternal crisis, a breakdown of male intimacy with his father. I trace how he struggles with the feelings of being unloved and unwanted, of being rejected and not good enough, and how Gabriel's cold engagement pushes him to search for male intimacy in another figure—namely, Elisha. Elisha emerges as an antithesis to Gabriel, and I argue that Baldwin endows the former with a salvific manhood—the divine and unconditional spirit of love and intimacy for his younger brother in Christ.

Chapter 2, "Flight, Freedom, and Abjection: Fractured Manhood and Tragic Love in *Giovanni's Room*," examines various male relationships in one of Baldwin's most controversial novels, *Giovanni's Room*. In particular, it considers David's relationship with different spaces—America, Paris, Guillaume's bar, and Giovanni's room—through the lens of Julia Kristeva's theory of abjection. Arguing that David and Giovanni's love is ultimately tragic due to the former's inability to love himself and his constant relegation of certain forms of gender expression to the idea of the abject, this chapter complicates the idea of salvific manhood while showcasing how spaces are endowed with conflicted meanings. Additionally, it begins the conversation of tragic manhood through its treatment of Giovanni and how he unravels with the divorce from David's love.

Chapter 3, "Alone in the Absurd: The Trope of Tragic Black Manhood in *Another Country*," racializes Albert Camus's theory of the absurd as it grapples with the phenomenon of Black male suicide in Baldwin's third novel. This chapter begins with a discussion of Rufus Scott's fatalistic wrestling with race, sexuality, and purpose, and argues that the absence of male intimacy precipitates the phantom protagonist's tragic fate while highlighting how topoi of invisibility and rejection operate within the American racial narrative. In particular, it examines the fraternal crisis plaguing Scott's relationship with his closest friend, Vivaldo, and posits that the latter's whiteness reveals a privilege of willful denial.

Chapter 4, "Theatrics of Mask-ulinity: Radical Male Intimacy and Black Power in *Tell Me How Long the Train's Been Gone*," explores the power of brotherly love from the perspective of kinship and community. Specifically, this chapter analyzes the peculiar bond between Leo Proudhammer and his brother Caleb, suggesting that the younger brother emerges as a salvific man as he helps Caleb to once again feel after being stripped of his manhood and humanity by the racism of the world. It also examines Baldwin's tenuous relationship with members of the Black Power Movement by positing Christopher Hall as a symbol for radical Black Nationalism. Viewing Leo and Christopher's relationship as a push to reconcile fictional and real fraternal crises, this chapter captures Baldwin's struggle as a man and artist writing within the 1960s.

Chapter 5, "Concrete Jungles and the Carceral: Exploring Confinement and Imprisonment in *If Beale Street Could Talk*," surveys Baldwin's claim about the severity of absented male intimacy. Focusing primarily on the various iterations of the idea of the carceral, from the prison–industrial complex to the abstract confining of Black male subjectivity, this chapter highlights the continual oppressiveness of racial absurdity. Primarily focusing in on the relationship between Frank Hunt and his imprisoned stepson, Alonzo, the analysis pivots on the salvific role the latter plays in the life of the former and how the prison experience gives rise to an irreconcilable fraternal crisis.

I end this work with "Somewhere in That Wreckage," which, as a sort of epilogue, critically examines different male relationships within Baldwin's last novel, *Just Above My Head*, while asserting its representational value as a culminating work. The conclusion grounds itself in analyses of Arthur Montana's relationship with various men, from his first male love, Jason Logan, to his brother Hall. Inevitably, it argues that Hall's narration, performed through a series of memories, testifies to a desire for fraternal reconciliation and teaches the reader new ways of remembering. Most importantly, it magnifies one of the goals of this project, which is to encourage us as literary critics and lovers of African American culture to strive for responsible mythologizing and to actively pursue a full understanding of James A. Baldwin.

Where there is separation, there is crisis. Where there is crisis, there needs to be intimacy. And where there is intimacy, there is the possibility for salvation. In each of Baldwin's novels there are salvific men, there are triumphs, and there are tragedies. *Salvific Manhood* journeys into these moments and, in the process, seeks to uncover the hows and the whys.

1

Wrestling for Salvation

Denial, Longing, and the Beauty of Brotherhood in *Go Tell It on the Mountain*

The song that lends itself to James Baldwin's first novel remains genealogically elusive. Musical and cultural historians have attempted to locate both its origin and generative author, and they must resign themselves to celebrating such mystery as the product of an African American oral tradition. What history does tell us, however, is how John Wesley Work Jr.—the famed historian as well as director of the renowned Fisk Jubilee Singers—played an instrumental role in (re)composing the song and bringing it to the attention of the country. At its heart, the song "Go Tell It on the Mountain" speaks directly to a tradition of Negro spirituals, a collective medium by which enslaved Africans or African Americans articulated faith, waged resistance, and composed survival through sonic utterance. Even more, the song's focus on the Nativity, or the birth of Jesus Christ, performs a symbolic framing of Baldwin's novel wherein the ideas of birth and celebration are intertwined with a narrative about manhood, a sort of coming-of-age tale bound by patriarchy and religion, liberated by a beautiful expression of brotherhood. Baldwin's *Go Tell It on the Mountain* offers its readers the opportunity to witness the birth of Black manhood within spaces committed to its denial, resolving itself through a profound rendering of Black male vulnerability and intimacy required for salvation.

Born originally as "Crying Holy" circa 1944, *Go Tell It* underwent several transformations, including the change in its title to *In My Father's House*, before becoming the 1953 work. When Baldwin first began writing, the preoccupation with the tense relationship between him and his stepfather colored the text. Nearly a decade later, however, it had evolved to include a plethora of relationships that spoke to a more holistic portrayal of James Baldwin and his young protagonist. To this last point, some context might be necessary. Like many authors, Baldwin's *Go Tell It* inevitably draws upon his personal life, transforming an autobiographical impulse into a work of art. And while these slippages might engender a favorable reading of the novel as autobiographical fiction, the central grapple of *Salvific Manhood* will be to highlight the larger thematic concerns of the text. Most of these concerns can be excavated from a treatment of the same-sex male relationships within the novel. Therefore, I argue that one of the fundamental aims of the novel is neatly embedded within John's relationship with God, Gabriel, Elisha, and self. Interestingly, women within the novel serve critical functions in John's pursuit of salvation; they are, after all, the ones who fortify him upon the threshing floor. Nevertheless, they remain peripheral to the larger play of manhood and masculinity. This identifies how patriarchy constructs gendered webs of exclusion, on one hand, and how the pursuit of an actualized manhood pleads for an understanding of exclusion because of it, on the other hand. While most of the women are presented as subsidiary characters whose stories are told for the purpose of contributing to John's and Gabriel's, this is also true of significant male figures like Elizabeth's Richard, Florence's Frank, and Gabriel's Royal and Roy. Beyond this consideration of gender, there are several elements that inform how Baldwin constructs or mediates relationships. To these, from the religious to the familial, we are asked to bear witness.

As early as the title, Baldwin's novel anticipates its own religious engagement. Such engagement is both guaranteed by the title and demanded by the subject. Baldwin could not have possibly explored the intricacies of a gendered and queered salvation without pulling from the doctrines responsible for so much of his moral self. And thus, quite naturally, many scholars enter the discussion of *Go Tell It* through the gates of the holy. In *James Baldwin's God: Sex, Hope, and Crisis in Black Holiness Culture*, Clarence Hardy advances a reading of Baldwin's first novel that is heavily grounded in a discussion of religiosity. According to Hardy, the novel "depicts a Black holiness culture that harshly restricts individuals' opportunity for growth." While *Go Tell It* does in fact reveal an individual's war with a religious institution or the constraints of that institution, Hardy's assessment of John's relationship to the church is somewhat limited. This is noticeable in the assertion, "Even as he enters into this religious world of holiness culture, John is not sure he wants to be trapped in such a narrow, parochial tradition separated from the joyful pleasures and thrilling demands of the world."[1] Such a thought captures the bulk of scholarship surrounding John's relationship with the church and serves as a basis for how the novel has come to be viewed. As Hardy continues to trouble John's religious relationship, however, he fails to explore the other symbolisms of the church and/or God within the novel. This, of course, was not his goal, but it provides an excellent space of intervention, where a new perspective may add to the breadth of criticism.

The centrality of religion in *Go Tell It on the Mountain* has influenced the ways in which readers understand and appreciate John's relationship with Gabriel. For many, Gabriel's relationship with the church cannot be separated from his relationship with John. This is a safe argument. For, as Michael Fabre points out, "The child [John] represents Elizabeth's sin to Gabriel's eyes, but also a means of projecting and of rejecting his own guilt."[2] The guilt alluded to speaks to Gabriel's first son, Royal. Royal, conceived in infidelity and subsequently rendered bastard by Gabriel's unwillingness to acknowledge fatherhood, is one of the many tragic characters in the novel. Also, Gabriel's distance from John is a matter of bloodline. In being merely a stepson, John is unable to fulfill God's promise to his stepfather. None of this is to be disputed, at least not in this instance. The reader, however, must also come to know that what forms Gabriel's relationship with John is not necessarily what shapes John's relationship to Gabriel. This is to suggest that while Gabriel's problem is hindered by some twisted spiritual investment mediated by an irresponsible history, John's issue is rooted in something far less religious. Thus, any analysis of the father–son relationship must take into account how very differently each man comes to understand the conflict. If one accepts the idea that "the novel can even more significantly be seen as an eloquent record of Baldwin's struggle to break away from his stepfather's God," then one must also question what that God represents, how it comes to be understood as such, and the effects it has on young Baldwin or his autobiographical protagonist.[3]

Probably one of the most fascinating and often-written-about relationships from *Go Tell It on the Mountain* is the relationship between John and Elisha. Offering a wonderful contrast to the discordant tie between John and Gabriel, this relationship magnifies a beautifully peculiar bond held between two of Baldwin's most endeared characters. Like the other relationships within the novel, John's connection to Elisha is tremendously influenced by the permeating rhetoric of religion. This in turn colors common readings of the relationship while obscuring the possibility of others. To be clear, most scholarship on John's unique brotherhood with Elisha reduces it to Baldwin's grappling with issues of sexuality, arguing that the ambiguity is, again, largely due to the strict confines of what Hardy terms the "Black holiness culture." The field almost unanimously writes John's attraction to Elisha as a flirtation with the homoerotic and homosexual, completely ignoring the possibility of pure homosociality or something that penetrates below the surface of sexual desire. Yet, while submitting that "Baldwin suggests a kinship between religious pursuits and sexual play throughout his work," the discourse is firm in its reading of both the physical closeness and spiritual connectedness of John and Elisha.[4] For instance, in the infamous scene between the two young men, most agree that "though they do not have a name for it, John and Elisha are wrestling with homosexual desire."[5] I mean not to propose that this moment between two adolescent men is not somewhat sexual, especially given Baldwin's autobiographical threading. However, there is more at work in this physical moment. And if we are to understand the significance of this "sexual play" within a religious space by two men in the nascence of their manhood, then we must pay particular attention as to what this means for John alone.

Geta LeSeur, writing in *Ten is the Age of Darkness: The Black Bildungsroman*, places *Go Tell It* convincingly within a tradition of coming-of-age novels written by African Americans. Citing John's push toward the limits of identity, she argues that the novel differs from crises of identity found in the white literary tradition as the particular dilemmas faced by Black youth are unique to their racial and sometimes class experience.[6] Louis

Pratt underscores this basic premise and asserts that, in a sort of Whitmanesque fashion, "Baldwin's novel becomes an exorcism, a purgation, a necessary constriction which leads, ultimately, to the unlimited expanses of self-identity."[7] Both LeSeur and Pratt capture the essence of the novel, as it is indeed the narrative of a boy who comes of age through a powerful pushing of identity. But, more than that, *Go Tell It on the Mountain* reveals how love, its absence and presence, and the search for it mediate John's existential crisis. In this regard, it is more than a reformed bildungsroman, more than an exploration of identity. John is neither lost nor invisible in the ways that such literary reasoning suggests; he is struggling because of a particular absence that his spirit ordains him to search for—a journey that continues in each novel Baldwin writes after the first.

If *Go Tell It* is in general a novel of human interactions, then it is in particular a narrative of male relationships. Above anything else, the most profound exchanges experienced by the protagonist, John, are had with the characters of Gabriel and Elisha. These two men represent something totally different for the peripatetic John, with Gabriel being a symbol of his departure and Elisha being a sign of his destination. This suggests that *Go Tell It* complicates the notion of the bildungsroman. The young protagonist does not simply come of age; in fact, the novel's chronology barely reaches past twenty-four hours. And while some may argue that John undergoes a spiritual transformation, I submit that the spiritual transformation is linked with a more symbolic travel. John's rebirth is less a matter of coming into a certain manhood and more an issue of demanding that which his manhood needs—namely, love. The rebirth is climactically connected to his fourteenth birthday because it coincides with Baldwin's entrance into the ministry. It is not, however, meant to boost the significance of a boy's search for identity and his ultimate cross into manhood. LeSeur was right; *Go Tell It* troubles the way existential crisis is patterned in the larger American literary tradition. However, it also muddles the ways in which it is displayed in Black literature. Inevitably, John's struggle, while magnifying certain identity markers like race, class, sexuality, and kinship, is definitively shaped by a desire of love. This is what defines Baldwin's novelistic corpus—the fictional writing of his philosophy of love. It begins, quite naturally, when he first began to work through it in his real life—in that moment of his youth when he danced on the cusp of manhood.

According to Colin MacInnes, *Go Tell It on the Mountain* "is a densely packed, ominous, sensual doom-ridden story, lit by rare beauty, love and human penetration. The theme is life and religion and how both, wonderful and terrible, can create and destroy."[8] MacInnes's idea of how "life and religion" are sources of creation and destruction aptly describes the life of the novel's protagonist, John Grimes. Thus, it is more so a novel relaying the story of John, whose dysfunctional relationship with his father (stepfather) leads him on a journey to fill a void. The metalanguage of paternity informs not only John's relationship with other family members in the novel but also the nature of his quest and the relationship he develops with Elisha. The metaphoric space-in-between John and Gabriel informs the young man's spiritual struggle. It is, in a sense, the proverbial fraternal crisis. It is the metalanguage of paternity, coupled with the rhetoric and religiosity of the novel, that shapes the notion of the fraternal. It, as explained earlier, relates to an idea of brotherhood. However, I suggest that my concepts of the fraternal and fraternal crisis, though deviating from more historical and literal understandings of "brotherhood" within the Christian and African American religious traditions, nonetheless serve this project well.

In addition to showing how God's love is absent from John's relationship with Gabriel, *Go Tell It* reveals the subsequent journey that John partakes of in order to find the love he so desperately seeks. This search for the fraternal is what many critics will conflate with a coming-of-age narrative. However, as shown later, it resounds with a more emotional element that Baldwin hopes to make clear. Consequently, as John begins his search, he is led to the figure of Elisha. Elisha emerges as a symbolic antithesis to Gabriel, as the former becomes a male embodiment of love John passionately longs for throughout the novel. I argue this as the criticality of *Go Tell It on the Mountain*.

Go Tell It begins with the proclamation of how everyone prophesied preaching as a part of John Grimes's future. He was to follow in his father's footsteps, to uphold the strong religious and ministerial tradition that consumed his father, Gabriel. The opening is framed in a week-old recollection of the Grimes's church and introduces, albeit in cursory fashion, many of the characters that will later move the novel's narrative. Nevertheless, it is after this brief contextual introduction that the novel truly begins, with the protagonist John Grimes waking up on his fourteenth birthday on a Sunday in March of 1935. The waking mood captures the crisis that will unfold throughout the day and hints toward the very schism that underwrites the entire novel.

The reader is launched into John's psyche as the thought of no one remembering his birthday plagues him: "For it had happened, once or twice, that his birthday had passed entirely unnoticed, and no one had said, 'Happy Birthday, Johnny,' or given him anything—not even his mother."[9] John's thoughts reveal one significant aspect of his struggle as a member of the Grimes household. He is tormented by the state of feeling invisible, unloved. Even more, the day is dramatized by the idea of birth, John's birth in particular. As readers continue, they learn that the silence surrounding John's birthday symbolizes the "problem" with his birth and the nature of his relationship with his father. Yet, before the reader experiences the tension directly, Baldwin uses an introspective John to build more dimensionality into his personal struggle.

As John lies in bed, the struggle with familial invisibility is coupled with the remembrance that he has sinned. And it is this unique combination of invisibility and sin, of lovelessness and religion, that colors the first section of the novel. He remembers,

> He had sinned. In spite of the saints, his mother and his father, the warnings he had heard from his earliest beginnings, he had sinned with his hands a sin that was hard to forgive. In the school lavatory, alone, thinking of the boys, older, bigger, braver, who made bets with each other as to whose urine could arch higher, he had watched in himself a transformation of which he would never dare to speak.[10]

For John, his coming-of-age is marked by a complicated or complex transformation unearthing the death of boyhood and the birth of a different type of longing. Not only does he become man through the symbolic sexual act, he becomes or begins becoming a different iteration of man. The transformation alluded to in this passage is one of the first indications of how John's crisis is one of manhood and masculinity. The reference of "the boys, older, bigger, braver" is layered. On one hand, it is a simple capturing of a boy on the brink of adolescence, a mentioning of the natural process of budding masculinity; after all, boys are rarely cemented in the doctrines of American heterosexual manhood despite their many practices. There are always these elisions, these moments when young men bend ego, wonder, or competition into the space of the homosocial. When that bending dares a more intimate dance, it approximates the other way this moment must be read: as an expression of a subtle homoeroticism. John's guised masturbatory moment is stimulated by the thoughts of young men *playing* with their sexual organs and signals that John's announcement of the birth of his manhood might also be potent with silences around how it is constructed. Additionally, the shame John feels is not simply the consequence of religious indoctrination. The thinking of other boys is not necessarily suggestive of homosexuality or homoeroticism. For, as John wakes cloaked in the shame of his sin and burdened with the feeling of being forgotten, what he recalls to the reader is that, on this day marking a cross from boy to man, his transformation happened alone. There would be no witness to his new masculinity, no one to share how he has *grown*. This is precisely the crisis that he faces—Who will help him settle into this transformation? And more importantly, who will usher him the love that his new manhood demands?

John's morning turmoil is neither random nor unfounded. He quietly lets the reader know that he has suffered for quite some time under this distance from people, men in particular. His relationship with God is also affected. But it is not a self-induced distancing. The difference that he feels from other men, namely Gabriel, has influenced the ways in which he interacts with other people. He goes as far as to think, "For he had made his decision. He would not be like his father, or his father's fathers. He would have another life."[11] Gabriel's essence seeps through the eyes and heart of John. The latter's wanting to be unlike his father tells of an issue not named right away in the novel. It is to come later as the day unfolds and John moves closer toward a new male figure. Although the tension with Gabriel is yet unnamed, John's musings delineate the core of what he longs for as a boy on the cusp of manhood. Remembering how John was praised for being a stellar student, the narrator recalls when John's school principal commented on his good work,

> That moment gave him, from that time on, if not a weapon at least a shield; he apprehended totally, without belief or understanding, that he had in himself a power that other people lacked; that he could use this to save himself, to raise himself; and that, perhaps, with this power he might one day win that love which he so longed for.[12]

The principal's affirmation served a purpose beyond praise: it held the key to a self-awareness John would need for his own survival or ascension. What Baldwin names and John understands as "a power that other people lacked" engenders a space where John's relationship with himself becomes a site of empowerment. It also becomes a battleground, a site of war, where he will inevitably need to be saved, if not by himself, then by someone very unlike his father. This is the deep subtext that will thread all of Baldwin's works together—the push for love, the pursuit of male intimacy, the search for the fraternal, where we will find one of Baldwin's first symbols of salvific manhood.

Given how religion saturates the novel from title to its most memorable scene on the threshing floor, it is easy to understand why scholars preoccupy themselves with John's relationship with and resistance to God. What must be remembered, however, is that John's main struggle is not mediated by John's sinfulness and the self-cognizance that comes with that sin. That is, the novel does not pivot on John's relationship with God or religion. Rather, it is the space-in-between John and Gabriel that shapes, colors, and breathes life into the work. The unspoken tension between John and his father, the distance between these two men, is the proverbial fraternal crisis. This crisis might evoke the biblical Cain and Abel, but it is important to remember the familial positions the two men occupy. Instead, we might read this crisis as one that queers the biblical story of Noah and his son Ham. Like Ham's discovery of his father's nakedness, Baldwin's John renders Gabriel exposed in so many ways. The sight of John is a reminder of his indiscretions, his failures in manhood and spirituality. Thus, to understand John's quest into manhood and to understand the events of the novel both religious and secular, one must come to recognize the essence of this breakdown in male intimacy.

John unofficially begins his birthday with his family at the kitchen table. After easing out of bed, he stumbles into a conversation between his younger brother Roy and his mother Elizabeth. Quite interestingly, on John's day, the most gripping discussion is not John's crossing into manhood but instead one centered on Gabriel's expression of love. After Elizabeth comments that Gabriel's physical punishing of the children is an act of love, Roy retorts, "That ain't the kind of love I understand, old lady. What you reckon he'd do if he didn't love me?"[13] This moment particularly relates to John's immediate struggle. While addressing his stepfather, it informs the reader that he (John) is fated to wrestle with this notion of love and how he is loved. Gabriel's "kind of love" is marked by physical punishment and is therefore coupled with violence. Roy's resistance to such a violent love, while merited, inevitably pales in comparison to the sufferings of John. Gabriel's "kind of love" expresses its violence differently for the two boys. Essentially, the love Elizabeth is able to salvage from the physical act of punishment remains invisible in the case of John. It is an invisibility guaranteed by the absence of blood kinship, a familial riddle strong enough to divide father from son.

John's struggle with being forgotten continues with his Saturday morning chores. His cleaning the carpet is steeped with the symbolism of how he is being punished. It not only highlights the seeming insignificance of his birthday but also speaks to his helplessness within his father's home. Baldwin takes the reader into the mind and perhaps the heart of his young protagonist.

> John hated sweeping this carpet, for dust rose, clogging his nose and sticking to his sweaty skin, and he felt that should he sweep it forever, the clouds of dust would not diminish, the rug would not be clean. It became in his imagination his impossible, lifelong task, his hard trial, like that of a man he had read about somewhere, whose curse

it was to push a boulder up a steep hill, only to have the giant who guarded the hill roll the boulder down again—and so on, forever, throughout eternity.[14]

The mythological allusion here is neither coincidental nor desultory. John's empathy for Sisyphus extends beyond the eternality of hard labor. While the sweeping of the carpet does express his disdain for a persistent dirt, it also relays his feeling as to why he must sweep in the first place. From a Sisyphean perspective, John views his chore as a punishment, a task given because he disrespected or disobeyed a god. The god, in this case, would be Gabriel. The cosmological reference here is important. It once again reminds the reader that John's relationship with his father is intimately connected to his relationship with religion and God. More importantly, it exposes why John resists the power of God throughout the novel and magnifies his spiritual rebirth in the climax. The question for John and the reader is, "Why is he being punished?"

John's Sisyphean task envelops more than the oppressive nature of his daily chores. One must remember that Sisyphus was punished not solely for his trickery of the gods but primarily for his audacity to think himself equal or as clever. Ironically, John will succeed where Sisyphus failed. However, in the actual moment of this task, John has yet to realize his own power. In a Du Boisian sense, he suffers from a kind of double consciousness, "this sense of always looking at one's self through the eyes of others, of measuring one's soul by the tape of a world that looks on in amused contempt and pity."[15] John's perception of self is directly filtered through Gabriel's eyes. He does not see God within him and, while somewhat formed by the idea that he has sinned, this has more to do with how his father describes him physically. As he cleans, he cannot help but remember how "his father had always said that his face was the face of Satan—and was there not something—in the lift of the eyebrow, in the way his rough hair formed a V on his brow—that bore witness to his father's words?"[16] The physical allusion to Satan here solidifies John and Gabriel's tension, but it speaks to the metaphoric distance between them as well. More importantly, the reader learns how that distance is necessarily promoted by Gabriel, how his viewing of John causes both an intimate and physical divide. And as John struggled with his father's perception and lack of love, he began believing that "In [his] eye there was a light that was not the light of Heaven, and the mouth trembled, lustful and lewd, to drink deep of the wines of Hell."[17] This longing to taste the "wines of hell" does not adequately portray John's nature. He is, at this point in the novel, characterized as a pretty mild-mannered and well-behaved boy. But it does suggest that John is finding comfort in the opposition caused by Gabriel. In fact, Gabriel's distance, one finds, is pushing him further into a darkness where he expects to find what he cannot find at home.

It is, therefore, after he labors futilely, confronts the similarities of Satan within his face, and obtains sympathy from a mother who has not altogether forgotten his birthday that John begins the journey that will underwrite this project and mirror more closely the eternal struggle for peace. This search does not symbolically begin until he leaves home on his birthday. Moments before, Baldwin signals this journey: "Suddenly, sitting in the window, and with a violence unprecedented, there arose in John a flood of fury and tears, and he bowed his head, fists clenched against the windowpane, crying, with teeth on edge: 'What shall I do? What shall I do?'"[18] John's emotion, a mixture of anger and hurt, echoes the unavoidable crisis building within his spirit. After Elizabeth gives him his birthday money, he assures her, "Yes, Mama. I'm going to try to love the Lord."[19] He leaves home—body tired from cleaning, spirit restless from questioning, but in search of something that he himself cannot name.

John's journey into the public space amplifies the metaphoric distance between him and his father. After lusting for the tastes of hell, his temporary flirtation with the secular is another indicator that he is accepting the distance of Gabriel, that he is seeking something different. He thought, "In the narrow way, the way of the cross, there awaited him only humiliation forever; there awaited him, one day, a house like his father's house, and a church like his father's, and a job like his father's, where he would grow old and Black with hunger and toil."[20] His father's house must not be taken literally, though the tangible space of home does play into his longing for something different. By house, John means to meditate over the structures—social and psychical—wherein Gabriel can move. From home to church to job, John's reading of his father's mobility is one of lament and shame, one bequeathed by a generous and torturous racial past. But alas, the forbidden city offered a place where John "might eat and drink to his heart's content and clothe his body with wondrous fabrics, rich to the eye and pleasing to the touch."[21] John's conception of the religious life is eclipsed by his vision of Gabriel. His father, in essence, represents all associated with the godly lifestyle. In contrast, the secular realm extended different elements that would make him happy and, in a sense, allot him some degree of freedom. So, at the top of a hill in Central Park, John, a Black Sisyphus standing in respite from the eternal punishment promised by the godly Gabriel, contemplates power and love, perdition and freedom. He lets the reader know that he is not content with his father's house, not pleased by religion alone, and that something is missing.

Baldwin's young protagonist, and by extension his young self, leaves his reflective post on the hill and stumbles into the core of the secular realm. The hill, an analogy to the mountain of "Go Tell It on the Mountain," allows John to sing a new tune of birth, where the future might be a bit brighter. Amid his descent, he stumbles into an older and somewhat crippled white man. He "struggled to catch his breath and apologize, but the old man smiled. John smiled back. It was as though he and the old man had between them a great secret."[22] Juxtaposing this encounter with Gabriel's sentiments "that all white people were wicked," of how John "was a nigger, [who] would find out, as soon as he got a little older, how evil white people could be," evidences how John and Gabriel's distance continues to grow.[23] And while Gabriel might reduce the physical bumping between a young Black boy and an older white man to a clash of two worlds, Roger Rosenblatt renders it "a single moment in *Go Tell It on the Mountain* when a kind of love flickers."[24] Although Rosenblatt's choice of "love" might be a bit of a stretch here, he hints toward the change in tone within the narrative. There is a certain comfort that emanates from the pages in this scene, a spirit of peace or acceptance rarely witnessed in the earlier moments of the novel. And for the first time, John seems connected with another human being, albeit ephemerally. This human connection is transported into the movie theater, where John identifies with the young white woman on screen as he longs for the coldness she ushers into the world. Sitting in the movie theater, John struggles with his own personal sufferings; he tries to harden himself to the world that has come to reject him. Through his connection with the movie character, he works through his own vulnerabilities. "He wanted to be like her, only more powerful, more thorough, and more cruel; to make those around him, all who hurt him, suffer as she made the student suffer, and laugh in their faces when they asked pity for their pain."[25] Suspended in this moment of rationalized vindictiveness, John bears his hurt to the reader. One understands, more now than before, that the burden he carries is pressing down unbearably upon his young shoulders. Still, knowing what home has to offer, he understands that this secular and white world is not his own, that he must return to face the ugliness within his father's house.

The fraternal crisis that so clearly defines Baldwin's first novel reaches its boiling point when the protagonist, John, returns home to discover his younger brother Roy has been stabbed. In no other scene in this novel does the reader witness such a breakdown of kinship between Gabriel and John. This moment, definitive for so many reasons, emphasizes the imbalance of love suffered by the character who might need it most—John Grimes. Despite the fact that Roy brought the violent misfortune upon himself, that John's behavior is diametrically different, or that it is the latter's birthday, it is John who suffers from his father's wrath, hatred, and frustration. The marked difference in Gabriel's gentle nature with Roy and irrational temperament with John further illustrates the divide between the two warring men of the novel. For instance, Gabriel, characterized as a stern and harsh man previously within the narrative, displays a softer and more nurturing side to his biological, injured son. As Roy lies in pain, "His father muttered sweet, delirious things to [him], and his hands, when he dipped them again in the basin and wrung out the cloth, were trembling."[26] The beauty of Gabriel's gentleness here is inextricably tied to the ugliness that is to follow. That he is indeed capable of a caring hand, able to transfer love with a compassionate touch, betrays his inability to fully love John, perplexes the violence of his "kind of love." This is evident in the way in which he tends to Roy, almost obsessively—not allowing Elizabeth, the boy's mother, to carry out what is traditionally thought of as a maternal act. Unfortunately, one also recognizes how Gabriel's love has its limits, how he reserves such endearment for Roy. The undeserving John, meanwhile, feels the absence of his father's love and the presence of his anger.

Gabriel's tone of voice is the first symptom of the severity of his fraternal crisis with John. Unlike the tenderness exhibited toward the hurt Roy, Gabriel proves unrelenting and unjustifiably unforgiving of John. As Baldwin writes, it was not only Gabriel's words or tone but also his face that caused discomfort within John.[27] For the first time, perhaps, John witnesses a truth his father cannot suppress, sees the true feelings of his father through his facial expression and the timbre of his voice. More importantly, John understands the reason for the space-in-between him and his father; he, in a sense, "saw now what he had never seen there before, except in his own vindictive fantasies: a kind of wild, weeping terror that made the face seem younger, and yet at the same time unutterably older and more cruel. And John knew, in the moment his father's eyes swept over him, that he hated John because John was not lying on the sofa where Roy lay."[28] John's epiphany conjures an epistemic stillness for the reader. The shared realization between John and reader renders a bit of emotional immobility, and while one has been privy to the truth of John's bastardy, John's awareness of his father's disconnect unsettles the prospect of hope. John's knowledge of how his father's hatred is rooted in a perverse wishing for John as scapegoat, for John to bear the cross Gabriel knew so well, for John to inherit the spoiled promise of American democracy that Black father is to pass to Black son, reveals how desperately Gabriel wants to save Roy and how, heartbreakingly, he does not wish to do the same for John. The unsettling continues as Gabriel digs deeper into the emptiness of John, telling Elizabeth, "You can tell that foolish *son* of yours something . . . him standing there with them big buckeyes. You can tell him to take this like a warning from the Lord. *This* is what white folks does to niggers." Gabriel's tirade is particularly telling in this scene. Ostensibly, his issues with race relations and whiteness are exhaled through his cautionary speech. His hate, the byproduct of enduring a life of racial absurdity, becomes reproduced and repackaged as a new offering for his family. Drawing attention to John's "buckeyes" collapses the protagonist into the author, conjures Baldwin from his own words while also speaking to the extent to which John has a capacity for sight greater than, and ugly to, his father. It also foregrounds Gabriel's prayers and his own existential struggles. Most relevantly, however, this outburst congeals the divide he holds with his son John, a divide that leads John to self-questioning, introspection, and a need to be saved.

Gabriel's misplaced anger confirms John's uneasiness. The attack on John's physicality, specifically his eyes, concretizes John's fears of ugliness in a way that only furthers the divide between the two. In "Conversion, the Self, and Ugliness," Hardy reminds the reader that "To be ugly in Baldwin's world is to be without love—in isolation from others; it is to live a life where there is only self-hate. In this world, ugliness becomes the physical manifestation of self-loathing. It represents the unattractiveness of a shame that distorts people's perceptions of themselves as they relate to the outside world."[29] Indeed, Gabriel's critique of John's physical self materializes into a painful double-consciousness. John questions not only his manhood but also his right to be loved. One sees this earlier in the novel when John bemoans his nakedness on the mantelpiece, ashamed to have himself bared to the world. Furthermore, one reads it within this textual juncture. Gabriel's disdain, his projection of anger, and his irrationality translate into a rejection John does not fully understand.

John's struggle thus becomes a product of his confusion. He cannot understand, due to an ignorance of his bloodline, why his father hates him so passionately. Consequently, he "examines himself in vain for the unaccountable blemish that could be the cause of his rejection. He finds part of the explanation in his own shortcomings; his Oedipus complex, his desire to leave the ghetto, the intelligence which singles him out, his resentment toward his father."[30] John's discovery is fragmentary in nature, for the explanation cannot be merely reduced to his Oedipus complex, longing for a life outside of poverty, or the intelligence and resentment separating him from his father. There is more to his father's refusal, more to be uncovered if one is to understand why Gabriel does not welcome reconciliation. Instead, he relegates John to a life devoid of fatherly love and ripe with isolation, where John is plagued by "the loneliness of the unloved, of the thinker who is set apart from the rest of his kind by the fact that he lives mainly in his own head, of the user of words, of the good boy whose goodness is measured by the fact that he does nothing that is not good; the loneliness of the bastard-outcast."[31] It is a peculiar state of being for John, to be a bastard without knowledge, to be hated for something beyond one's cognizance and control. And yet, we wonder how Gabriel arrives at this point, and we must be careful not to reduce the fraternal crisis to a simple defect in his personality. To be certain, the true question is not whether Gabriel is ugly toward his stepson John but "why" he is ugly. The answer to this query complicates the notion of fraternal crisis and purposes the prayers voiced within Baldwin's first novel.

The tense exchange between John and Gabriel surrounding Roy's injury should solidify a certain disdain for the father figure. However, despite Gabriel's misplaced cruelty, the reader cannot completely write him off as a bad character. This is largely due to how Baldwin couches Gabriel's hatred in historical remembrance and cultural context. Ironically, one searches for a deeper reason for his dysfunction, tries to understand why he is unable to love a very lovable young man. One asks, in the same questioning voice of Colin MacInnes, "How is it that it is impossible to loathe—even despise— Gabriel?"[32] Simply put, one understands his hatred is not directly personal, that it stems from a greater phenomenon and not just a desire to make John's life unbearable. One forgives him, in essence, "because he suffers and—worst of all suffering—endures its agonies without enlightenment. And then, though pride in a general way may be detestable . . . one cannot but respect—if not admire—his pride: it is so total and so terrible in its effects on him."[33] Indeed, Gabriel's emotional incompatibility with John, his unwillingness to father him with the same nurturing hand or spirit extended to Roy, has less to do with John and is more reflective of a past he has not fully resolved. Gabriel represents a certain stern religiosity characteristic of a midcentury Black religious tradition, but he also embodies "a man victimized and burdened by the sins of his past. The South—'the blood stained land'—is the scene of his personal fall from the glory of God as well as the space in which his embattled Black manhood has been so ruthlessly socialized."[34] To be clear, the fraternal crisis is rooted in a time predating

John's birth and can be traced to a space much farther south geographically and culturally. John's dilemma therefore becomes greater than his present and is comprehensible through the prayers of Florence and Gabriel.

Gabriel's problem with paternity does not begin with his northern New York family. It is compounded by personal historical baggage first unpacked within Florence's prayer. As she stands in the sanctuary, vulnerable to the mercy of God, she recounts her childhood and reminds the reader of how misfortune befell her family. Born to a mother who knew plantation life intimately, the Grimes children were reared in a racially hostile South. African Americans bore no dignity for white countrymen who took pleasure in the raping, lynching, and castration of Black bodies. Undoubtedly, this made growing up as Black and male a particularly difficult task during Gabriel's adolescent years. Couple the racial disharmony of the time with the reality of how Florence's desire to escape the South mirrored that of her father, who "had departed that way one morning not many months after the birth of Gabriel."[35] While little textual space is dedicated to Gabriel's father, his absence is noteworthy, for in the somewhat dated epistemologies of Black family, the absence of the father weighs heavily on the upbringing of a *man-child*. Inevitably, Gabriel's juvenile acts of rebellion and delinquent expressivity, his irresponsibility and male privilege, indicate his own search for a father, one that he would later find in the rigid cosmology of Christianity.

Gabriel's search for a father is an interesting precursor to John's quest for fraternity. The difference lies in their different perceptions and appreciations of religion. For Gabriel, the religion of the South was too strongly tied to racial oppression and the institution of slavery. It symbolized how Blacks were rendered impotent by white exploitation and violence. The scene of his baptism profoundly captures his fierce grappling with religious power and addresses a fundamental internal struggle that extends beyond a straightforward discussion of religion:

> He was slowly led into the river, where he had so often splashed naked, until he reached the preacher. And the moment that the preacher threw him down, crying out the words of John the Baptist, Gabriel

began to kick and sputter, nearly throwing the preacher off balance; and though at first they thought that it was the power of the Lord that worked in him, they realized as he rose, still kicking and with his eyes tightly shut, that it was only fury.[36]

Gabriel's fury, and by extension his struggle against baptism, reveals a fear and resistance to the systems and structures of control prominent within an American South dancing on the heels of Reconstruction. Symbolically, he fights fervently against being submerged under a regime of Black powerlessness and subjection to "white" sovereignty. At this stage in Gabriel's youth, religion is merely metonymic for a hierarchy of domination and inferiority, an idea easily traceable within his discourse on whiteness throughout the novel. It is not until he believes himself capable of harnessing such power that his attitude toward theology changes. He realizes in a moment of great weakness how religion may hold the Father for which he searches.

Gabriel's search for a father reaches its end in the moment of his weakest hour. Unable to endure the fruitlessness of his corrupt life, unable to suffer through the continuous lack of fulfillment, he finds himself alone in the wilderness and under the darkness of self-reflection. Standing at a familiar tree, one symbolic of the very tree in the biblical story of the Garden of Eden, "He faced the lone tree, beneath the naked eye of Heaven."[37] And like the tree, within the quietness of nature, he was cognizant of his own loneliness, of how isolated he was as a boy without a father or a foreseeable future, as a Black man without love in the brutal reality of the South. Here, he witnessed his own existential break, the point in life when the state of being alone is too much to bear. There was no one there to hold him, no voice to ease his suffering mind. Yet, within this valley of weakness, he sought his Father:

He felt that this silence was God's judgment; that all creation had been stilled before the just and awful wrath of God, and waited now to see the sinner—*he* was the sinner—cut down and banished from the presence of the Lord. And he touched the tree, hardly knowing that he touched it, out of an impulse to be hidden; and then he cried: "Oh, Lord, have mercy! Oh, Lord, have mercy on me!"[38]

His cry for mercy extends beyond a desire for religion. The plea for mercy is a cry for salvation. And not the mythical longing to be forgiven for sins or transgressions. No, this cry is the supplication of a man who knows that he is at the lowest part of life; he knows that if someone or something does not *save* him, his existential crisis will end tragically. The silent pursuit of God, the lonely reach for his Father, is a desperate attempt to save himself. For as Gabriel bears himself under this tree, his supplication does not spring from a selfless hope to be a shepherd for others; his prayer is not to become messenger. Rather it is, and must be seen as, a hopeful quest to save himself. He is crying for salvation.

The irony of Gabriel's breakdown at the tree reflects the purpose of this project. It captures the Black male's need for vulnerability and emotionality coupled with the rare space where the need can be satisfied. Essentially, Gabriel's quest is no different from John's. In his youth he too longed for an intimacy strong enough to compliment his manhood. One must remember that his life was not devoid of love or compassion: his mother and the troubled Deborah bestowed unconditional love upon him. However, the love of women is not enough, at least for Baldwin. For the latter, there is something particular about Black manhood, something that requires a different type of intimacy, a peculiar form of love. This may be due to the complexity of American masculinity or Baldwin's personal draw to maleness. Regardless, Gabriel's search for God is a testament to this fact. Only in the silence and solitude is he able to bear himself, to peel back the hardness of his manhood and open his heart to salvation.

> "I wept," he said later, "like a little child." But no child had ever wept such tears as he wept that morning on his face before Heaven. . . . They came from deeps no child discovers, and shook him with an ague no child endures. . . . He was screaming, each cry seeming to tear his throat apart, and stop his breath, and force the hot tears down his face, so that they splashed his hands and wet the root of the tree: "Save me! Save me!"[39]

His vulnerability seems uncharacteristic, especially given how he treats John and Roy as the men expected to follow in his footsteps. But it also keeps the reader from completely despising him as a male figure within the novel. There is a gentleness in his catharsis which inadvertently softens him and portrays a deeper humanity. More importantly, this emotional exchange with God highlights how emotion and intimacy are profoundly connected to Black men's search for salvation. Inevitably, Gabriel's connection with his cosmological Father is emblematic of man's search for male intimacy. It suggests that Baldwin, while appreciative of the role of women, understood fraternity as transformative, particularly for young boys burdened by a world incessantly bent on the literal and metaphoric emasculation and castration of Black men. Gabriel's cry to God is but a search for love, a love endowed with the redemptive power of manhood.

If one takes Baldwin's words to be literal, and there is no reason not to do so, it is after this emotional bonding with God that Gabriel begins "his life as a man."[40] Baldwin is careful and sincere in this textual space. Gabriel's newfound manhood, while perhaps reducible to an idea of being born into a new Christian self, immediately follows a poignant emotional purging. The tree, and the silent nature that surrounds it, carved salvation into a space necessary for Gabriel's figurative crossing. Furthermore, the prospect of redemption required the presence of *maleness*, figuratively textualized as the spiritual presence of God. God, as Father, becomes the only entity able to save Gabriel's weary soul. From the time of his spiritual rebirth, Gabriel moves by the mantra, "Order my steps in your Word." His critique of his Elders in the faith, of God's male ministers, stems from his own relationship with salvation. To him, they no longer maintained the balance between savior and sinner; they "had been in the field so long that they did not tremble before God any more."[41] His reduction of character to a measure of "trembling" iterates the fragility of men who have been saved. He, so new to the cloth, still suffers the shakes of a newborn who thought itself near death. To tremble is but to remember that the power one now enjoys, the manhood through which one speaks, was a gift bestowed by someone or something willing to hear one's cry. These men had been men so long they forgot their power passed through the hands of another, namely, their Father. And yet this is the lesson that Gabriel must come to remember throughout the novel; he too will let the seasoning of his manhood (religious self) dilute his memory of how important it is to love. The love given by his Father will be eclipsed by the very power it enables. He, as *Go Tell It* shows us, will lose the capacity for Fatherly love.

Gabriel's incapacity for fatherly love surfaces through his antipaternity. This is not to suggest an inability to become father or an antagonism toward fathers; rather, by antipaternity I mean to identify how Gabriel is unwilling to father his sons by blood or marriage. Ultimately, the antipaternalism leads to a fraternal crisis, a breakdown between Gabriel and the younger men of his life, namely John and Royal. The symbolic space-in-between these men, while largely due to Gabriel's nature, may also be viewed as a consequence outside of his control. For instance, as stated previously, Gabriel's male distance may be attributable to the lack of a father figure during his childhood or his soiled relationships with the elder men of faith. After all, how can he expect to showcase a love that he was never given himself? Despite these plausibilities, other scholars attribute his emotional coldness to his relationship with religion in general. In assessing Gabriel's relationship with his son John, Fabre draws upon the traditional strictures of Old Testament Christianity in arguing, "Mutual love is forbidden, it seems, as much by virtue of psychological fatality, holiness as opposed to happiness, as by a divine order, the saint being in reality a damned soul."[42] Within the "old" logic of Christian religiosity, the saint's love is usurped by the demands of his or her deity. Holiness precludes reciprocation of love unless God is the recipient. In essence, Gabriel's relationships with his sons are mediated by his relationship with his Heavenly Father. Again, the reader sees the metalanguage of paternity as God's *fatherhood* affects the ways in which his son builds relationships with other men.

Other scholars read Gabriel's relationship with religion differently. Instead of it reflecting the strongholds of religious practice, for Sondra O'Neale, the relationship captures how the "schism between white-practiced Christianity and Black American art was always axiomatically present."[43] Her reading of religion in *Go Tell It on the Mountain* pivots on the idea that "Baldwin should be seen as the last Black American writer to exploit as a major theme the Black man's relationship with Christianity. Conversely, he may be considered the first Black American writer to distance himself from the lone enduring Black institution, the Black church . . . by his overtly persistent portrayal of its lack of authentic Christian commitment."[44] O'Neale's criticism conflates the role of religion in the novel with the role of religion within Baldwin's life. While this is plausible, I argue that it has more to do with the unspoken tension between Gabriel and John and not that between Baldwin and the church. Their fraternal crisis parallels Baldwin's tension with his devoutly religious stepfather, but it also speaks to Baldwin's struggle to expand the notion of Christian love, not necessarily to assert a new "human love" outside of its parameters. This precisely accounts for part of John's rejection of Gabriel's God and his inevitable acceptance of a different (still very Christian) theology later on in the novel. For this reason, Baldwin is not distancing himself from the church per se; he is simply removing the crumbling bricks from the discriminating walls. Viewed under this light, *Go Tell It* becomes more than the story of John and his quest for love; it serves to show Gabriel's need for redemption.

Baldwin's Gabriel is complicated by the realities of Southern racial oppression, the centrality of Black religious institutions, and the innate humanity of individuals. At any point within the novel, he is caught between a perverse Kantian ethic, where his action is dictated by a moral law transcendent of his own rationality, and the emotional compulsion of humanity, the will to violate the religious doctrine of the day. In other words, he is "a man of strong emotions torn between the demands of the flesh and those of the spirit. His tragedy (or pathos) is that he can neither reconcile those demands nor live without reconciling them. His dilemma produces, alternately, denial, rage, and projection onto others of his flaws."[45] Gabriel's struggle, then, alongside echoing his need or possibility for redemption, reveals how "Baldwin argues for an acceptance of and tolerance for human weakness over moral purity, in part because purity is not possible in a fallen world."[46] And this subtle challenge to Christian romanticism is part of Baldwin's agenda as he writes the fraternal crisis as the consequence of Gabriel's blind devotion. More important, Gabriel must be flawed so that Baldwin can magnify the cracks within the religious tradition so responsible for his voice. Through Gabriel's failures and shortcomings, and through using him as a metonym for Christian thought, Baldwin identifies a root of human crises, particularly those existing between men.

For Baldwin, Gabriel's fall is a necessary one, not only to illuminate experiences from his personal childhood but also because *Go Tell It*'s novelistic success depends on it. From a literary standpoint, Baldwin must exploit Gabriel's flaws as he delineates the breakdown that happens with John. If readers are to understand the fraternal crisis, they must recognize why John's father is so reluctant to love him. Through the prayers, this all becomes clear as one understands Gabriel's need for redemption. Again, we are unable to dismiss his character due to how the crisis is inextricably linked to the emptiness that he battles. The reader sympathizes, albeit temporarily, in knowing that "he stands in need of deliverance from himself. He preaches his sermons, makes love to his prostitutes, and marries his women—all for the convenience of the moment. He is incapable of pursuing his own quest for identity . . . because he has lost touch with humanity."[47] The problem, therefore, is found within Gabriel and not John. By extension, the space-in-between men is carved by an unresolved issue of identity within the father figure, the unrest of a deep-seated longing. Perhaps this is the greatest of Gabriel's flaws throughout the novel, that inability to feel a connection of love with those closest to him. And while the women, namely Florence and Elizabeth, suffer from his emotional detachment too, "the most glaring evidence of this shortcoming is nowhere more obvious than in his failure to establish a genuine relationship with his two sons."[48] Inevitably, it is John who carries the burden of his father's shortcoming. His younger brother Roy does not express the same type of longing for male love. However, John's ignorance of his father's history precludes the possibility of understanding, as it might have changed his perceptions for better or for worse. If he had known how his father failed early on as a father, perchance he would have rechanneled his hatred.

What John failed to know would hurt him, and that was that Gabriel had fallen in multiple ways in the life he lived before moving north. After giving his life to Christ, becoming a faithful servant of the Lord, and solidifying his obeisance by marrying a somewhat dejected woman (Deborah), his godliness was tested and it failed: "So he had fallen: for the first time since his conversion, for the last time in his life. Fallen: he and Esther in the white folks' kitchen, the light burning, the door half-open, grappling and burning beside the sink. Fallen indeed: time was no more, and sin, death, Hell, the judgment were blotted out."[49] Here, in this passage, Baldwin continuously deploys the word "fallen" in an effort to emphasize how this godly man has fallen short of that moral purity discussed earlier. His reiteration is not meant to alert the reader to Gabriel's hypocrisy; rather, he hopes to capture how romantic notions of Christianity prevent the "imperfection" of humanity. Additionally, the trope of visibility appears pervasively in this scene; the act of performing it within a space racialized as white as opposed to the marginally invisible spaces of Black people, the presence of light, and the open door all speak to the nakedness of Gabriel's humanity. Baldwin's intention is for the reader to "see" the true essence of John's father. Nevertheless, despite the textuality of Gabriel's adultery, this is neither Gabriel's gravest sin nor his greatest fall: "Most strangely, and from deeps not before discovered, his faith looked up; before the wickedness that he saw, the wickedness from which he fled, he yet beheld like a flaming standard in the middle of the air, that power of redemption to which he must, till death, bear witness."[50] He was redeemed in his faith, and it carried him away from the shame that tugged at his soul. No, he took refuge in the sanctity of his marriage and convinced himself that "their married bed would be holy, and their children would continue the line of the faithful, a royal line."[51] Yet, his faith-garnered peace did not "forgive him his transgressions" and did not save him from the seeds he had sown.

Gabriel's night of sinful pleasure begot him a son with Esther. But after hearing this, knowing that God forgave him for his adulterous act, he could not bear the truth of such news. Consequently, Esther goes north silently, vowing to make her bastard son a better man than his shameful father. She dies sometime after, the boy is sent to live with her family back in the South, and Gabriel watches "his son grow up, a stranger to his father and a stranger to God."[52] Even more, Gabriel's son's physical proximity, coupled with the symbolism of his name, Royal, consistently mocks God's minister. This is evident in one of the earliest encounters between the two where, coming across the young boy playing with others in the street, "Gabriel, wishing to smile down into the boy's face, to pause and touch him on the forehead, did none of these things, but walked on. Behind him, he heard

Wrestling for Salvation   43

Royal's explosive whisper: 'I bet he got a mighty big one!'"[53] Royal's sexual quip is at once a confession of male adolescence as well as an ironic play on Gabriel's manhood. Moreover, the utterance becomes subversive when Gabriel hears it, for the potential mightiness of his *manhood* is undermined by the reality of his antipaternity. As Royal grows, so does Gabriel's predisposition to fraternal crisis; his antipaternal nature evolves to the point of mirroring the elders he once critiqued. One notices the stronghold of antipaternity through how difficult it is for Gabriel to speak to Royal. For instance, in a moment capturing the racial tension of the South, the two men encounter each other on the unsafe streets and "Gabriel could not speak at once; he struggled to get his breath."[54] Silence, or rather the struggle to speak, connotes on a deeper level how that small aperture separating father from son grew into a profound space-in-between men. The bloodline connecting them has long dissipated by the time of this last meeting, and all Gabriel can hope to offer is that divine fraternal love he preaches about every Sunday. Unfortunately, be it the provinciality of his faith or the bastion of his ego, he does not even offer Royal that, and a couple of years later his firstborn is dead. Deborah, the lone figure in the novel unable to give life, becomes the bearer of death. While discussing the heavy heart of the boy's grandmother, she drops the news of his murder. Gabriel, unable to muster that peace so reflective of his character, "began to cry, not making a sound, sitting at the table, and with his whole body shaking. . . . Then it seemed that there was weeping everywhere, waters of anguish riding the world."[55] His cries are both inevitable and telling: they represent the overwhelming emotionality of the situation as well as Gabriel's hidden humanity. More important, Royal's death is didactic in that it captures Baldwin's fear regarding the absence of male intimacy and fraternal love. To be clear, men, particularly Black men, who are unable to forge intimate connections with other men, often fall victim to tragic fates. Such is the lesson here and in many narratives written by Baldwin. And the question becomes, How does Baldwin negotiate John's need for salvation and Gabriel's inability to save?

The reader is also emotionally affected in this moment, but not singularly by Royal's death or Gabriel's catharsis. No, the reader must ask, What will become of John? Knowing that tragedy possibly awaits the boy denied his father's love and knowing that John bears no bloodline to carry his father's love to him (as is the case with Roy), Baldwin introduces another route to salvation. If John is to avoid falling victim to a tragic fate, he must search for the fraternal elsewhere, for Gabriel's history with Royal and his favoritism with Roy reveals that he is unable or unwilling to give John the love he seeks.

Immediately following the incident surrounding Roy's misfortune, John finds himself at the church, attempting to work through the realization that his father Gabriel does not love him as he needs to be loved. Ironically, the church serves as a space of refuge, a place where he can cleanse the day's disappointments from his wearied soul. And despite John's antagonism toward religion or Gabriel's God, the church functions as a transformative space, a necessary end to his search for the fraternal. As memoirist, Baldwin uses the religious institution to work through his autobiographical narrative and to prioritize the significance of Black cultural space. However, as artist, he uses the church as a metaphoric space for reconstitution. Baldwinian *salvation* extends beyond the Christian context and necessarily touches upon humanity's capacity and responsibility to *save*. For this reason, the church symbolically delineates Baldwin's agenda by textualizing all human interactions within this "holy" cloak of human obligation. He is fundamentally preoccupied with the well-being of John's manhood and less concerned with John becoming a man of the cloth, though this is important. Regardless of its autobiographic or artistic purpose, the church in *Go Tell It* affords John the opportunity to find the male love he could not find at home.

Male intimacy first appears for John through Elisha. Elisha represents a younger antithesis of Gabriel but also the image of Christian godliness. Even more, he represents a redemption for John from lovelessness. If John's relationship to Gabriel evokes the biblical story of Noah and Ham, then his relationship with Elisha speaks readily to the biblical narrative of David and Jonathan. Framed through this biblical sensibility, John and Elisha's fraternal bond gives way to the redemptive power of love. More specifically, this male-to-male love, cloaked within the ritualistic play of young manhood, offers up a new logic of salvation. And we must accept this truth of John's journey. If *Go Tell It* is read as bildungsroman, if it is read through the inevitable conflicts of social geography through the North and South migration narratives, or as an endeavor into the tensions born of generational difference, beneath it all, it centers on a quest for love that will be delivered through a Baldwinian intimacy. Indeed, aside from Gabriel's fleeting moment of tenderness with Roy, there is no "flickering of love," and if Roger Rosenblatt is right, "until the end of the novel, when John discovers the beginnings of brotherly love in Elisha, there is no other occurrence filled with as much pure affection."[56] Rosenblatt's categorization of John and Elisha's love, keeping with the religiosity of Baldwin's text, evokes the notion of brotherhood as commonly used within Christian discourse. Nevertheless, anyone who reads the intimacy of their exchanges understands how something is brewing beneath the textual surface. Their brotherhood, while grounded in a Christian ethic, also rises above it in its appeal to human emotionality and tenderness as opposed to religious or moral law. It is reconstituted as something not uniquely religious but peculiarly human. In a sense, its transformative essence is channeled through Elisha, whose very presence and voice have a profound effect on John's disposition. Or as Baldwin communicates, John "felt unaccustomedly bold and lighthearted; the arrival of Elisha had caused his mood to change."[57] For the first time in *Go Tell It*, John seems genuinely happy in someone else's company, and, perhaps for this reason, critics focus so heavily on that relationship.

The seeming homoeroticism within John's relationship with Elisha pervades many critics' analyses of *Go Tell It on the Mountain*. Arguing that Baldwin uses this brotherhood as a way to indirectly work through his own sexuality, scholars are likely to view the religious bond as a guise for a more sexual impulse. Some, like Bryan Washington, go as far as to say that *Go Tell It* is a "novel that will not (cannot) articulate homosexual desire" while ignoring the metasexual push for the fraternal, whereas others argue that the work performs "a crucial discursive task by suggesting the possibility (if not viability) of Black men's same-sex relationships."[58] Washington misses, along with those quick to dichotomize the novel's relationships into being either heterosexual or homosexual, the queering of human sexuality performed by Baldwin's work. This is to suggest that while John's relationship with Elisha "contrasts sharply with the presentation of heterosexuality in the novel", it also distinguishes itself from relationships so easily classified as homosexual.[59] Certainly, homoeroticism factors heavily into the novel and into this relationship in particular, but how does it function?

In "The Reclamation of the Homoerotic as Spiritual in *Go Tell It on the Mountain*," Margo Crawford uncovers the ways in which queer sexuality factors prominently within Baldwin's novel, but she does so without a diminutive reading of same-sex relationships.[60] Nuancing the intricacies of the father–son relationship through a lens that couples queer expressions of intimacy with spirituality, she not only underscores how Gabriel's relationship with John functions as a metalanguage of paternity but also reveals the slipperiness of the homoerotic in *Go Tell It*. Accordingly, "the homoeroticism between this young boy, John, and another young Black male, Elisha, is the brotherly love set against the traumatic relationship between the father figure and the son."[61] Within this idea, Baldwin's grappling with sexuality becomes both personal and purposed as homosexuality evolves from a simple state of being to a method of becoming. Inevitably, John's relationship with Elisha emerges as a symbolic riposte to his failing relationship with his father. And the reader, keenly aware of the sexual tension between the two characters (at least on John's end), must additionally recognize Baldwin's other preoccupation within this moment. Above anything else, while John basks in the iridescent light of a newfound masculinity, the two together capture how the space-in-between men is often reconciled through a symbolic wrestling, a wrestling where men must fight for the intimacy that their spirits long to possess.

The proverbial wrestling scene in *Go Tell It on the Mountain* has more often than not been reduced to a homoerotic tussling. This is largely due to Baldwin's imagery and the intrusion of autobiography into the novel. Descriptive language lends itself to symbolic interpretation as the male exchange escapes the heteronormativity so characteristic of young adolescent masculinity. Speaking of Elisha, Baldwin subtly inserts the forceful sensuality attributable to male virility. For instance, at the initial stage of wrestling, "With both arms tightening around John's waist [Elisha] tried to cut John's breath, watching him meanwhile with a smile that . . .

became a set, ferocious grimace."[62] Illustrating the physical seriousness of the exchange, Baldwin uses words that also function in sexual play. Elisha's "tightening" arms evoke, perhaps perversely, images of contracting muscles, and his convenient position around John's waist adds to the sexual imagery. Furthermore, the buildup of intensity as indicated through the travel from a smile to a grimace hints toward the escalation of sexual energy. Baldwin continues this purposeful elision of nonsexual boyhood with homoerotic sport by coupling anatomic words like "biceps," "shoulders," and "belly" with sexually suggestive verbs like "thrust" and "squirmed." Nevertheless, the most profound innuendo comes from John's rise in power, where he "was filled with a determination not to be conquered, or at least to make the conquest dear."[63] Here, Baldwin capitalizes on the power dynamics prevalent within sexual practice and discourse. John's resistance against being "conquered," when viewed in the context of his sexual awakening, connotes an aggressive proclamation of manhood, a manhood that is not developed enough to do the conquering. The quiet submissiveness embedded within John's struggle reflects male resistance to vulnerability while also hinting toward the internalized heterosexism widespread within queer communities of color. To be conquered would mean to be out-*man*ned, not to be simply outmatched physically. John and Elisha's struggle thus becomes a struggle for male position and, by extension, sexual privilege. John has not fully negotiated his manhood in an all-male intercourse. Nevertheless, despite the strong presence of sexuality, the wrestling match transcends both the physical and sexual to become a metaphoric representation of John's search for the *fraternal.*

John's wrestle with Elisha on the church floor is seductively homoerotic and offers itself to a myriad of queer readings. Was this Baldwin's "coming-out" moment; was he attempting to voice the quiet parts of his sexual being? Undoubtedly, a part of this text hints toward Baldwin's personal wrestling with sexuality and advances a case for same-sex intimacy. But what else is going on within this male interaction and lies buried beneath the surface? After expending energy and time trying to conquer and not be conquered, the boys find themselves at a physical impasse. In an instance, they are suspended in each other's embrace, wrapped so tightly in each other's masculinity that it becomes "a deadlock; [Elisha] could not tighten his hold, John could not break it. And so they turned, battling in the narrow room, and the odor of Elisha's sweat was heavy in John's nostrils. He saw the veins rise on Elisha's forehead and in his neck; his breath became jagged and harsh, and the grimace on his face became more cruel; and John, watching these manifestations of his power, was filled with a wild delight."[64] The language in this scene is suggestive of many things. On one hand, it continues to iterate inclinations toward homosexuality, while on the other, it carves out a space for male intimacy that reaches beyond constricting constructions of sexuality. The deadlocking of John and Elisha approximates the Bible's tale of David and Jonathan. While John and Gabriel's fraternity is undeniably shaped by a symbolic space-in-between them, for John and Elisha, such a space is removed, if not an impossibility. Where Noah would curse his son for the witnessing of nakedness, Jonathan offers his to David without discomfort: "And Jonathan stripped himself of the robe that was upon him, and gave it to David, and his garments, even to his sword, and to his bow, and to his girdle."[65] Elisha's metaphoric nakedness upon the church's floor moves from his willingness to engage John—so closely in the flesh. Literally, he participates in the removal of space often characterizing fraternal crisis and, more symbolically, begins to situate himself as a redemptive force in John's life, a trace of salvific manhood. For Baldwin, John is not simply working through an existential crisis of sexuality; he is wrestling with a crisis in manhood. He discovers in his vigorous fighting with Elisha a capacity for *fraternity* in excess of Christian brotherhood. His struggle, emblematic through words such as "power," "cruel," "exasperate," "battling," et cetera, is symptomatic of an internal war with manhood/masculinity. While his "fight" is with Elisha, one remembers how he has just engaged in a symbolic war with his stepfather Gabriel. A war that, predicated on a prize of love, he lost. However, with his subsequent battle, he is able to conjure strength and power where he could not before, is able to push and pound against Elisha's manhood.

Baldwin colors the exchange with a physical intensity preventing a reductive reading of human sexuality. If, and this is a priori, Baldwin sought only to capture the possibility of homosexual relationships, the wrestling match might have been a bit more delicate. Instead, it is rife with "violent" imagery, indicating a more serious battle for John. I am not suggesting that his relationship with his sexuality is not tumultuous; rather, I hope to illustrate how, in addition to issues of same-sex attraction, Baldwin is playing with a notion of nonsexual male intimacy. As the boys become deadlocked, as they are unable to tighten or break their holds on each other, they are symbolically held together—through a bond that is, similar to Christian brotherhood, unbreakable. And this is what defines John's ultimate search: a space where he can be both vulnerable and strong in his manhood, where the shackles of society's perceptions loosen their hold on Black masculinity and intimacy. He locates in Elisha the fraternal element lacking in his relationship with Gabriel, discovers that gentle masculinity so desperately longed for and witnessed between Gabriel and Roy. Baldwin punctuates Elisha's importance through his employment of this homoerotic fraternalism and by "[exploring] the 'funny child['s] desire for Elisha, [he] locates a homoerotic spirituality that emerges as a liberation theology, one that inveighs against the racism and homophobia in the religious doctrine John has inherited."[66] Inevitably, Elisha's character emerges at John's cross-roads to establish itself, within the metaphoric space of the church, as one endowed with a salvific manhood.

Baldwin intentionally has the most intimate scene of the novel take place in the church. By doing so, he evokes all of the meanings associated with the Black religious tradition and his own relation to Christianity. As a space, the church signifies salvation and carries with it the possibility of spiritual cleansing. Incidentally, this coincides with John's personal mission to be cleansed from the spiritual turmoil of his father by finding someone able to act as an agent of salvation and also perform an act of reconstitution. Free-dom, in the sense of self-expression, is sanctioned within the walls of the religious institution as evidenced by the ways in which Baldwin describes the various activities. According to Byerman, "The church gives the body and its movements a freedom that is forbidden outside its boundaries. The young (and old) bodies kept under surveillance by the preacher and his minions are allowed full expression when within the gaze, and thus control, of church authorities."[67] His claim is inherently contradictory, as the "full expression" of freedom cannot possibly coexist when regulated by a Foucauldian gaze. Surveillance, authority, and control automatically undermine individual expression and give the illusion of autonomy in the presence of dependency. Nevertheless, his understanding of the church as a freeing space connects wonderfully with Baldwin's subtext, where John and Elisha's physical interaction on the church floor reveals a full expression of manhood.

Byerman's observation also substantiates the idea of physical freedom in arguing that "Physicality, even to the point of something like orgasm, is not so much denied as directed toward the purposes of the church."[68] In this regard, the church functions as a necessary end for John's search for the fraternal. It serves as a site for confrontation in that individuals are able to work out their personal conflicts under the auspices of religious governance. Sin acts as a marker of individual struggle and "serves as the mechanism that brings 'the sinner' before the altar in an act of contrition that subverts the power dynamics of relationships between fathers and sons . . . saints and sinners, and saved and unsaved—relationships that are constantly being produced and reproduced in cultural and familial contexts."[69] For Baldwin and his protagonist John, sin is a metaphor for individual crisis, a signifier of disconnect or dilemma. It does not necessarily embody a negative essence nor does it relate to a violation of religious tenets. Instead, it functions as a liaison between he who suffers—the "sinner"—and that which cleanses—"the church."

Religion and the church, then, perform a symbolic role in *Go Tell It on the Mountain*. They must not be taken up in their literal representations lest the reader miss part of Baldwin's pursuit. Surprisingly, they become both the obstacles and prisons for individual captivity, alongside the bridges and conduits for human liberation. In the epilogue of *James Baldwin's God*, Clarence Hardy illumines this tension through the assertion, "Even as Baldwin warns . . . of the risks of safe havens and easy choices, he celebrates how the individual has the capacity to break the social control of religion and loveless fears of social convention."[70] For Hardy, fragility in Baldwin's work speaks to how the latter uses literature to protest the structural constraints and oppressive forces within the larger society. Conversely,

Hardy also argues that "Baldwin's sentimentalism belies all his protests to the contrary" because, as he puts it, "this emphasis on the individual yields a cramped notion of freedom limited to seeking the humane and the tender intimacies of personal relationships instead of radical social change."[71] Notwithstanding Hardy's analysis of how the individual challenges social conventions, I disagree with the relationship between Baldwinian sentimentalism and protest. For me, the appeal to the sentimental reifies Baldwin's preoccupation with individual loneliness but also allows room for metaphoric extension. The individual becomes a referent for a much larger community, be it Black men, Black people, or Americans. Regardless of what the church symbolizes for the reader, it holds a specific purpose for John. For him, the church (outside of Gabriel and through Elisha) affords the opportunity and space for male intimacy and vulnerability. Under the guise of religious brotherhood, men are able to resolve the metaphoric space-in-between them and enjoy the type of closeness witnessed during John and Elisha's wrestling match. More important, it adorns Elisha with a salvific signification. He comes to be John's saving grace.

When John departs from home and the tense exchange with Gabriel, his travel is more of a search than a flight. While he hopes to flee Gabriel's oppressive paternity, he seeks male love more abundantly. Thus, when he stumbles into the church and subsequently wrestles with Elisha for the latter's intimacy, the search for the fraternal becomes more apparent. Furthermore, it is in this moment that the reader learns that if anyone is to save John, it will be Elisha—the figure in the novel most endowed with the salvific manhood John seeks. In "Religious Symbolism and Psychic Reality in Baldwin's *Go Tell It on the Mountain*," Shirley Allen reminds us, "Baldwin has already prepared the reader for Elisha's role as John's guardian angel by giving some history of their friendship and emphasizing Elisha's holiness."[72] Allen's reading reinforces Elisha's divinity while foregrounding its role in John's redemption. Importantly, John is not some wayward child who needs to be redeemed from a traditionally sinful life. Rather, "His need for affirmation [redemption] comes not only from his fear of eternal damnation due to his attraction to other boys, but also from his hatred of a father who finds him morally and physically reprehensible."[73] If Henderson is right, while his homosexual urges play a role in John's *need* for affirmation, what most notably plagues him is this breakdown in male intimacy with his father. Again, this is what fuels John's journey, what solidifies Elisha's pivotal role in his life at the church on the night of his birthday. It is there, on the same holy floor that deadlocked him into a beautiful brotherhood with Elisha, that John undergoes his transformation. For this reason, the threshing floor signals the end of a journey for the itinerant John.

After Baldwin takes the reader through a series of prayers ranging from the familial adults in John's life to the religious saints of his congregation, he begins the final section of his novel with John on the threshing floor. Placing John's threshing-floor experience toward the end of the novel symbolizes the finality of his search for the fraternal. All events, historical flashbacks, and illusions lead up to this decisive moment where John has been paired with the angelic Elisha and finds himself ready, in a sense, for salvation. While the church has its symbolic meaning, the fraternal is not denoted by physical location. Nevertheless, space is important as he must travel through, within, or over a particular experience in his effort to eliminate that metaphoric distance between men. Accepting this notion, we see the threshing floor is extremely important as it shapes his final crossing into a particular man-hood. Henderson's understanding of "clearing space" provides a more ready explanation for its significance. Arguing that "the ceremonial rituals per-formed in these places that connect character to space/place in each instance point to the cycle of repression and oppression associated with each charac-ter's attempt to reconcile the self with the self," she identifies how the thresh-ing floor is a site for personal confrontation.[74] If her reading is accurate, and "Baldwin's novel stages this site as a conversionary space where the secular and sacred meet as the individual prays for spiritual renewal before God and the congregation," then perhaps viewing John's transformation as a deliver-ance from Gabriel's power as opposed to John's sexual sin makes more sense.

Baldwin, without warning, places John under the spirit of God to be renewed and reborn into a new man. On the same floor where he found his angelic guardian, John "was invaded, set at naught, possessed. This power had struck John, in the head or in the heart; and in a moment, wholly, filling him with anguish that he could never in his life have imagined, that he surely could not endure, that even now he could not believe, had opened him up."[75] The initial impact of this description reveals how the process for reconciliation, for redemption, is not a peaceful one. Much like his violent wrestling with Elisha, it takes much energy and courage to embark on eliminating the distance within the humanity in which one suffers. John finds himself falling into the heart of this distance, which Baldwin writes as a religious darkness, in order to build the strength one needs to live anew. Because of this fall, John is not able to self-resurrect; this is Baldwin's purpose: to reveal how man is always in need of another for his salvation and to demystify the idea of the autonomic acquisition of freedom. John does not understand this as of yet; in fact, his desire to resurrect himself is neatly articulated by the text: "He tried to assure the voice that he would do his best to rise; he would only lie here a moment, after his dreadful fall, and catch his breath. It was at this moment, precisely, that he found he could not rise; something had happened to his arms, his legs, his feet—ah, something had happened to John!"[76] Recognizing his inability to rise strikes terror into John's heart; he is beginning to understand the process of salvation. Relatedly, Henderson asserts,

> In Baldwin's narrative, John does find a sense of purpose on the thresh-ing floor in his "sin," but he does not know how to speak the language of redemption that facilitates his movement from sinnerhood to saint-hood: this help comes not only from Elisha, whose "perfect" body . . . and spiritual tongue make him an able-bodied surrogate for John, but also from the "Prayers of the Saints," whose spiritual evocations at the altar reveal the impact of the past on the present and the cultural and social anxieties that inhibit self-love and acceptance.[77]

Henderson begins to outline the interdependence of salvation. John remains unable to do it alone; he must have someone there to pull him through, to speak him through the darkness. And while the Saints are integral in this scene, the critical helper is none other than Elisha. It is his voice that will reach out to John and encourage him to continue his trek toward redemption, but not before John experiences, more painfully, the task that lies before him.

Go Tell It on the Mountain's threshing-floor section is easily one of the most analyzed scenes in the novel. John's fall and subsequent redemption seduce the reader in ways that escape the previous two sections. Additionally, one realizes that all has led up to this point, this defining moment of John's young life, his cross into manhood and his confrontation with self deep down under the power of some unnamable spirit. At times this moment is alarming, as such a beautiful rebirthing process should not be so laden with terror, but alas the reader knows that for ultimate redemption, in keeping with the Christian tradition, Baldwin needs his John to undergo a traumatic experience. Therefore, one finds John's redemption preceded by a terrifying descent into darkness:

> Ah, down!—and to what purpose, where? To the bottom of the sea, the bowels of the earth, to the heart of the fiery furnace? Into a dungeon deeper than Hell, into a madness louder than the grave? What trumpet sound would awaken him, what hand would lift him up? For he knew, as he was struck again, and screamed again, his throat like burning ashes, and as he turned again, his body hanging from him like a useless weight, a heavy, rotting carcass, that if he were not lifted he would never rise.[78]

I quote this passage at length in an effort to show the darkness of John's descent and to illustrate the dread felt as he is continuously struck by the Spirit. Additionally, this passage highlights John's budding understanding that his redemption is not a solitary process, that if he is to rise, someone will have to aid him. Baldwin cleverly, or possibly subconsciously, imagines this descent with an eerie allusion to lynching. The burning of the throat; the dangling, decaying carcass; and the helplessness of the Black body speak to a violent imagery of racial sport. Essentially, the text vacillates between the literal and metaphoric. All at once, it conveys an individual's search for redemption through his personal narrative while metaphorically showing how that same individual comes to represent a people, Black people in particular, and its quest for redemption. Baldwin's slippages between individual and cultural narrative magnify the power of his literature to confront historical atrocities through the seemingly autobiographical. This is further evidenced as John encounters a variety of traumatic moments under the power of the spirit.

John's time on the threshing floor is divided among a series of experiences relating to the different figures of his life. He faces his mother and the indiscretions of her past, his aunt Florence and her fall from grace, Roy and his predisposition for trouble, and more. However, the most definitive exchange he endures is with his father, Gabriel. Interestingly, the first person that comes to him in his fallen state is Gabriel. Baldwin relays the following:

> ... in the silence, then, that filled the void, John looked on his father. His father's face was Black—like a sad, eternal night; yet in his father's face there burned a fire—a fire eternal in an eternal night. John trembled where he lay, feeling no warmth from him from this fire, trembled, and could not take his eyes away.[79]

Upon seeing his father, John thought Gabriel was there to help him rise, only to discover such was not the case. As indicated by the passage, John received no warmth from the life that burned in Gabriel, and this warmth is naturally symbolic of love. Baldwin uses this encounter to reify the severe fraternal crisis plaguing John and Gabriel's relationship. That which would be able to bond them—love—is conspicuously absent, and, as if John needed a reminder, he is once again introduced to the truth of his disconnect. Of course, this moment is a bit different, given the situation and John's suspended state of despair, but also because here the struggle with his father becomes more pronounced. John "knew that he had been thrust out of the holy, the joyful, the blood-washed community, that his father had thrust him out."[80] At this point, the battle between the two is inevitable. Not only does Gabriel withhold his love, he also attempts to withhold John's salvation. Fortunately, John is not left alone to fight this battle; his angel, his guardian, his key to the fraternal emerges to help him fight against Gabriel's will.

Michael Fabre, in his pivotal essay on the father–son relationship in Baldwin's first novel, reminds the reader of how "John mobilizes an 'accomplice in salvation' in order to speak to God through this intermediary without respecting the hierarchy in which his father figures among his immediate superiors."[81] I argue that in this critical juncture on the threshing floor,

Elisha actualizes his salvific manhood and his capacity to redeem. For amid John's banishment from his father, when he flirts with the possibility of a representative death, Elisha encourages, "Get up, John. Get up, boy. Don't let him keep you here. You got everything your daddy got."[82] With a series of descents into what seems to be unforgiving darkness, John continues his battle with his father in different ways. His battles grow more difficult on that threshing floor as he witnesses isolation in forms never before known, sees and experiences death with all of his senses. Yet still, when he could bear no more, when his spirit seemed too weakened to continue its journey, "he began to shout for help, seeing before him the lash, the fire, and the depthless water, seeing his head bowed down forever"; he called out, "Oh, Lord, have mercy on me. Have mercy on me."[83] At his lowest moment in the darkness, the voice of Elisha, so aptly described as the "ironic" voice by Baldwin, tells him, "Go through. Ask Him to take you through."[84] Moments later, after John finds the voice to ask for his salvation, after he finds himself in the presence of the Lord, "Ah, how his tears ran down, how they blessed his soul!—as he felt himself, out of the darkness, and the fire, and the terrors of death, rising upward to meet the saints."[85] Quite expectedly, the first voice he hears is Elisha's, his angelic guardian encouraging him to stand and confirming that it was indeed Elisha who talked him through the darkness. Elisha's mediation of John's journey to God on the threshing floor further recalls David and Jonathan's strong intimacy. In a proclamation of male intimacy in direct conflict with the notion of the space-in-between men often texturing male fraternal crises, they proclaim, "The Lord be between me and thee, and between my seed and thy seed forever."[86] The biblical staging of male intimacy witnessed between David and Jonathan climaxes in the shared knowledge of God as that which is between them, the strength of their bonding love. The way Baldwin re-creates this moment, even if subconsciously, reaffirms Elisha's role as a salvific figure. As Jonathan offers to share his birthright with the beloved David, Elisha extends his hand and voice to assist John in the journey toward God. And God is, remember, love.

Go Tell It on the Mountain ends its chronicling of John's quest to overcome a fraternal crisis with two meaningful confrontations following his rebirth.

The first comes immediately after he has risen, when John finds himself face to face with his father. Baldwin cements the irreconcilable nature of the divide by mentioning Gabriel's reaction. He simply utters, "Praise the Lord," but Gabriel "did not move to touch [John], did not kiss him, did not smile. They stood before each other in silence."[87] Silence characterizes the end of a pursuit for John. He no longer desires to resolve the tension between them and has no need for the love Gabriel conveniently withholds. In fact, "John struggled to speak the authoritative, the living word that would conquer the great division between his father and himself. But it did not come, the living word; in the silence something died in John, and something came alive."[88] Essentially, John's need for Gabriel's love has died and in its place now dwells that beautiful brotherhood shared with Elisha. Indeed, Gabriel's opportunity to redeem John was supplanted by the power and openness of Elisha's fraternity. And last, standing on the steps on his home being told by his father to go inside, he "looked at his father and moved from his path."[89] As if to solidify John's newly discovered manhood, Baldwin has his protagonist defy his father's word and instead make permanent the fraternal bond developed with Brother Elisha. If readers ever doubt the divinity of the latter's manhood: "[Elisha] kissed John on the forehead, a holy kiss," and as he walked away, the sun "fell over Elisha like a golden robe, and struck John's forehead, where Elisha had kissed him, like a seal ineffaceable forever."[90] Elisha assumes the position of the biblical Jonathan once more. All of the elements are there—the defiance of a father, the intimate sealing of a bond: "And they kissed one another, and wept with one another."[91] Elisha's kiss is symbolic in this final moment. It does not, as Carolyn Sylvander claims, become "a kind of spiritual translation of the physical attraction suggested between the two young men."[92] For me, John's intimacy with Elisha is inseparable from the spiritual. Instead the queering of salvation presents itself within the tense and beautiful friendship between the young men. Again, while the presence of homoeroticism certainly is readable, this kiss is symbolic of that fraternal bond sought by John from the onset of the novel and established through an intimate relationship that reaches beyond sexuality.

John's fraternity with Elisha, while giving way to the possibility for homosexual attraction, is transcendental in nature and resonates with Baldwin's mission to combat the loneliness of his own life with male intimacy and vulnerability. *Go Tell It* foregrounds the Black religious tradition, the intricacies of Black family life, and the secular–sacred duality plaguing individuals forced to negotiate race, gender, and sexuality in a pre–Civil Rights America. More important, it is a novel situating the Baldwinian pursuit of the fraternal by highlighting the longing for male intimacy, crises in same-sex relationships (romantic and platonic), and possibilities for redemption through the evolution of salvific characters. What Baldwin's first novel teaches us is that Black men suffer from a metaphoric space-in-between with other men, that they have no space to express their emotional selves, and that they inevitably search for that love when they cannot find it at home. And while John was blessed enough to experience the salvific manhood of Elisha, not all would be so lucky. Eventually, Baldwin's exploration of the complexity of Black men's search for love and acceptance transforms into new ways of examining these relationships; some will be triumphant, some will be tragic, but they all will be reflective of his personal search to find love, companionship, brotherhood, and acceptance in a world determined to withhold it.

2

Flight, Freedom, and Abjection

Fractured Manhood and Tragic
Love in *Giovanni's Room*

If James Baldwin's novelistic introduction to the world came through *Go Tell It on the Mountain*, and the world understands how it is so intimately tied to Baldwin's personal life, his African American culture, and his wrestling with religion in pursuit of a new theology, then his second novel— *Giovanni's Room* (1956)—might come off as a bit of an anomaly. While *Go Tell It* spoke from a discernibly Black space and is expectedly located within the United States, the following novel makes a drastic geographic shift. Despite these differences, and in celebration of them, *Giovanni's Room* continues a Baldwinian journey into the nuances of male intimacy and vulnerability. Fraternal crises abound within it, the space-in-between men emerges with a different texture and form, and the idea of salvific manhood takes on new life in the face of human tragedy.

Baldwin's *Giovanni's Room* challenged the American literary tradition by foregrounding issues of sexuality and love in ways previously undone. Set within the 1950s, the novel is a first-person account of a man whose struggles to make sense of individual freedom are channeled through a journey that nuances the complexity of human love by complicating the notion of same-sex desire. With the Parisian city and culture as a literal backdrop, the novel's landscape plays off the romanticism of the popular imagination and captures for the reader a fantastic dance between manhood and sexuality, freedom and imprisonment, love and tragedy, et cetera. *Giovanni's Room* at once creatively critiques the oppressiveness of heteronormativity, offers a discourse exploring the relationship between Black and queer identities, and troubles the American concept of freedom. Even more, however, it relays the gripping narrative of love punctuated with topoi of betrayal, hopelessness, and death amid an individual's wrestle with and against male intimacy. While on the surface it appears to be a convenient *deviation* from *Go Tell It on the Mountain*, Baldwin's second novel continues to reveal the pervasiveness of the author's preoccupation with loneliness.

In his introduction to *A Historical Guide to James Baldwin*, Douglas Field remarks,

> While Baldwin's first novel, *Go Tell It on the Mountain* (1953), was hailed as a masterful exploration of Black culture, his second novel, *Giovanni's Room* (1956), portrays a homosexual relationship in Paris with no African American characters. Although it was hailed as a seminal work of homosexual literature, Baldwin repeatedly steered readers away from interpreting *Giovanni's Room* as a work of gay fiction.[1]

What is important in Field's observation is the treatment of the novels, specifically how each was hailed differently. Whereas *Go Tell It* was extolled because of its signification of Black culture, *Giovanni's Room* gained its acclaim through its dealings with sexuality. Further, to perhaps explore the polysemy of Field's words, his seemingly straightforward acknowledgment of praise speaks to how each novel was claimed and relegated to a particular literary space. *Go Tell It*, with its emphasis on the African American experience per se, has been interpellated as a racial text—one whose merit lies in its compelling negotiation of Black cultural idioms. Conversely, with its erasure of race (all white characters), *Giovanni's Room* became interpellated as a text of gender and sexuality—one whose gems are rooted in the troubling navigation of same-sex or "alternative" intimate desire. Field's statement may not have intended this interpretation but like Baldwin's novels, it cannot escape the privilege of its reader. This is to suggest that authorial intentionality goes only so far within the literary world, and this is something Baldwin learned quickly with the publication of his second novel.

One learns, through William Cole's recitation of a 1954 letter from James Baldwin, how the latter understood *Giovanni's Room*: "It's a love story—

short, and wouldn't you know it, tragic. Our American boy comes to Europe, finds something, loses it, and in his acceptance of his loss becomes, to my mind, heroic."[2] In his letter to Bill Cole, as evidenced in both the quoted statement above and in the absented text, Baldwin understood his novel as something beyond sexuality. While same-sex desire decorated part of the narrative, its fundamental concern was with the discovery and loss of love. Yet, despite Baldwin's pronouncement that this was a novel concerned with the many facets of love, "he was soon to find out that very few readers would see his novel the way he did. It would merely be a homosexual novel to most people, even publishers."[3] Such was the truth that Baldwin had to swallow, his newest piece of fiction *hailed* into an unfounded literary space of queer studies and stripped of its most personal preoccupation. From the moment of the novel's publication in 1956, popular opinion would label it a creative exploration of "deviant" sexuality conveniently devoid of the problems of race. Or as Leslie Fiedler asserts, "*Giovanni's Room*, whatever its limitations, is a step in this direction—that is to say, a step beyond the Negro writer's usual obsession with his situation as a Negro in a white culture, an obsession which keeps him forever writing a first book."[4] It is this understanding, the idea that Baldwin avoids or goes beyond a perceived "obsession" with The Negro Question, coupled with the projected thought that he was pushing a queer-rights agenda, that colors the controversy and tension of his novel. It would become, in a sense, the most peculiar production of his canon as it complicated what the world had understood as Black literature and pioneered a new field within the literary world.

The question of race or racelessness when it comes to Baldwin's second novel has been used to justify its underwhelming treatment in African American and Black literary studies. Arguing that Baldwin's focus on gay sexuality comes at the expense of echoing the type of rich cultural exploration found in *Go Tell It on the Mountain*, African Americanists approach Baldwin's work with an intentional blindness to *Giovanni's Room*. To be clear, "while [*Giovanni's Room*] has gained a central place in (white) gay culture and is often a focus of attention in (white) gay studies, in the context of African American literary and cultural studies, historically it has been alternatively dismissed or ignored altogether, stumblingly acknowledged or viciously attacked."[5] This historical dismissal, as Ross sees it, has led other scholars to reimagine the field of African American Studies and to resituate *Giovanni's Room* within a particular function. For instance, in "Straight Black Studies: On African American Studies, James Baldwin, and Black Queer Studies," Dwight McBride reads the novel "as a text that both provides a challenge to traditional modes of analysis for African American literary production and suggests a broadening of what African Americanist critique might mean."[6] For McBride, E. Patrick Johnson, and other thinkers pushing the field of Black queer studies, Baldwin's work becomes a much needed literary nexus where the "Black and queer can speak to each other."[7] *Giovanni's Room* thus emerges as a critical text within the field of African American Studies, one demanding a specific intercoursing of race and gender analyses and necessitating, as McBride highlights, a new methodology for examining African American literature.

In a letter to Bill Cole, Baldwin revealed *Giovanni's Room* was first titled *Deep Secret: One for My Baby*. The original title, as relayed to Cole in the 1954 letter, reveals that despite Baldwin's claim that it was not about African Americans, it was in part about one African American—Baldwin himself. Aside from the retitling, there are other symbolic markers suggesting that the novel deals, however tangentially, with Baldwin's struggles with intimacy. Take, for instance, the book's dedication: "For Lucien." The elision of a last name here raises questions of reference and signification. Which Lucien is Baldwin referring to in this ambiguous dedication? For many, the parallel between Giovanni's murder of Guillaume and the real historical homicide perpetrated by Lucien Carr seems an appropriate fit. Scholars have and will inevitably read the novel's tragedy as inspired by this figure and thus suitably dedicated. However, understanding how the other tragedy within the novel relates to love or unrequited love, one is apt to read the dedication as a reference to Lucien Happersberger. As noted by David Leeming, "In Lucien, Jimmy found the 'Love of [his] life.'"[8] Couple this with the known reality and the confession by Lucien that things never reached a level of romantic intimacy with Baldwin, and the latter's dance with love becomes tragic. This is further evidenced with his choice of the novel's epigraph: "I am the man, I suffered, I was there." Employing Whitman's words, Baldwin reminds the reader that *Giovanni's Room* is indeed his *Deep Secret*, or, as he states, "*Giovanni's Room* comes out of something that tormented and frightened me—the question of my own sexuality. It also simplified my life in another way because it meant that I had no secrets."[9] Again, while speculative, the epigraphic ambiguity points to a deeply personal admission by Baldwin. *Giovanni's Room* is a text of loaded ambiguity, one that relies heavily on shifting signifiers and symbols demanding a closer and more nuanced reading. And though it is easy to dismiss the personal slippages as a desire for personal distance, there is also the question of strategy and why Baldwin felt inclined to mask the racial, personal, and sexual. Regardless, I mention the biographical intrusions here to further substantiate how *Giovanni's Room* speaks to notions of fraternal crisis and salvation. Whitman's words capture the journey Baldwin will offer us through the tormented David.

Baldwin's decision to write a narrative of sexuality through white characters, while controversial for different reasons, must also be seen as strategic. The country, still decorated with the residue of the Second World War, was not particularly psyched about the question of gay sexuality. Even more, as an African American writer, Baldwin had to consider what power Black raciality would have over the novel. Inevitably, he deviated—somewhat—from a theme of blackness so that another topos might be treated within the literary world. He understood, as Ross indicates, "If the characters had been Black, the novel would have been read as being 'about' blackness, whatever else it happened actually to be about. The whiteness of characters seems to make invisible the question of how race or color has, in fact, shaped the characters—at least as far as most readers have dealt with the novel."[10] Ross's subjunctive reading is convincing, as blackness maintained a peculiar place in midcentury discourse. African American writers dealt with this racial dilemma in all of their work, consistently attempting to rescue themes, tropes, plots, and meanings from the usurpation of race. This is not to say that their work did not carry a certain preoccupation with race; how could it not? Rather, I mean to suggest there were literary moments where race interfered with interpretation, where its metalanguage consumed other discussions of oppression or otherness. Thus, the whiteness of *Giovanni's*

Room must be taken into a particular context and understood as a choice by Baldwin both aesthetic and necessary.

Giovanni's Room also presents the question of strategic detachment, indirectly addressed by Cyraina Johnson-Roullier in her essay "'The Bulldog in My Own Backyard': James Baldwin, *Giovanni's Room*, and the Rhetoric of Flight." Noting Baldwin's desire for personal distance, she argues that the novel "maintains a firm grip on the artistic and the imaginative—making of it a fictional, rather than a purely autobiographical, treatment of the plight of the homosexual in the middle of the twentieth century."[11] Baldwin's fictional gripping reflects less an interest to establish a fiction of sexuality and more a desire to maintain his own *Deep Secret*. At the time of writing, despite his own inner reconciliation, Baldwin was not yet ready to release his personal truth to the world. Instead, he planted autobiographical seeds in the grounding of the novel, hoping that readers might be able to witness his personal investment even amid the whiteness. Despite the strong ties to Baldwin's personal life and the lack of resolve surrounding his sexuality, *Giovanni's Room* as a literary text performs a continued conversation first begun in *Go Tell It*. At its heart, the novel concerns itself with the question of fraternity and fraternal crisis. In the various male–male relationships throughout the work, the symbolic space-in-between shows itself to be a consistent foil to healing, comfort, and most importantly, salvation. This is to suggest *Giovanni's Room* is as much about salvific manhood as its predecessor is, and, much to the torment of the reader, it offers the complex dark side of such a subjectivity. Nevertheless, it also begs the question of racial identity, as Baldwin's strategic departure from the themes of *Go Tell It* almost guarantees it as a focus.

The peculiar absence of Black characters in the novel does not preclude a reading of race. Citing the need for aesthetic and personal distance, alongside the problem of literary blackness, scholars propose the novel to be a "literary masquerade" where whiteness is merely a cover necessary for gay sexual discourse. In "James Baldwin's *Giovanni's Room*: Expatriation, 'Racial Drag,' and Homosexual Panic," literary critic Mae Henderson asserts, "In James Baldwin's *Giovanni's Room* (1956), geographical expatriation combines with the literary act of racial expatriation—or what I call "racial drag"—to create a space for the exploration of the homosexual dilemma within and beyond the social and geographic contours of post–World War II America."[12] Henderson's view of expatriation as racial distancing further advances the argument regarding the symbolic nature of whiteness within the novel. And while the geographic setting may simply be the result of Baldwin's sojourns in Paris, the same cannot be said of how he locates whiteness within the novel. Considering Henderson's claim, the "racial drag" of Giovanni's Room highlights Baldwin's proclivity for employing an autoethnographic methodology in his fiction. To mask, reveal, and perhaps work through his "truths," he uses personal narrative as an inspiration and backdrop for his creative fiction. And in keeping with the African American employment of Bahktinian double-voiced discourse, such a tactic for individual expression still carries an appeal to the universal. Undoubtedly, if even unconsciously, part of Baldwin's motivation stems from this thinking, and the reader is benefited by such knowledge.

If Baldwin's second novel is another example of literary masquerading, and if its "racial drag" reflects a systematic distancing, the question of autobiography becomes critical. More specifically, if one can easily identify the writer within his work, if that Barthesian death of the author never manifests and if the Foucauldian detachment from the text is barely actualized, what is one to assume about Baldwin's intention? Perhaps the novel, again similar to the one preceding, takes its form from personal experience. And if so, was the author intentional in masking; was he really performing drag? For Stanley Macebuh, Baldwin's "somewhat obsessive preoccupation with his own private world . . . was in itself an indispensable, if not mandatory, exercise in self-therapy. In a sense, indeed, Baldwin had become, technically, a 'writer' long before he found anything to write about—anything, that is, that went beyond an embellished autobiography."[13] "Embellished autobiography" as an idea captures the unique way Baldwin uses the personal within his fiction. It speaks to what I term "literary découpage"—the autoethnographic method of guising autobiography under other markers of identity. I argue that Giovanni's Room, along with Baldwin's other fiction, performs this literary découpage through a variety of mediums. He hides his personal narrative under a plethora of cutouts—European geographies, white racial identities, unreconciled sexualities, socioeconomic privileges, moralities, et cetera. However, if one begins to nuance this découpage, to peel back the layers of covering by performing literary analysis alongside biographical referencing, the original object, once hidden by the decorative elements of identity, mirrors Baldwin's life and his own preoccupation with loneliness. In this regard, Macebuh's observation is valid—Baldwin's writings never escape their motivations, always point back to the author himself. Literary découpage thus becomes a useful concept for unpacking the work that the novel performs. It also serves as a useful critical methodology for the approach and treatment of autoethnographic fiction that vacillates between the autobiographical and the universal. Inevitably, readers who view *Giovanni's Room* as a representation of découpage will be able to position it as a part of and not a deviation from Baldwin's other novels. And even more, they might be able to glean a greater understanding of the subtext pervading the novel and how it is a logical continuation of *Go Tell It on the Mountain*. Indeed, viewing it from this lens evidences that Baldwin's wrestling with iterations of male intimacy, the fraternal, and salvific manhood are continued after his first major piece of fiction.

Literary découpage, as a concept, encourages scholars to revisit the question of *Giovanni's Room*'s construction and by extension its literary success. Take, for instance, Robert Bone's crucial denouncement of Baldwin's work. In an essay exploring Baldwin's novels and his position as "the most important Negro writer to emerge during the last decade," Bone argues, "*Giovanni's Room* (1956) is by far the weakest of Baldwin's novels."[14] He continues, "There is a tentative, unfinished quality about the book, as if in merely broaching the subject of homosexuality Baldwin had exhausted his creative energy."[15] Bone's critique, which comes after Baldwin had published three novels, speaks to the ways in which many critics have misread the conversation of sexuality within his work. Indeed, what Bone reads as a "tentative, unfinished quality" is a reflection of the complex narrative of human relationships and intimacy. The denouement he seeks is but the romantic hope for closure on an issue Baldwin was just beginning to trouble. For as an author and as a man, Baldwin was neither prepared nor willing to punctuate his second novel with some appeal to clarity or finality. In "broaching the subject of homosexuality," he understood the limits of the genre and the scope of his creative endeavor. Such finitude would undermine his project and his life by suggesting that resolve could come in three hundred pages.

Geography carries a strong symbolism within the novel, with a marked vacillation between U.S. and European national and cultural space. The narrator, David, is an American expatriate whose flight from home can be likened to his attempt to flee from himself and his sexuality, in particular. As Gabriel Welsch suggests, "the novel meditates on American identity, as its expatriate protagonist mulls over the very nature of his masculinity, a cipher for American identity as he understands it. Also, the impact of collective and individual history makes David's decisions fraught and destructive."[16] Welsch's reading, aside from capturing the symbolic link between nationality and sexuality, additionally reveals how place functions as a layering for sexuality. This is to say Baldwin does not simply use America as a metaphor for a certain type of sexuality but also shows how the history of it as a geographic and colonial space also informs the limits of sexual expression. Much like the continent, David's body is cartographed by a narrative of conquering and an absence of freedom. As a result, like Baldwin and other expatriates, he flees the oppressiveness of a home space in search of something more liberating.

America to Paris: Expatriation or Exploration, Flight or Freedom?

In *Giovanni's Room* Baldwin restages the complexities of manhood, an American manhood in particular, by first restaging the space or place of fraternal crises. Similarly to *Go Tell It*, the space of the home plays a critical role in delineating the struggles of the men in the novel; the home space is reconfigured consistently. Additionally, where *Go Tell It* used the church to allow for gender play and negotiation, *Giovanni's Room* relies on the Parisian club or nightlife scene. On one hand, this examples Baldwin's evolving idea of a queered notion of salvation, as religion's presence need not have physical immediacy. Like the geographic distance achieved between his first two novels, there is an ideological one assumed as well. Beyond space as popularly noted, however, the novel plays with the space of manhood a bit more readily. Here, space is both America and American. It is both Paris and Parisian. The male body in *Giovanni's Room* comes with its own topologies, and, in a sense, the reader's journey depends on the careful navigation of this Baldwinian terrain. The question then, asked by this sequel of sorts, is, How does male intimacy and vulnerability map onto these various spaces? Or, How do the spaces within the work help us to better understand the iterative possibilities of fraternal crisis, and how do they retexture the idea of salvific manhood with a new staging of tragedy?

When young Baldwin reached an age of exploration, when the pressures of adolescence and sexual identity reared their heads, when the theology of his youth gave way to disillusionment, he left home. "Home" was a floating signifier to a degree, as it simultaneously denoted the church, the actual household of his youth, and his Harlem community. And by the age of twenty-four, he was ready to extend his flight over the ocean, joining the ranks of previous African American artists who took refuge in France after leaving their American home. However, unlike others, Baldwin maps his personal expatriation onto his fiction, and "through the elaborate searches that many of his fictional characters undergo to find a home, [he] explores issues of nationality, home, and, more specifically, *home place*."[17] Arguing that *Giovanni's Room* is fundamentally concerned with the "construction of place," Kathleen Drowne hints toward the idea that the departure from America, with its isolation and oppression, led Baldwin to Paris and to the exploration of identity within his second novel.

America carries a very particular symbolism within *Giovanni's Room*. David's expatriation is less an indication of a cosmopolitan spirit or a desire to explore and more the reflection of a need to escape and a propensity for flight. What he flees from are the cultural elements of an America that denies him the freedom to be himself, a geographic space that appears more constricting and asphyxiating with each passing day. His reality, in America, is one of homelessness, where the instability of his father's house and his discomfort within it mirror his personal feelings of displacement and being alone. As a result, his journey throughout the novel, aside from the obvious push to reconcile a warring sexual self, is defined by an effort to identify and create a "home." Baldwin takes leisure in expanding the idea of home, being sure to complicate the prevailing idea of physical space, items, and bodies. For him, like geographic space, "home suggests more than merely the place where one lives. In fact, home for David is perhaps the most ephemeral of places."[18] Drowne capitalizes on how Baldwin utilizes David to reimagine the home space and the ways in which the protagonist is torn between the American homeland marked by birth and the new home he searches for within his very flight. His flight to Paris, his sojourn in the European city of romance, is a telltale sign that America is at odds with who he sees himself to be. Or, to put it more specifically, "his longings for a homeplace in America are not without contradiction; in truth, he fled to Paris to escape this home and its impossible (heterosexual) expectations of him. David tries to convince himself that physically distancing himself from his U.S. birthplace amounts to leaving it behind psychologically."[19] Drowne understands David's flight as a psychological dilemma, reads it as inextricably linked to his wrestling with sexuality. More importantly, her reading magnifies how Baldwin signifies America, how he writes it as this "impossible" place for a warring David, and how it demands its own rejection as pronounced in David's flight.

In *Stealing the Fire*, Horace Porter argues that the "chief artistic aim of the novel, from Baldwin's point of view, is the dramatization of an American consciousness in particular, and perhaps unusual, circumstances."[20] This is symbolized through David's unreconciled sexuality, his metaphoric flight from his homeplace, and his peculiar relationship with Giovanni. Like America, he is unable to resolve a troubled history, one that engenders a profound shame and self-restlessness. The American flaw—and, by extension, David's struggle—then becomes the inability to acknowledge an inherent tension within, to accept the truth pervasive in one's history and unavoidable in one's present. Thus, the flight within American consciousness and David's life; it is a "willful American blindness toward the past, whether it is the past of an individual American or the nation at large, a perspective that involves a refusal to accept the fact that a man's life, like that of a nation, is to an extraordinary degree marked by a series of past decisions."[21] The slippage between individual and nation renders David's flight as both personal and symbolic. It parallels America's "willful blindness" and captures why geographic spaces emerge as characters within the novel. Even more, it extends the reading of space beyond the contours of autobiography, signaling again how literary découpage is at play within Baldwin's work.

For some scholars, *Giovanni's Room* differs little from *Go Tell It on the Mountain*. In fact, many argue that "when [Baldwin] attempts a novel of homosexual love, with an all-white cast of characters and a European setting, he simply transposes the moral topography of Harlem to the streets of Paris."[22] While cultural similarities abound between the progressive spaces of Harlem and the mythical spaces of Paris, such a reading is reductive. Others, citing Baldwin's continuous use of the autobiographical and his literary autoethnographic bent, view Paris as a logical setting given Baldwin's travels in his midtwenties and the extensive time he spent there during his writing career. Even still, other scholars understand the strategic use of the personal within the novel and view geographic spaces as a symbolic wrestling with another demarcation of identity—namely, sexuality. For instance, Johnson-Roullier asserts that "Baldwin uses his newfound understanding of 'Americanness' in such a way that he is able to see far enough beyond the communal obligation to write about race . . . that he frees himself to write about another, and in some ways, for him, more pressing problem—that of homosexuality."[23] The freedom outlined above does reflect Baldwin's desire to write about sexuality but not at the expense of race. Indeed, the racial drag of the novel is necessitated, as mentioned before, by how literary blackness functions as a *Black hole*, in a sense. By this, I am suggesting that its presence within a piece of fiction is inevitably ecliptic; it indirectly consumes all other themes, topoi, or motifs. Therefore, while the Parisian landscape liberates Baldwin's pen so that it might touch on same-sex male intimacy, its employment was not for the erasure of race. Quite the contrary, it was strategically used to minimize the erasing potential of blackness so that the author could write a love story without fearing racial pathologization.

The setting of *Giovanni's Room* has led to a large amount of scholarship surrounding the significance of place and space within Baldwin's work. The novel's Parisian landscape causes a peculiar but warranted critical engrossment. Critics posit different readings, varying from the autobiographical to the mythical, of how Paris functions within the novel and the symbolism that it necessarily embodies. James Campbell's *Exiled in Paris* offers the reader an excellent window into what Baldwin does with Paris and why he chose to employ it:

> Baldwin set *Giovanni's Room* in Paris partly because he just happened to be there, but also because the mythical freedoms the city grants its temporary residents are central to the behavior of the book's narrator, David. He is enabled to follow, for a short season, his natural desire— which, if he permits it, could lead him to the grail of all Baldwin's stories: love.[24]

What Campbell highlights here are many of the divergent views on the question, Why Paris? Beginning with the obvious, Campbell cites how, to the syllogistic demise of others, Baldwin chooses Paris because, simply, he is in Paris. This simple yet concrete fact might be enough to end any discussion surrounding Baldwin's choice of setting, but Campbell understands, as do I, that Paris also occupies a certain symbolic position within the novel. The city, historicized as a sanctum for romance and mythologized for the lifestyles enjoyed by its residents, symbolizes freedom in a stark contrast to the rigidity of American liberty. Baldwin is careful not to overindulge in the myth of Parisian freedom, however. He does not write a novel that flirts with the vulgar or makes a mockery of the moral. His Paris, David's refuge, though ripe with sexual and social "deviance," was not one defined by "licentiousness; [. . .] the freedom Baldwin sought was the freedom to fulfill oneself, to be whole."[25] In this regard, Paris serves as more than a sexual pit stop for a confused American tourist and erects itself as a welcoming space for he who seeks respite or resolution from a past (think history) that refuses to remain at rest.

If America represents the "impossible," then Paris, naturally, represents possibility. Baldwin creates for the sexually torn David a space where his personal history and, more specifically, the tension of that history can be forgotten, if only for a moment. The myth of Paris, the freedom interwoven within its national consciousness, affords David a space of resolve and reconciliation vastly different than his American homeplace. His expatriation ensures, rather ironically, a beautiful confrontation with himself and forces upon him a vision of sexuality to counteract his blindness. Inevitably, his newfound freedom dichotomizes his feelings into that of a never-before-experienced liberation and an unwelcome imprisonment. Even more, Paris becomes for the reader a necessary element for Baldwin's novel, for without it and all that it comes to mean, David's pursuit of himself and the ability to love is lost within a constricted American space. Baldwin understood this, and for this reason, to simply read Paris as the product of an auto-biographical motivation would rid the novel of its very meaning; how else would one understand the complexity of David's search and longings without the intricacies of his flight?

Aside from the familial dysfunction experienced by David at the hands of his father and his aunt, his flight from the United States stems from a dialectical desire to escape and find himself. America, steeped in a history of sexual conservatism and oppression, rendered David "Other" to his bisexual body. Through the relationship between David and his childhood friend Joey, *Giovanni's Room* captures the protagonist's early struggles with sexuality and the symbolism surrounding his journey across the ocean. Remembering a particular exchange, David recounts how while amid "normal" male bonding something stirred in the two of them that was previously foreign or unexplored. In acknowledging how he grabbed Joey's head after joking about something rather ridiculous, he recalls, "But this time when I touched him something happened in him and in me which made this touch different from any touch either of us had ever known. And he did not resist, as he usually did, but lay where I had pulled him, against my chest."[26] The difference in touch marks the beginning of a new sexual awareness for David and perhaps Joey as well. Furthermore, the language surrounding resistance, how this moment's essence was "usually" negated by a "resisting" Joey, hints toward the possibility of the desire for intimacy being latent. However, as with most battles involving resistance, when the resisting party relinquishes its fight, the war is generally over. Here, the space-in-between men is removed, albeit temporarily, as Joey comes to lie upon David's chest. As a result of Joey's acquiescence, David's internal struggle with sexuality (read: heterosexuality) ends and signals a new battle, one punctuated, according to David, when "Joey raised his head as I lowered mine and we kissed, as it were, by accident."[27] David's confession of "by accident" begs curiosity. Surely he does not hope to suggest the unintentional touching of lips is due to a closeness or clumsiness of bodies. Rather, "by accident" connotes the unintentionality of young male minds and spirits to disrupt the heteronormativity of American space through same-sex intimacy. David's fraternal moment with Joey, while a catalyst for a new sexual awareness, also becomes indicative of his future fraternal crises.

When David left America, his experience with Joey was but a distant memory, some residue from his childhood. It may, in fact, have been forgotten or suppressed with his "normal" practice of heterosexuality. But the moment—reawakened as his feet touched new soil, that of France—contains the heart and hurt of his sexual dilemma. He remembers the night with a vividness that reflects that while remaining unspoken, his intimate encounter was nonetheless definitive:

Joey's body was brown, was sweaty, the most beautiful creation I had ever seen till then. I would have touched him to wake him up but something stopped me. I was suddenly afraid. Perhaps it was because he looked so innocent lying there, with such perfect trust; perhaps it was because he was so much smaller than me; my own body suddenly seemed gross and crushing and the desire which was rising in me seemed monstrous. But, above all, I was suddenly afraid. It was borne in on me: *But Joey is a boy.*[28]

David's recognition of Joey's boyhood and its relationship to his surfacing fear reveals certain aspects of his sexual struggle. The passage above captures both the draw of Joey's body, the gravity of same-sex attraction for David, as well as the contrasting repulsion. His dilemma is of longing and loathing; he is at once caught within a web of intrigue and disgust—the "beautiful creation" that is Joey's boyhood begets the grotesqueness of his own. When he labels his growing desire as "monstrous," he reifies heterosexist ideology relegating homosexual desire to a position of abnormality. Moreover, his self-imposed resistance, his unwillingness to touch Joey, comes under the idea of "the preservation of innocence."

David's appreciation of Joey's beauty and his repulsion at his own monstrosity, his longing to feel but unwillingness to touch, his desire for intimacy but "respect" for innocence, catapulted him into an internal war beyond words. Regardless of the unreconciled nature of the event, however, it symbolizes the moment in his life when his flight from self and sexuality truly commences. This is his fraternal crisis. Unlike the crisis with John Grimes in *Go Tell It on the Mountain*, David's conflicting relationship with same-sex desire precipitates a breakdown of male intimacy. An inability to reconcile a culturally inherited conception of manhood with a natural longing for male touch leads him into behaviors of rejecting Joey and himself, of creating that proverbial space-in-between men. More importantly, David's resistance and response evoke Julia Kristeva's *Powers of Horror: An Essay on Abjection*. Considering his body "gross" and his desire "monstrous," David does more than reject intimacy with Joey; he marks it as abject. This marking, the unique result of unconscious behavior and intentionality, echoes Kristeva's conceptualization of abjection:

> There looms, within abjection, one of those violent, dark revolts of being, directed against a threat that seems to emanate from an exorbitant outside or inside, ejected beyond the scope of the possible, the tolerable, the thinkable. It lies there, quite close, but it cannot be assimilated. It beseeches, worries, and fascinates desire, which, nevertheless, does not let itself be seduced.[29]

If one reads David's exchange with Joey through this lens, the rationality behind his rejection becomes apparent. David views Joey's body and the potential that it holds as something to be feared, for "in [Joey's] thighs, his arms, and in his loosely curled fists" dwelled a power strong enough to crush his idea of manhood.[30] Even more, the young David believed the sharing of male intimacy as castrating, a threat better avoided. In his own thinking, "The power and the promise and the mystery of that body made me suddenly afraid. That body suddenly seemed the Black opening of a cavern in which I would be tortured till madness came, in which I would lose my manhood."[31] Baldwin reveals the essence behind David's state of being afraid. Although moved by possibility, he also feared the loss of his manhood. Therefore, as Kristeva suggests, the potential consequence of the threat is so grave that it pushes the idea of succumbing to desire into the realm of impossibility. It becomes unthinkable for David to continually submit to the temptation of Joey's body, to violate the laws of manhood governing his behavior. His desire, tempted by the previous night's tasting of sexual male intimacy, does not allow full seduction; instead, "Apprehensive, desire turns aside; sickened, it rejects."[32] And for David, rejection extends beyond the intimate moment, demands distance from the threat, and ensures intolerance, or, as he puts it, "I began, perhaps, to be lonely that summer and began, that summer, the flight which has brought me to this darkening window."[33] Who knew that the expressed need to distance himself from Joey could later synecdochically represent his need to leave America?

Gazing from a Parisian window and contemplating Giovanni's fate, David understands that his sojourn in France is but the flight from America. Viewed in this regard, his flight is marked by a geographic distinction that parallels the physical—to leave Joey and all he embodies, David must leave America. Nevertheless, he complicates his own understanding of flight when he recognizes,

> When one begins to search for the crucial, the definitive moment, the moment which changed all others, one finds oneself pressing, in great pain, through a maze of false signals and abruptly locking doors. My flight may, indeed, have begun that summer—which does not tell me where to find the germ of the dilemma which resolved itself, that summer, into flight.[34]

Here, David offers the reader an honest awareness of his sexual dilemma. Instead of deferring to the idea previously alluded to, that his sexual ambiguity was created through his intimate exchange with Joey, he intimates that its derivation exists elsewhere. The physical exchange was but a tool of awakening, the avenue by which he became cognizant of the "germ of the dilemma." And this is evidenced in his understanding, "Of course, it is somewhere before me, locked in that reflection I am watching in the window . . . It is trapped in the room with me, always has been, and always will be, and it is yet more foreign to me than those foreign hills outside."[35] David confesses in this moment, albeit retrospectively, how his dilemma of sexuality roots itself within his very nature. Through this acknowledgment, Baldwin not only challenges the idea of homosexuality as a social construction but also uses David to speak to how despite familiarity (read, perhaps, sexual practice or acceptance), there is a naturality to same-sex desire or attraction. Additionally, as David muses over his dilemma and locates its germ within himself, he magnifies the inevitable conflict one is doomed to encounter in a world where same-sex intimacy is defined as abnormal. The reader, then, prematurely develops a compassion for David by understanding his plight to be bigger than his own will. And thus we understand that his *flight* to Paris is defined by a search for something within and without himself.

Though the novel tells the story of David and his clumsy occupation of different spaces, this occurs only through his relationships with other characters. Individuals are tied to specific spaces and, while presenting some meaning with their individual bodies, cannot be read without a consideration of those spaces. David's closest friend before meeting Giovanni is a "Belgian-born, American businessman named Jacques."[36] David admits, "In some ways I liked him. He was silly but he was so lonely; anyway, I understand now that the contempt I felt for him involved my self-contempt."[37] Despite his Belgian birthright, Jacques represents the American home space from which David fled. His loneliness, a clear product of an inability to find love, coupled with his middle-aged and somewhat flamboyant disposition, touches on the crisis of manhood and masculinity that David first experienced in the States. In Jacques, David witnessed, or thought himself to, the stereotype of same-sex desire, particularly when it ages. Jacques's tie to America, his performance of sexuality, reminded David of that gross and monstrous feeling of manhood that he had experienced conflictingly with Joey. There seemed to be a desperation adorning Jacques, an unattractive quality that scared and threatened David. That elusive threat, so present within Jacques's signification, grows within Paris and is augmented by the freedom afforded by the geographic space.

The reader learns of the strong contrast between Jacques and David within a bar owned by a man named Guillaume. Guillaume's bar, a "noisy, crowded, ill-lit sort of tunnel," captures David's thoughts regarding masculinity and the disparaging ways in which he views men unlike himself.[38] Describing the venue, he notes, "There were the usual paunchy, bespectacled gentlemen with avid, sometimes despairing eyes, the usual, knife-blade lean, tight-trousered boys. One could never be sure, as concerns these latter, whether they were after money or blood or love."[39] His initial reading of the men suggests a perception of difference and, by extension, distance. David dares not imagine himself a part of Guillaume's community and is content to assume a "stranger in the village" persona. To be different is a necessity for him; his well-constructed manhood proves too fragile to be a member of this community's collective. In fact, his feelings toward an employee who at times is said to blur gender lines evinces his disdain for any variance of manhood: "People said that he was very nice, but I confess that his utter grotesqueness made me uneasy; perhaps in the same way that the sight of monkeys eating their own excrement turns some people's stomachs."[40] David's language, a clear indication of his repulsion, highlights his crisis of manhood. Although within a city known for its freeing potential, he maintains a stronghold on his "American" sensibilities. And at this point in the novel, his flight is still heavily grounded in the geographic—he has yet to escape the psychological confinements of his past, has yet to taste of a new state of being.

David's performance of a particular brand of manhood and masculinity, sine qua non to the novel's development, is critical to understanding the multiple ways different spaces function within the novel. Through David's expressions, Guillaume's bar becomes signified as a refuge for the monstrous and grotesque and as a sanctum for those men who either reject or are rejected by traditional forms of masculinity. Nevertheless, it also serves as a meeting ground, a site of convergence where men from different walks of life are forced and lured into dances of love and death. And thus David, markedly distinguished through his unique performance of gender, occupies the space as an outsider of sorts. Neither old and desperate like Jacques nor young and manipulative like the other patrons, he represents the prototypical American tourist, a foreign body in the Parisian free world.

His masculinity, with its firm grip on tradition, instills him with a peculiar power—he is both vintage and avant-garde, an ancient artifact reconstructed within new American accent(s). And in knowing the gravity he holds in such spaces, he moves in ways that dictate the movements of others. Take, for instance, his relationship with Jacques. He admits,

> I knew . . . that Jacques' vaunted affection for me was involved with desire, the desire, in fact, to be rid of me, to be able, soon, to despise me as he now despised that army of boys who had come, without love, to his bed. I held my own against this desire by pretending that Jacques and I were friends, by forcing Jacques, on pain of humiliation, to pretend this. I pretended not to see, although I exploited it, the lust not quite sleeping in his bright, bitter eyes and, by means of the rough, male candor with which I conveyed to him his case was hopeless, I compelled him, endlessly, to hope.[41]

I quote this passage at length for a variety of reasons. The first is to highlight David's knowledge of the power he possesses with Jacques and inevitably with others like him. He understands himself as an object of desire, knows that Jacques's gaze is sexual in nature. Indeed, it is David's foreign manhood, his traditional masculinity perfectly wrapped in American fabric, that entices others. Second, through this admission, David tells the reader of his propensity to exploit. He uses his desirability to manipulate the lust of the gazer. In this regard, David positions himself as a passive predator, as a man who takes advantage of those longing to taste the fruits of his manhood.

Something else arises from David's commentary on Jacques and his disgust for that different breed of man found in the bar. His ostensible disdain, witnessed within Guillaume's establishment, speaks to how he views the space as one of abjection and its people as, by nature, abject. Again, the debasement of male difference, the feelings of revulsion to *la féminine* indicates how the protagonist's fraternal crisis remains unresolved, even after flight. Keith Mitchell's essay "Femininity, Abjection, and (Black) Masculinity in James Baldwin's *Giovanni's Room* and Toni Morrison's *Beloved*" echoes this assertion through its deployment of Kristeva's theory of the abject. Accordingly, "David's encounters with women, maternal figures, and effeminate nonheteronormative characters illustrate his sexual ambivalence and his desire to rid himself of what he sees as the castrating and feminizing implications of same-sex desire."⁴² When examining David's acts in this vein, the reader understands his relationship to feminine men to be rooted in an unchecked fear, not a perverse hatred. His fear, elusive as it may be, links itself back to American cultural practices and sexual ethos. His gendered body rejects or attempts to reject any threat that would alter how it is received or perceived by others. Unfortunately, for him, his same-sex attraction was not left back in America and rages with desire despite his best efforts to deny it. Inevitably, he engages in a Foucauldian waltz of fascination and revulsion, and his body, that emblematic prize of manhood, leaves him susceptible to the powers of others. And in being a receptor of the male intimate gaze, his movement becomes weakened and regulated by his desire.

In Guillaume's bar, David's manhood creates an interesting irony. Although it garners him some semblance of power, it also renders him extremely vulnerable. He, using Jacques as a marker, deludes himself into thinking that he has great control. However, as the reader knows, his sojourn to Paris and his frequenting of the bar exemplify the crisis he faces with manhood. Sexual vulnerability trumps his confident disposition as his sexuality reeks of ambivalence. Quite naturally, Guillaume's patrons are able to smell and sense his irresolution, happily making him their prey. Trapping David within a dialectic of predator and prey, between states of power and vulnerability, Baldwin accentuates David's fraternal crisis, a crisis in which its symptoms are readily traceable to his experience with Joey but in which its germ, through David's own admission, begins and belongs to him alone. Understanding this, his friendship with Jacques endangers him, places him upon the precipice of temptation. It reunites him, in a sense, with that very thing from which he sought flight and encourages a confrontation that David's fragile sexuality may not be strong enough to endure. That confrontation comes through the figure of Giovanni.

David is introduced to Giovanni, the newest barman, through the gaze and lust of Jacques. Giovanni stands as another potential conquer for the Belgian American embodiment of David's disgust and surely as an interest beyond employment for Guillaume. He, like David, also differs from the regulars and "was so exactly the kind of boy that Guillaume always dreamed of that it scarcely seemed possible that Guillaume could have found him."[43] His difference, the source of his dreamy nature, is but the adornment of manhood also found decorating David—masculinity that seemingly betrays same-sex sexuality. And whether for the longing of the absence within themselves or for the genuine attraction to that deemed masculine, men like Jacques and Guillaume fawn over men like Giovanni. Jacques's pursuit of Giovanni, though not surprising or out of character, causes David discomfort. Perhaps this is because Giovanni is different: he reflects David back to himself and allows for the first time some pretense of community. Maybe Jacques's advancements renders him uncomfortable because David can see himself in Giovanni and dares not imagine, more than he has already, the idea of being pursued by those he views as abject. Even more conceivably, judging from his proclamation, "I was suddenly ashamed that I was with him," perchance David's uneasiness stems from the idea that Giovanni's presence removes him from the illusion of the Parisian free space and obliges him to remember his fraternal crisis.[44] Standing in front of what the reader will later learn to be a bisexual body, David is cast back into that moment with Joey, back into the American cultural space, and back into the knowledge that he is torn between "being" a man and wanting to be with one.

Standing in Guillaume's bar in front of someone who wears "manhood" as well as he does, David becomes more cognizant of the breakdown in his own masculinity. The predator–prey predicament gives way to the more pressing fraternal crisis that he had thought himself to have escaped. In this moment, the safety Paris afforded is vanquished by the intrusive realization that despite his distance from America, despite his geographic divorce from the land that gave birth to his crisis, he cannot escape himself. In Parisian spaces represented by places like Guillaume's bar, David deludes himself into thinking that he has found resolve, praises himself into believing the very mask he has constructed. The homosexual men of Paris resurrect his dying heterosexuality, reconfigure a manhood shattered through experiences like the one with Joey. Persuading himself, David states, "Most of the people I knew in Paris were, as Parisians sometimes put it, of *le milieu* and, while this milieu was certainly anxious enough to claim me, I was intent on proving, to them and to myself, that I was not of their company."[45] Ironically, by dwelling in a space sexualized as homosexual/bisexual, and by surrounding himself with men defined by same-sex attraction, David is able to maintain his own heterosexuality. Indeed, his ability to "resist" the advances of the likes of Jacques, Guillaume, and the "grotesque" men who challenge gender constructions keeps his sexuality intact, and it solidifies, if only in theory, that he is "not of their company."

Paris becomes for David a superficial reconciliation of that inescapable fraternal crisis he had faced within the States. The milieu provides a way in which he reimagines himself and amends a fractured manhood bifurcated by competing expressions of masculinity. Men in *le milieu* are necessary for David's conception of self and critical to his ability to overcome his same-sex desires. Furthermore, "the homosexual nonsubjects of *le milieu* not only reflect David's own subjectivity, creating him as a real man; they also stand in for the erasure of boundaries that render the entire real/ not real logic unworkable."[46] Casting Parisian gay men as abject and then allowing their abjection to *stand in* as the true Other to a heterosexual Self, David authenticates them as subjects and in doing so, through his unique difference, redefines himself as something different. It is the free play of signs and symbols that marks the freedom he enjoys in Paris—that is, until he meets Giovanni. Guillaume's bar thus functions as a site of confrontation when David and Giovanni meet for the first time. On one hand, the mask so well constructed by David, dependent on the abjection of others, is cracked by the manly posture and presence of Giovanni. On the other, the space, defined by David's disinterest and his manipulation of that, now holds a potential object of desire. Giovanni's presence, therefore, signals the reemergence of David's fraternal crisis and generates his need to be saved, his search for the fraternal.

Despite Guillaume's bar's being situated in Paris, David's need to be saved from America or what it represents is still very present. He flees America not because of its familiar topography but out of the desire to wrest himself from its limitations on his personal freedom. The mythology of Paris, and his designation as foreigner within its spaces, allows him the benefit of starting over, of creating a new identity less constrained by a traditional ethos of masculinity. Where America breaks, Paris bends—proves itself flexible in considerations of gender performance. More important, America as home space presents David with an unavoidable confrontation. There is a spirit of permanence there, of fixation—something that anchors his very being. As such, his manhood demands a certain consistency, for the way he projects himself will come to define him, to mark him, to claim him. This is precisely why his relationship with Joey, despite his longings, cannot be. To pursue same-sex intimacy beyond that exceptional night would ordain him into a new manly order—one that reads him as he comes to read the very men in *le milieu* of Paris. Conversely, being but a traveler to Paris, he is not bound by the same ties of space. His time and experiences in the "Parisian demimonde" are characterized by a whimsical transience. His itinerancy appropriates a privilege of impetuosity—he needs not to be overly concerned with his actions, need not overthink his behavior, as it will not leave permanent scars upon his person. In Paris, his acts speak of the carefree tourist who sojourns and indulges outside of his or her nature. However, this is the problem for David as he gazes upon Giovanni; he realizes that his problem in America is yet his problem in Paris.

David's need to be saved begins to reveal itself in his conversation with Giovanni exploring the differences between New York and Paris. Suggesting that the fundamental difference between Americans and the French has something to do with an idea of time, Giovanni offers David a new perspective for viewing his national exceptionalism. For Giovanni, "Americans are funny" in their conception of time and in their approach to constructing their national image. He tells David, in a spirit of ridicule, "As though with enough time and all that fearful energy and virtue you people have, everything will be settled, solved, put in its place. And when I say everything . . . I mean all the serious, dreadful things, like pain and death and love, in which you Americans do not believe."[47] His point here captures the American propensity for order, its obsession with cataloguing and compartmentalizing. Time, for America, becomes a vehicle for perfecting an already imperfect narrative, a way to forget the brutalities of its history. It allows America to dwell within its neatly constructed *states* of disbelief, to erase those "dreadful things" contradicting its self-perception. Within this conversation, "Giovanni casually alludes to what Baldwin considers America's fatal flaw, its unwillingness to deal honestly with its own history."[48] In a space of debating nationalistic difference, Giovanni's commentary is understood to be an indictment of American historical amnesia, perhaps around its treatments of particular populations of people, something else emerges.

The debate with Giovanni displays the truth of David's farraginous sense of self. America as place is folded into the individual nature of David as man and prevents the possibility of a neat separation. Unable to detach himself from the land of his birth, he is thrown into his own proverbial crisis and forced to recognize how despite his flight, he has not truly left America. Evidenced by Giovanni's revelatory proclamation, "Ah, you are really an American," David finds himself, perhaps for the first time within his Parisian excursion, face to face with the reality that he cannot help but embody the breakdown of his American manhood.[49] In this light, when Giovanni hints toward America's "fatal flaw," he also identifies David's shortcoming. Like America, David is unable to admit his history, and his engrossment with time in Paris unearths his effort to settle the crisis engendered by his intimate exchange with Joey. The residue of David's past becomes readable within his interaction with Giovanni. That which was once hidden surfaces in the most unexpected ways, and David's body in Guillaume's bar appears as a corporeal palimpsest—bearing traces of a history he tried so vigorously to erase. Inevitably, thanks to Giovanni, he seeks salvation from his American past and his Parisian present.

Salvation, for David, extends beyond his American self. Although he becomes more cognizant of his fraternal crisis rooted in America, his struggle, previously ignored within the Parisian space, resurfaces. When forced to confront his American history, he opens himself in ways never exposed and *le milieu* witnesses the transformation. Unbeknown to him, the dialogue with Giovanni has softened his nature, comforted him to the point of lowering his guards. Giovanni's manhood seems somewhat inoculated to the tolerance David has offered other men and produces a level of transparency, even within their abstract chat. The young Italian's seductive essence warms David's being in such a way that his sexuality, usually "above suspicion," bares itself naked to the other patrons of the bar. In an instant, he is vulnerable in his exchange with the barman and with those who in moments past attempted to deduce if he were open to that type of exchange. Uncomfortable, unmasked, and intrigued, David comes to be the recipient of the milieu's gaze like never before.

Baldwin's conflicted protagonist grows even more uncomfortable the moment he realizes that the power dynamics between him and *le milieu* have shifted. His nakedness, an unwelcome gift from Giovanni, makes him a vulnerable spectacle in a space that has been scrutinizing him since he arrived from across the ocean. He recognizes this when Giovanni leaves momentarily, when he professes, "I watched him as he moved. And then I watched their faces, watching him. And then I was afraid. I knew that they were watching, had been watching both of us. They knew that they had witnessed a beginning and now they would not cease to watch until they saw the end."[50] And while he is no stranger to the gazes, without the mask of his masculinity (read: heteronormative and tolerant sexuality) he is targeted in more ways than one. In fact, his fear actualizes when an effeminate man with strong hands asks him about liking the barman. His reaction, approaching an extreme drama of emotion, reveals itself in his private thoughts: "I did not know what to do or say. It seemed impossible to hit him; it seemed impossible to get angry. It did not seem real, he did not seem real."[51] Here the reader is privy to the collapse between the real/ not real logic suggested by Reid-Pharr. To extend Reid-Pharr's argument, David's logic becomes unworkable through the body of Giovanni. The Italian man tending bar in the Parisian demimonde stands cloaked in a manhood that mirrors his own and forces a self-recognition that was once avoidable. In a sense, he disrupts David's matrix of manhood and exposes it as the Parisian simulacrum that he created it to be. Guillaume's bar thus becomes a space of elision, a site of convergence where David's Parisian self is peeled back to uncover a self from whom he cannot seem to flee. Perhaps no better exchange than the one with Jacques in this moment captures the profound vulnerability of David. Who knew that his innocent conversation with Giovanni would have such consequences? He certainly did not foresee the breakdown of his nicely constructed world, did not anticipate the speed at which he traveled from hiding his true self to witnessing its *spectacular* dance with visibility. Yet, while trying to clean up the mess caused by the germs of his dilemma while proclaiming to the half-mad, half-curious Jacques, "There's been no confusion," he showcases his own bewilderment.[52] There is indeed confusion for David. He cannot make sense of how unresolved his fraternal crisis remains, cannot understand how everyone, or so it seems, now knows his deep secret. It is Jacques's admonishment that lets him know the severity of his crisis: "Confusion is a luxury which only the very, very young can possibly afford and you are not that young anymore."[53] Jacques is right: there is no time for confusion, and David needs much more to be saved. Before, it was in America; now it is in Paris.

Ironically, the source of David's reemerging crisis also holds the key to its resolution. Giovanni proves himself a salvific figure for the suffering protagonist, as he is capable of saving him from America, Paris, and now himself. More importantly, his salvific endowment, the curious manhood that laid bare David's Parisian simulacrum, was but the peculiar result of a history not too different from his American friend's. Indeed, the commonality in their histories, albeit distinct, presents Giovanni as the most able of the Parisian men to save David. In the former, the latter can see himself, find himself, and lose himself while playing in the field of same-sex desire. Their exchange, beyond the intimate, would be of a symbiotic salvific nature—what Giovanni is for David, David would be for Giovanni. Inevitably, in learning of Giovanni's past and his present struggles, the reader understands that the men can only escape their histories and presents by taking refuge in each other and that if either wishes to survive their crises, they would have to save each other. David comes to learn this as he hears more of Giovanni's life story.

The moment readers recognize David's need to be saved, they also realize the same for Giovanni. Much like David, Giovanni's narrative is characterized by fraternal crisis and flight. Similarly, Giovanni fled his original home space due to a breakdown in traditional ideas of manhood suffered within an intimate encounter. The reader, along with David, does not come to know the exact reason for the barman's flight, however, until much later in the novel. Caught within an intense emotional catharsis, Giovanni informs David, now his male lover, of the day he left home: "I will never forget that day. It was the day of my death—I wish it had been the day of my death."[54] His recollection combines metaphoric gesturing and literal longing. Symbolically, the day represents the loss of something dear to his individual livelihood and perhaps because of it, he wishes for the more real ending of his life. He continues, in an effort to shed light on the trauma of the day, "I remember I was weeping . . . That was the first time in my life that I wanted to die. I had just buried my baby in the churchyard where my father and my father's father were and I had left my girl screaming in my mother's house. Yes, I had made a baby but it was born dead."[55] The following day, Giovanni fled his small village in Italy and came to France. His flight, more externally traumatic that David's, was precipitated by a fraternal crisis. The stillborn birth of his son signaled a collapse in how he perceived his own manhood. And partly as the result of a historical coupling of human reproduction and masculinity, his manhood was rendered ineffective on that day. Consequently, he fled his home, wife, and dead son, hoping to escape his newly discovered impotency. Home would remain a constant reminder of how unmanly he was, would hasten the developing space-in-between him and his own manhood. Therefore Italy, like David's America, signified a space of internal division and unsettledness. Any expectation of personal peace required a departure from the place that, so fraught with signs of "masculinity," demanded a confrontation with the idea of a fragile sexual self. He, too, found a freedom in Paris.

Comparable to David's, Giovanni's flight to Paris does not completely resolve his fraternal crisis. While it does afford him the opportunity to re-create himself from the fractures of his Italian manhood, he consistently tiptoes on the precipice of another crisis. Like his American counterpart, Giovanni dangerously flirts with the predator–prey dialectic. His unique expression of manliness, at odds within the Parisian demimonde, places him in a position of power and powerlessness. Guillaume's bar paradoxically frees and imprisons him in that it permits his stability while objectifying his masculinity. As such, he engages in power struggles defined by his manipulation of le milieu, their incessant lusting, and his own same-sex desire. In fact, his current job and position within the Parisian scene is owed to the imbalance of power between him and the noble-named Guillaume. He later tells David, "I saw that he could be useful if I could only find some way to make him keep his hands off me. . . . It appears that I am good for business. For this reason, he leaves me mostly alone."[56] Thus, not unlike David, he positions himself as different from this community of sexual "Others" in order to benefit from performative distinctions. Using their desire against them, he is able to obtain financial security. Nevertheless, his dialectical play differs drastically from the true American's as his economic livelihood depends on this community. This places him in a somewhat more vulnerable position, one in which the power or control favors, to a certain degree, those whom he despises. "The white bourgeoisie, the French Guillaume and the Belgian (American) Jacques, are competing constantly to claim both Giovanni's labor power and his sex, a process that necessarily restricts Giovanni to the realm of the corporeal and the dirty."[57] With only his physical body as leverage, he has little room for play. Consequently, he must play, in keeping with Reid-Pharr, as slave—never able to escape the sexual component of his crisis. Unlike David, whose Americanness and financial independence guarantee a certain freedom of play, Giovanni must move carefully and strategically. He must meet the demands of le milieu if he expects to enjoy his sojourn in Paris. For this reason, he, too, must be saved in Paris. And in meeting David, someone of like gender expression and historical struggle, he finds his salvific man and the key to his salvation.

At first, the reader questions the compatibility of David and Giovanni; after all, they do come from very different worlds. David, a symbol of American Puritanism and sexual conservatism, grounds himself in an appeal to a moral neatness that escapes the Parisians. Conversely, Giovanni, a representative of impulsive pursuits of freedom, holds fast to the expressive critique of convention and the possibility for question. Where David offers stability, Giovanni offers dynamism; both men bask in the balance yielded by each other's difference. Thus, when David finds himself in an unrecognizable sentiment, when he "ached abruptly, intolerably, with a longing to go home . . . home across the ocean, to things and people [he] knew and understood; to those things, those places, those people which [he] would always, helplessly, and in whatever bitterness of spirit, love above all else," he presents his deepest vulnerability to Giovanni.[58] And while his sentiment goes unspoken, while Giovanni remains unsuspecting in his sudden urgency to return to the hotel, he opens himself for an invitation to love. His longing for home, to be among those he loved, is but his heart's confession that he wants more than the transience of Parisian delights. Emptiness pervades his spirit, and he cries out to Giovanni from the hollow spaces of his longing manhood. The irony lies in how different Giovanni is from him. Accordingly, "Giovanni is the last person in the world with whom a man of David's moral ambiguities could safely afford to have anything to do. . . . He is David's nemesis, and in a more limited sense his salvation, precisely because he refuses to conceive of any meaningful existence that is devoid of a conception of sin."[59] Macebuh's aforementioned observation homes in on how Giovanni's difference allows him to serve as David's salvific man. His disregard for conventional morality and the rigidity of an American ethos carves the space for him to invite David to his room—a room, the reader should note, that will become their sanctum from crises.

In her essay "'An Irrevocable Condition': Constructions of Home and the Writing of Place in *Giovanni's Room*," Drowne writes, "David and Giovanni retreat from the larger cage of Paris to the private but even more suffocating air of the room that does serve, for a time, as a refuge from the unfriendly and judgmental forces threatening their already precarious relationship."[60] Drowne's statement evidences the importance of Giovanni's room as a contrasting space to Guillaume's bar, the Parisian demimonde, and each man's respective home geographies. The small space outlined in "clutter and disorder" permits the pursuit of intimacy where other spaces denied it. Its seclusion promises secrecy and, in that, encourages the men's erasure of the symbolic space-in-between them. For David, reminiscent of the closeness he once felt with Joey, it represents a harbinger of what is to come. Therefore, in his unease he thinks, "If I do not open the door at once and get out of here, I am lost."[61] By lost, David reifies the fear he first experienced with Joey. Intimacy with Giovanni threatens, much like that with Joey, the logic of his manhood. He fears the complete erasure of his Parisian simulacrum, the destruction of his heterosexual self, and, more importantly, his manly self. However, the draw of Giovanni is too much to resist, and the compulsion to touch him or be touched by him challenges the internal fraternal crisis from which he suffers. He admits, "But I knew I could not open the door, I knew it was too late; soon it was too late to do anything but moan. He pulled me against him, putting himself into my arms as though he were giving me himself to carry, and slowly pulled me down with him to that bed."[62] David's struggle in this moment represents his confusing battles with himself. Although committed to maintaining his well-constructed American manhood, he naturally longs to submit to his sexual desires. Inevitably, his compliance to retreat into Giovanni's room is acquiescence to intimacy. And this is precisely what he needs.

Giovanni is able to do that night what Joey had been unable to years before—compel David to come back. This, of course, is largely due to the combination of David's maturity, a difference in geographic location, and his need for intimacy. Space, above everything else, is critical to understanding the possibility of their relationship. Paris still represents David's playground, and, in that sense, David rejects the idea of permanence. While dwelling and loving in the refuge of Giovanni's room, he enjoys a surreal detachment from reality, or, as he recalls, "I remember that life in that room seemed to be occurring beneath the sea. Time flowed past indifferently above us; hours and days had no meaning."[63] "Time" has a dual function in this recollection. On one hand, it refers to the blissful state of isolation where the men's investment in each other blinds them to the minute elements of day-to-day activity. However, on the other, it is redolent of the first meaningful conversation between David and Giovanni. Remembering that conversation, the idea of time is strongly linked to history and, more specifically, to the "triumphant parade" of settling, solving, and putting things in place. Its absence here relates to an unpassing of history, for David. The surrealism, suspension, and submersion "beneath the sea" prevent the possibility of trace, of evidence, of real occurrence. Indeed, the reality of life holds no meaningful tie to the one they experience together. Giovanni's room, despite its tangible realness, is but another simulacrum constructed by David—only slightly different from the world he created through *le milieu*. Thus, contrasting David's thought of how "In the beginning, [their] life together held a joy and amazement which was newborn everyday" with how "anguish and fear had become the surface on which [they] slipped and slid, losing balance, dignity, and pride," the reader learns that the love eliminating that symbolic space-in-between them is as fleeting as the season.[64] Resolution to their fraternal crises is impermanent.

David's thoughts surrounding the fragility of his relationship with Giovanni and chronicling its descent from the beautiful into the ugly confirm the reader's suspicion and Giovanni's fears that their love will not endure. I argue that the collapse in their relationship stems from David's unwillingness to construct or imagine a real life grounded by male intimacy. His American identity and Puritan morality refuse him the possibility for same-sex love. In his own confession, "Even at my most candid, even when I tried hardest to give myself to him as he gave himself to me, I was holding something back"—David acknowledges an inability to fully invest in a same-sex relationship.[65] In an effort to justify his approaching separation from Giovanni, he uses Hella, the convenient itinerant woman of his life, to reauthenticate his heterosexual self. Reauthentication proves difficult as all the while he is made to concede to the profound emotional bond he has developed with and for Giovanni. Musing over the various distractions he pursues in hopes of freeing himself from Giovanni's room, he divulges to himself, "And no matter what I was doing, another me sat in my belly, absolutely cold with terror over the question of my life."[66] The question of his life is nothing but the attempt to identify and make sense of the germ of his dilemma, to locate meaning in the powerful attraction he has to men. Giovanni's danger lies in his ability to push David past the purity of his American innocence. The inability to dismiss Giovanni as easily as he did Joey begets a series of thoughts surrounding his future ability to control his sexual impulses toward men. Out of this thinking springs "sorrow and shame and panic and great bitterness," and, according to David, "with this fearful intimation there opened in [him] a hatred for Giovanni which was as powerful as [his] love and which was nourished by the same roots."[67] It is within this moment that the willingness to save and be saved changes for David. Though already pulling away or holding back from Giovanni, his new fear pushes him to a rejection of their love altogether. The consequences of this highlight the tragedy of the narrative.

David and Giovanni's retreat into the room purposes itself as a refuge from the nonunderstanding predatorial worlds that sought to claim them. Within that space they become each other's sanctum, bask in the beauty of unrestricted fraternity. For the both of them, the fraternal crises once defining their lives and flights dissipate in the presence of a powerful bonding love. Nevertheless, as this love truly begins to show itself, as the men became more salvific for each other, David pulls back. His withdrawal is first witnessed through his critique of the room. Commenting on the clutter and disorder, he proclaims, almost epiphanically, "This was not the garbage of Paris, which would have been anonymous: This was Giovanni's regurgitated life."[68] By equating Giovanni's life with garbage, David begins the process of abjecting the man who claims his love. Giovanni is relegated to an idea of filth, coupled with dirt to contrast the clean and pure innocence of David's American manhood. Abjection, thus, is a necessary step for distancing himself from Giovanni and the room, of re-creating space-in-between them. Once he begins the process of abjection, it is hard for David to stop; the room incites fear within him. He continues,

> But it was not the room's disorder which was frightening; it was the fact that when one began searching for the key to this disorder, one realized that it was not to be found in any of the usual places. For this was not a matter of habit or circumstance or temperament; it was a matter of punishment and grief.[69]

Although he treats his thought as a realization and not a construction within the process of abjection, David alters the symbolism of Giovanni's room. It no longer is that paradisical hideaway from a persistent and intolerant world; rather, it changes into a space of torture and misery. The American protagonist realizes, now more than ever, that the burden of salvation tilts more in his direction and that he is "to destroy this room and give to Giovanni a new and better life."[70]

The severity of the fraternal crisis plaguing David's relationship with Giovanni surfaces in a variety of scenes following his initial critique of the disorder of the room. He, for instance, has sex with Sue, a random woman within the novel, in an attempt to escape the room and, more importantly, Giovanni's love. However, it escalates once he returns to the room and finds his male lover emotionally distraught after being fired from his job for not giving in to Guillaume's advances. Giovanni, rendered vulnerable beyond words, professes his need and love for David to such a degree that the latter feels trapped within the situation. David's subsequent critiques of the room, of its "encroaching walls," speak to the suffocating nature of their love and how desperately he sought to increase the space-in-between them. Even more, David realizes in this moment how his cleverly constructed Parisian simulacrum now threatens the heteronormative reality existing outside of it. His situation with Giovanni, as the room was undergoing transforma-tion, was inching toward a permanency he neither desired nor knew how to handle. Giovanni demanded more and more of his time, dragged him "to the bottom of the sea," and in speaking of the growing attachment, he reveals his own weakness to the reader: "He could not endure being very far from me for very long. I was the only person on God's cold, green earth who cared about him, who knew his speech and silence, knew his arms, and did not carry a knife. The burden of his salvation seemed to be on me and I could not endure it."[71] David's confession captures both his acknowledg-ment that he is Giovanni's salvific man as well as his incapability to honor the "obligation." Through David's transparency, Baldwin thus complicates the idea of salvific manhood. He highlights how the nobleness within the endowment is not enough to compel the bearer to accept it. Unlike Elisha in *Go Tell It on the Mountain* and unlike Giovanni, in a sense, David rejects his ability to save; he does not feel strong enough to bear the burden of loving Giovanni unconditionally, of honoring the purity of their frater-nal bond. Instead, he engages in acts of betrayal and lies, waiting for the moment when he can fully place space-in-between them and precipitate a crisis that neither of them expected.

The proverbial fraternal crisis of *Giovanni's Room* culminates when Hella returns to Paris resolved and ready to create her life with David. Her arrival represents the convergence of David's American innocence and his Parisian freedom. Additionally, his inability to manage his life with Hella with his life with Giovanni shows the impossibility of his situation. To be clear, the heteronormative world that he "desires" does not allow for the Parisian simulacrum he has constructed. And inevitably Paris, as a site of conflict for David, necessitates his decision. After spending days with Hella, a superficial effort at heterosexual reauthentication, David visits Giovanni's room to punctuate the fraternal crisis with finality. Rejecting David's assertion that he must leave him for Hella and that it should be no surprise, Giovanni offers one of the most penetrating emotional ful-minations of the novel:

> You walk around with your hands in front of you as though you had some precious metal, gold, silver, rubies, maybe *diamonds* down there between your legs! You will never give it to anybody, you will never let anybody *touch it*—man or woman. You want to be clean . . . You want to leave Giovanni because he makes you stink. You want to despise Giovanni because he is not afraid of the stink of love.[72]

Giovanni's emotionality in this scene stems from the realization that David's flight from him is neither about Hella nor the "real" disorder of the room. His flight, as the intuitive Italian reminds the reader, is rooted in the per-ception of same-sex desire. David never truly resolved the fraternal crisis that emerged when he was with Joey; he never decoupled male same-sex attraction from dirt and filth. The "stink of love" connotes the messiness of same-sex or homosexual desire, signifies how it challenges the rigid constructions of human emotion.

For David, to love permanently, fully, is to risk the loss of his manhood. The "stink of love" beckons that fear he has so neatly withheld from his Parisian simulacrums. He does not fear losing Hella, does not fear losing the love of his father; no, David fears the loss of himself. He admits this in his response to Giovanni:

> What kind of life can two men have together, anyway? All this love you talk about—isn't it just that you want to be made to feel strong?

You want to go out and be the big laborer and bring home the money, and you want me to stay here and wash the dishes and cook the food and clean this miserable closet of a room and kiss you when you come in through that door and lie with you at night and be your little *girl*. . . . That's what you mean and that's *all* you mean when you say you love me. You say I want to kill *you*. What do you think you've been doing to me?[73]

Thus, for the first time in the novel, Baldwin gives the reader a very direct insight into David's wrestling with same-sex desire. While hinted at throughout the narrative and while definitely implicated within his relationships with different people, this is the first time that David is honest about his fear. To love men is to risk the ridiculous idea of losing his manhood. To love Giovanni is to violate that Puritan ethos so crucial to his American self. It is to soil his American innocence by deeming the Parisian simulacrum of homosexual love as permanent, as more than a touristic sojourn. This is not something David is able to accept or allow. He is content with the fluid movement between reality and simulacrum, between acceptability and flirtation. However, to delve into the stink of love is to blur the lines between what he sees as his simulacrum and his real, is to make same-sex desire more real than his protected American manhood. His problem comes from his inability to view love outside of a heteronormative and heterosexual paradigm—for in order to love, there must always be a woman, must always be the essence of *la féminine*. This is the sine qua non of his fraternal crisis.

The events that follow the last real emotional exchange between David and Giovanni have been exalted, within Baldwinian scholarship and queer studies discourse in general, as the marker of tragedy. Undoubtedly, the murder of Guillaume by a tired and overwhelmed Giovanni is tragic, as is the eventual execution of Giovanni and its peculiar link to the withheld love of David. But, above anything else, I read the tragedy of *Giovanni's Room* within the embodiment of David. The entire novel pivots on Baldwin's preoccupation with American innocence and how it prevents the possibility of a complex and fully developed manhood. All of David's relationships, even his love-filled one with Giovanni, are meant to be backdrops to the relationship he has with himself. His ultimate struggle, then, is magnified through his flights from Joey, America, Hella, and Giovanni. It is, if one reads the novel carefully, not directly concerned with the question of same-sex desire or homosexual love. His struggle and his novelistic journey, I argue, are defined by his quest to love himself. *Giovanni's Room,* then, as a novel of flight, hopes to tell the tragedy of man's inability to love self in a world bent on skewing his reflection. For David, the world gave him one idea of manhood, and his goal is to free himself from the control of that idea. Baldwin does leave this tragic narrative with hope, however—pushing one to the point of looking within. It is the last lesson David shares: "I look at my sex, my troubling sex, and wonder how it can be redeemed, how I can save it from the knife. The journey to the grave is already begun, the journey to corruption is, always, already half over. Yet, the key to my salvation, which cannot save my body, is hidden in my flesh."[74] Giovanni's death symbolizes the unfortunate casualty of war experienced when one dares to love someone battling to love themselves. Tragically, Giovanni's need to be saved came prematurely, as David's salvific manhood was primarily reserved to save himself.

3

Alone in the Absurd

The Trope of Tragic Black
Manhood in *Another Country*

There is but one truly serious philosophical problem, and that is
suicide. Judging whether life is or is not worth living amounts to
answering the fundamental question of philosophy. All the rest—
whether or not the world has three dimensions, whether the mind
has nine or twelve categories—comes afterwards.

—ALBERT CAMUS, *The Myth of Sisyphus*

On a cold December night in 1946, a young African American man by the
name of Eugene Worth climbed atop the rails of New York City's George
Washington Bridge and hurled himself into the Hudson River. Worth's
suicide, for many, was simply the reoccurring signifier of how treacherous
the New York cityscape could be, of how the city of bright lights promised
despair to those whose daring to dream proved too unfulfilling. For our
young adult Baldwin, Worth's suicide meant so much more. As one of his
closest friends, and as the man whom he loved both intimately and platon-
ically, Eugene carried a huge personal loss for Baldwin. Outside of the hole
left in Baldwin's twenty-two-year-old heart, Worth's death also spoke to the
peculiar struggles faced by African American men in 1940s America. Even
more, it highlighted the vulnerability of Black manhood, how fractured it
had become by the cruelty of this world. Baldwin would use that pain, and
rage, and torment to work anew on a book entitled "Ignorant Armies." At a
point, the novel stilled itself, and we later learn it is because it contained two

of Baldwin's most important novels: the first, *Giovanni's Room*; the second, *Another Country*. That these two novels were born from the same fodder, and that they read very differently in subject matter and context, reaffirms the quiet assertion underlying this project; Baldwin's novels, despite their seeming difference, collectivize to tell a most poignant narrative. And perhaps in no better place, the narrative of salvific manhood and fraternal crisis pronounces itself in *Another Country*. Sadly, Baldwin's loss, and his desire to make sense of it via the literary, forces us to reckon with the question, What is the price of absurdity for Black men? What does it mean, or how does it mean differently when they perform their own tragedy?

Eugene Worth's suicide forced Baldwin into personal depression and a philosophical grappling much akin to Albert Camus's meditation on the role of suicide. The latter's decision to pursue the question of suicide as a philosophical consideration born out of existential plight suggests how either he had become a man so disillusioned with the constructions of life that he found merit in questioning its worthiness or he had, like other men and women before him, witnessed the dangers of dancing with darkness through the fates of those who dared to stop themselves from breathing. Whether the product of his own bouts of depression or the result of spectatorial engagement, the inquiry alone was both timely and important. Camus's contribution to existentialist philosophy encouraged the literate and living to look more deeply at the begetting agent of suicide. The question of it, of the intentional act of individual erasure, reveals how concerns of meaning and worth, and the depth of those ideas, produce an amazingly dangerous seduction where human beings either move closer to recognizing their mortality or are pushed to fight for life. Camus's quandary lies within his "hope" to discover, as he states, "the means to proceed beyond nihilism."[1] And yet, this interrogative dilemma is not unique to the realm of philosophy, does not reside solely within the minds of those notably deemed existentialists; rather, it is a concern that deeply pervades the body of human literature and flows powerfully from the pens of those artists bold enough to ask the question, What, if anything, is the meaning of life?

American literature, particularly that written post–World War II, saw itself grappling more and more with the existentialist's plight. African American writers, in particular, found literary existentialism useful in their efforts to capture the peculiar nature of blackness within an American context. Novels such as Ralph Ellison's *Invisible Man* (1952), Richard Wright's *The Outsider* (1953), and Toni Morrison's *The Bluest Eye* (1970) distinguished themselves in coupling a commitment to explore the traditional topoi of African American literature with creative–philosophical examinations of the complexity of Black identity. However, no African American novel published in the immediate decades following the War captures Camus's paradox of the absurd with the disturbing poetic textuality of James Baldwin's *Another Country* (1962). Exploring what Camus has deemed the "one truly serious philosophical problem," Baldwin's third novel placed the issue of suicide back into the American imagination while complicating the question that it necessarily evoked. *Another Country* lays bare the tragic consequences of absented male intimacy while hinting toward its salvific potentiality.

Another Country, using Eugene Worth as a model for the tragic and phantom protagonist Rufus Scott, is at once a literary representation of Baldwin's efforts to understand the suicide of his beloved friend and his desire to draw attention to the disposability of Black manhood within this country. Baldwin, while never purporting the novel to be what Camus claims for *The Myth of Sisyphus*—an "[attempt] to resolve the problem of suicide"—knows that it has something in common with Camusian absurdism.[2] Baldwin understood it as a "reflection of the 'incoherence' of life in America."[3] Indeed, the very question that moves the text is the preoccupation with trying to make sense of suicide as a legitimate response or an appropriate answer to the question of (in)sufferable living. The novel emerges as a stark interjection to Camus's philosophical meanderings within the problem of suicide. It asks its readers to consider how the trope of tragic Black manhood messies and challenges the Camusian idea asserting that suicide does not settle the paradox of the absurd and that it is merely another form of evasion. Reading *Another Country* through the trope of tragic Black manhood complicates the discourse surrounding suicide by tracing how absented male intimacy undermines Rufus Scott's wrestling with race, sexuality, and purpose. Additionally, it highlights how the phantom protagonist's Sisyphean will-to-endure is systematically stripped by racial and social structures of power, structures that reveal how white bodies, through expressions of privilege and withholding, are complicit within these tragedies. Such complicity encourages and demands a rereading of suicide that counters Camus's philosophical underpinnings and interventions.

Another Country, from the same source who gave us *Giovanni's Room*, continues a Baldwinian pursuit of salvific manhood. Whether plagued by illegitimate personal guilt or recognition of the discordance between Black manhood and American idealism, Baldwin's partial novelizing of Worth's life builds off the fractured manhood witnessed in *Giovanni's Room*. Whereas in *Go Tell It on the Mountain* Baldwin traces the complexities of Black manhood through an intraracial lens largely focused on the home space and the church, and whereas he seemingly reaches across extremes to chronicle white same-gendering love, desire, and American identity in *Giovanni's Room*, *Another Country* brings these two worlds together in a gripping survey of how fraternal crisis and salvific manhood operate within an interracial frame. This novel offers a continued expansion of what I see as Baldwin's investment in truly understanding the possibilities and limitations of male intimacy. In *Another Country*, Baldwin asks about the price of love, insisting on an interrogation of how different characters come to love and to express such love, and magnifying how we often fail to offer the very gifts we were endowed with to share. In picking up where *Giovanni's Room* cuts off in its promising of tragedy, *Another Country* showcases the power of intimacy and love through the consequences of its denial. In the end, Baldwin gifts a sobering reflection, which takes the heaviness of *Giovanni's Room* to a new depth of despair.

Baldwin prefaces *Another Country* with a musing from Henry James, who is attempting to make sense of a population or demographic of people "beyond his divination":

> They strike one, above all, as giving no account of themselves in any terms already consecrated by human use; to this inarticulate state they probably form, collectively, the most unprecedented of monuments; abysmal the mystery of what they think, what they feel, what they want, what they suppose themselves to be saying.[4]

While Baldwin is not concerned here with the Ninevites, as James names them, the musing captures a significant challenge within Baldwin's novelistic pursuit. Simply, one of the goals of *Another Country* is to present subjects whose realities are seemingly beyond the divination of the American readership. That these subjects are temporally and thus existentially distinct from James's Ninevites means nothing as, like his muse, Baldwin understands his characters, and his central character in particular, to occupy the same fate of inarticulateness. His task from the outset, then, lies in rendering Rufus Scott legible. The difficulty, as Baldwin revises from James's observation, emerges from the way in which Black life, or Black male life to be specific, has no "terms" from which to communicate itself. Baldwin's struggle, then, in scripting the lived and postlived reality of Rufus Scott stems from the absence of precise and sufficient language. Rufus, much like Eugene Worth, is unknowable. The novel's driving plot hinges on the quiet effort to make certain parts of him known, to reveal what he feels, what he wants, what he supposes himself to be saying.[5] What James identifies as "abysmal the mystery" Baldwin perceives as the necessary chase—to stretch the language of the time beyond its limitations into a portrait of a man grossly misread through a state of being unknowable.

Inasmuch as the beginning of book 1, "Easy Rider," highlights how Baldwin intends to wrestle with particular subjectivities who are otherwise unknowable, its epigraph employs W. C. Handy's lyrics to foreshadow part of Rufus's fate. The simultaneous signifying of Rufus Scott as "easy rider" and the framing of his life through "I told him, easy riders / Got to stay away, / So he had to vamp it, / But the hike ain't far" establishes a bluesing of both his ontological self and the life he is to experience.[6] Signifying Rufus as an "easy rider" might be read through a literal genealogy, where his vocation as a jazz man mirrors blues musicians whose lives were often characterized by the ways in which their instruments clung easily to their persons. Here, the instrument is both tangible and abstract—a literal relationship where the physical instrument hangs effortlessly to its musician, as well as a synecdochical relationship where the instrument symbolizes the music as an essential part of the man. However, "easy rider" might also be extended to signify the ways in which Rufus attempted to navigate through life, carefree and easygoing. If the former, then Handy's evocative presence speaks directly to how blues music, at its core, reflects the darkness witnessed and experienced by the musicians burdened to play it. But if the latter, the epigraph lays bare the warning necessarily tethered to Black manhood—the terrain of this life is not meant for "easy riders." In a more nuanced reading, Baldwin's use of Handy suggests a marrying of the two. He is at once signifying on the blues tradition and the role or struggle of the musician within it, and making a statement about how the existential reality for Black men in midcentury America antagonizes those who wish to be easy riders, who wish, that is, to move through life like a slow-moving train.

The very first line of the narrative, "He was facing Seventh Avenue, at Times Square," exemplifies Baldwin's desire to offer a layered portrait of an unknowable subject.[7] Perhaps even more, however, with the time being stamped as midnight, Baldwin means to suggest some level of obscurity. What the text thus offers in its opening are the shadows and silhouettes of Baldwin's beloved subject. By situating Rufus in Times Square, a symbol of commercial and social interest, Baldwin hints toward Black male longing for both investment and visibility. However, this positioning is overshadowed by both the time of night and the politics of place, as Rufus has recently left the movies and a movie theater experience that was more revealing than entertaining. Within the space of the theater, "Twice [Rufus] had been awakened by the violent accents of the Italian film, once the usher had awakened him, and twice he had been awakened by caterpillar fingers between his thighs."[8] As with the Handy epigraph, Baldwin's scripting holds double meaning. On one hand, the state of being awakened relays the simple state of physical exhaustion or time spent within the space. On the other, it begs for the quality of disillusionment. Rufus's awakening links his physical exhaustion with an abstract disillusionment. The awakening from sleep— the disturbing of his sanctuary, that is—comes through multiple mediums: violence, authority, and violation. The "violent accents" suggest a violence outside of his person, that which is both foreign and other. Additionally, and somewhat similarly, the second awakening comes from a figure endowed with power within the very space affording him sanctum. And last, somewhat climactically, his disillusionment comes through acts of violation where his body becomes a site of pillage. These details significantly highlight his state of loss, reflect how he occupies spaces characterized by unsafety and abjection. The expression of his psychic state in this moment evidences his sense of loss: "He was so tired, he had fallen so low, that he scarcely had the energy to be angry; nothing of his belonged to him anymore—*you took the best, so why not take the rest?*"[9] At once tired, depressed, and with an inability to express justified emotion to his circumstance, Baldwin's Black man has been stripped of agency and autonomy. In a world yet to be painted, we learn of his dispossessed manhood. The italicized "*you took the best, so why not take the rest?*" ominously ushers in the trope of tragic Black manhood. And as if to punctuate how this trope enjoys a life of eternality, Rufus "stumbled down the endless stairs into the street."[10]

Despite the heaviness of *Another Country's* opening scene, Baldwin carefully complicates Rufus's struggle. In addition to his learning of the world's "violence" toward and "violation" of him, there is also mention of the possibility of safety. As potential escape from his awakened state of destitution, the idea of friendship is constructed as a space for refuge. That human intimacy might serve as respite from the "violent accents" of society reflects the strong but riddled subtext of the novel. Nevertheless, we must not ignore how "[Rufus] had been thinking of going downtown and waking up Vivaldo—the only friend he had left in the city or maybe the world."[11] Ultimately, Rufus's decision to not access the space of friendship identifies the impaired relationship between manhood and intimacy, in addition to a very real obstacle Black men face when in need of articulating their suffering. The tension between Black men and the necessary expression of vulnerability is systemic and tragic. Similar to his inability to express anger in the movie theater, he is unable to express a softer emotion like vulnerability. These inabilities ought to be understood as consequences of dispossessions, as traces of violence and violation where Black male subjects have been dispossessed of their right and energy to articulate themselves, to make known their sufferings.

The first portrait of Rufus Scott is one of aimlessness and destitution. Baldwin wastes little time in informing the reader that his protagonist is in some form of trouble. Through the use of flashback, he outlines how Rufus arrived at his current state. And by taking the reader back to Rufus's last performance as a member of a jazz band, he reveals the moment when the drummer's life began to change as well as the subtle question that pervades the text. Capturing the symbolic and collective power of music, what might be understood in a Fanonian sense as a sort of artistic collective consciousness, Baldwin outlines the relationship between artist and witness. For Baldwin, and for Black people more expansively, the artist assumes a unique role in the battle against suffering. He emerges as the conduit of pain, the medium for plight. His goal is to use his artistry to alleviate the darkness of his witnesses. What makes this possible within the community, and this is evidenced by the blues tradition, is that the artist communicates to the suffering that they are not alone, that what they are experiencing is endurable, and that there is "some meaning in the suffering." And perhaps it is this Nietzschean idea of survival that emboldens the artist's sound in *Another Country*. Whatever the case, Baldwin's racialization of the artist's function establishes and demands new lenses for the viewing of Black manhood in crisis. More specifically, creating a space where artists must play or communicate for each other moves the level of suffering into a metadiscursive space. Ultimately, the novel's play with Black male need and vulnerability, collectivity, and voice flays Camus's reckoning with suicide. What philosophically fails for Camus becomes a more than viable option for Baldwin, for blackness.

Baldwin's revision of Camus's quandary reveals itself through the poignant relationship between Rufus and another, though younger, musician. Using his instrument to speak to the audience, to the world, and, more importantly, to Rufus, the young saxophonist unveils a critical part of the trope of tragic Black manhood. His youth and the narrative to be conveyed through his instrument magnify the pervasive and haunting presence of suffering for Black men. Tragic Black manhood, while realized or maybe discernible in men of maturity, nevertheless roots itself in the earliest articulations of Black boyhood. Thus, when the saxophonist plays his story, he simultaneously manifests himself as ontological metonym, a reflection of the young adulthood engendering Rufus's current struggles in manhood. Listening to the young man as he assumes a solo, Rufus observes,

He stood there, wide-legged, humping the air, filling his barrel chest, shivering in the rags of his twenty-odd years, and screaming through the horn *Do you love me? Do you love me? Do you love me?* [. . .] This anyway, was the question Rufus heard, the same phrase, unbearably, endlessly, and variously repeated, with all of the force the boy had.[12]

In describing the boy as "shivering," Baldwin once again captures the coldness of this world. But this coldness is not solely projected outside of the boy's body; rather, it has become the very condition of his personhood. His circumstance comes to be reflected through the "rags" that decorate his existence, his time on this earth. That his clothes do not properly shield him from the cold reality metaphorically iterates how blackness or Black manhood is insufficiently protected from the very spaces it claims as home. Additionally, instead of speaking or singing or crying through his music, Rufus's surrogate is "screaming." Through the juxtaposition of such a powerful mode of expression and the tender question of "Do you love me?", Baldwin complicates and punctuates the Black male capacity for an expressive vulnerability. Rage, anger, and frustration subsume tenderness, softness, and gentleness. And while Black male tragedy necessitates an expression of the former emotions, its panacea, as I argue, requires the latter. Ironically, the artist's performance as empath pushes us toward tender expressions of vulnerability, a vulnerability identifiable through Rufus's reception of the saxophonist's musical utterance.

The vocal musicality in this moment foreshadows Rufus's journey through the rest of book 1 and through the memories of the other characters of the novel. The *saxophonic question of love* and Rufus's ability to understand it are symptomatic of his own struggle with love, with the prospect of being alone in the cold New York cultural space. In questioning love's presence, or in identifying its absence, the saxophonist melodizes the tragedy of Black manhood. Such tragedy emerges precisely in the space of lack and absence, at the site where the utterance of Black male longing is answered with a hollow and deafening silence. Indeed, it is this absence of love, the questioning of worth, that precipitates the racial and gendered battles with loneliness. The ground is inevitably cold. Baldwin paints this cultural coldness through a more detailed dark musicality, one bringing clarity to the screaming saxophonic question of love:

> And yet the question was terrible and real; the boy was blowing with his lungs and guts out of his own short past; somewhere in that past, in the gutters or gang fights or gang shags; in the acrid room, on the sperm-stiffened blanket, behind marijuana or the needle, under the smell of piss in the precinct basement, he had received the blow from which he never would recover and this no one wanted to believe. *Do you love me?*[13]

The description of the boy's past, whether imagined by Rufus or real in nature, testifies to the cultural reality for many Black men coming of age in the New York environment. Not only do we *hear* the deplorable conditions of his past and possibly his present, we come to learn of the inseparability of the question of love and material conditions. One cannot claim to love those whom one renders marginal, abject, or invisible. Moreover, he who has come of age in the wastelands of the nation's urban spaces easily discerns the denial of love. Circumstances of poverty, while suffocating, deafening, and blinding, do not occlude the dispossessed from feeling absence, distance, coldness, or withholding. Therefore, the saxophonist's powerful evocation of violence, allusion to repugnant sexual practices, reference to abuse of drugs and criminality, and representation of filth all coalesce into a portrait of destitution that strongly parallels Rufus's being. Inevitably, the saxophonist becomes defined by a multifaceted performativity, where he enacts a manifold surrogacy through the expression of a metonymic manhood and the collective racialized consciousness for a more general population of people.

The expression of impoverished material reality, while definitely central to his music, is eclipsed by the strained relationship between the saxophonist and social intimacy. In her essay "Baldwin's Bop 'N' Morrison's Mood: Bebop and Race in James Baldwin's *Another Country* and Toni Morrison's *Jazz*," Keren Omry argues, "The raw, sexualized image that characterizes the music is mingled with the musician's stark loneliness, a human hunger that is satisfied by the musician's ability to transcend his isolation and—through the music—to communicate with the other band members."[14] Omry identifies several critical elements occurring in what I read as an intimate exchange between Rufus and the saxophonist. First, in identifying "loneliness" as a human hunger, Omry universalizes the tender vulnerability often expressed by Black musicians in search of the fraternal. Black males' longing for company and camaraderie, for investment and visibility, is not born out of the margins that constrict them. Rather, this is intrinsic to human comportment. Men, and women, are born longing, even if into a world that will promise to deny it. Furthermore, she understands music's functionality in Baldwin's work as a strong and necessary response to isolation. Here one envisions the intimate exchange between Rufus and the other musician. The music holds, even if temporarily, and communicates to the listener that he or she is not alone. More quietly, Omry alludes to Baldwin's desire for the reader to glean that while actual circumstances may be different between Rufus and the saxophonist, their stories are very similar. This is why Rufus hears him so clearly within the music, why he understands this pleading question of love. The saxophonist's solo was never shared solely to tell his story; it was also to offer the reader a glimpse of Rufus's struggle with loneliness, to show how the beat of his life echoed the saxophonic question of love, "*Do you love me? Do you love me?*"

Rufus's struggle with loneliness and the longing to be loved materializes in a variety of different relationships. Baldwin's intention, I argue, is to use these different relationships in order to magnify the "germ of his dilemma." While the act of asking the proverbial question "Do you love me?" is significant, the reader is also forced to wonder, "To whom, exactly, is he asking this question?" In asking this and daring to answer it, honestly and responsibly, the reader understands Rufus's loneliness as not some abstract feeling of alienation that can be experienced by a random individual feeling lost in an overwhelming world. Instead, his loneliness is decidedly racial: it is the product of a social environment intolerant of his blackness. In a sense, Rufus is at war in the very land he calls home, feels disconnected and rejected from the very space that ought to be his sanctum. By stumbling into this particular consciousness of being, he experiences a crisis in his manhood where all that he knows and loves about himself is attacked from multiple angles. This is iterated by his earliest psychic confession, where the reader learns how "nothing of his belonged to him anymore." From a Camusian perspective, this signals his exposure to the absurd, for "in a universe suddenly divested of illusions and lights, man feels an alien, a stranger. His exile is without remedy since he is deprived of the memory of a lost home or the hope of a promised land. This divorce between man and his life, the actor and his setting, is properly the feeling of absurdity."[15] Rufus's feeling of the absurd, earlier hinted toward through his ability to relate to the saxophonic question of love, crystallizes into more concrete interracial moments where his blackness, the core of his manhood, is literally attacked, questioned, or conveniently ignored. That Rufus endures the divorce between his manhood and his life is also into-nated by him becoming a disembodied subject. Arguably, the racialized body consistently tortured and tormented by a state of terror within the western world could proverbially represent Camus's philosophy, particularly if one reads it through that lens. Nevertheless, it is Baldwin's scripting of Rufus's journey in *Another Country* that demands of absurdist philosophy a new way of reading the experiences of people of color. Considering this, Rufus's divorcement from his "promised land" and his encounter with Black male loneliness signals a confrontation with racial absurdity. Rufus, then, as a Black male subject systematically disembodied by an oppressive racial economy must, if he is to survive or stave off his own tragedy, find a space of intimacy, a place to bare his vulnerability and to have it held.

While the theater moment that begins *Another Country* emerges as the definitive moment of disillusionment for the struggling Rufus, the disillusioning process can be traced to a series of spaces, experiences, and relationships. Similar to the "violent accents" of the film, his time at boot camp, characterized by a violence against his person and the subsequent attack on his right to or possession of agency, is ironically ushered in through the body of a white woman who has sojourned to the North. His conversation with Leona, this "blonde girl" whose socioeconomic origin coupled with her race and gender situates her as the quintessential repre-sentation of Southern violence, precipitated the painful memory. Leona's "damp, colorless face, the face of the Southern poor white, and her straight pale hair" signifies for Rufus a forbidden and dangerous engagement.[16] Given Leona's whiteness, Rufus's thought of indulgence is itself a taboo pursuit. Even more, her poor class identification erects the ever present threat of violence that can be linked to poor whites in crisis who often resorted to anti-Black racial violence to protect their fragile investments in white privilege. Without coincidence, then, Leona's face metaphorizes itself as the perpetual racial absurdity often rooted in the South. Rufus sees in her face, and perhaps hears in her voice, that which he met in the South. The perversity of racial absurdity offers Rufus a memory of the space Leona signifies as a response to her admiration of the imagined liberating space of New York. As if countering her sense of wonder with the space he calls home, his recollection extends to her a proclamation of how awful her space is:

> He remembered, suddenly, his days in boot camp in the South and felt again the shoe of a white officer against his mouth. He was in his white uniform, on the ground, against the red, dusty clay. Some of his colored buddies were holding him ... The white officer, with a curse, had vanished, had gone forever beyond the reach of vengeance. His face was full of clay and tears and blood.[17]

Although claiming little textual space, this incident and its memory are very critical to understanding Rufus's feeling of absurdity. Perhaps, and this is a priori, this event marks Rufus's first serious encounter with the racism of 1950s America. Even if he had experienced the burden of race within New York, surely the cultural geography of the South enlightened him to the serious racial divide still present in the land of his birth. The white officer signifies the onslaught of a world bent on rejecting Rufus's Black manhood. By coupling Rufus's tears and blood with the quiet longing for vengeance, Baldwin displays the impact of this racial encounter on Rufus. Being kicked in the mouth, as the text suggests, splinters off into various meanings. Rufus literally is the victim of physical racial violence, his Black body the site of tangible torture. Additionally, the boot to mouth represents how Black men were refused, denied, and stripped of voice. The officer's vanishing and his metaphoric escape into the "forever beyond" symbolizes the inability to locate or directly identify the source of anti-Black racism and violence. Racial absurdity, in its abstractions, positions racist subjects as the mediums of a more powerful and dangerous ideology at play or work. Rufus is unable to enact revenge on the white officer because his agency is a perpetually shifting fiction, an ideology of violence with multiple sites and hosts. Although named as white and male, the officer emerges as, in antithesis to the saxophonist, a metonym for a more general community. As such, Rufus's experience racializes the absurd, and the "life" from which he divorces can no longer simply be viewed as some abstract world in which anyone might share his experience. Additionally, because of the double function of white male subjectivity in this moment, his crisis becomes inextricably fraternal and existential—a symbolic space-in-between men where the painful divorce man suffers from his life is brought about by an oppressive subjectivity. Inevitably, this encounter echoes the idea of how "at any streetcorner the feeling of absurdity can strike any man in the face"; the face of Rufus just happened to Black.[18]

If Rufus's recollection of the violent South remains tethered to his first encounter with Leona, then, undeniably, their relationship becomes the unfortunate site for his wrestling with racial absurdity. As a white, blonde, older woman from the South, she carries with her the multiple layered racial scripts of her past and past localities. Baldwin carefully scripts the intercoursing of Rufus's Black male body with her gendered white Southernness by having them meet the night that he performs his last jazz gig. Immediately following his performance, they accompany each other to a party, further punctuating the occasion. While drinking on the balcony and after dismissing their worries about the other partygoers, they submit to the magnetism pulling their bodies together. And though spontaneous sexual acts are often a staple of the midcentury American bohemian narrative, something in their exchange proves disturbing. To be clear, Baldwin's description of the sexual scene emphasizes both the vulnerability and the violence of Rufus's touch. He offers the reader troubling and telling insight as Rufus thinks, "He wanted her to remember him the longest day she lived. And, shortly, nothing could have stopped him, not the white God himself nor a lynch mob arriving on wings. Under his breath he cursed the milk-white bitch and groaned and rode his weapon between her thighs."[19] Considering the symbolic power of Leona's subjectivity, Rufus's seemingly violent engagement must be read through the language of vengeance. Playing off the idea of memory, Baldwin chooses to complicate the relationship between past and present. Using Leona as a portal to the temporal reality of his boot-camp memory, his wish for her to "remember" him, as perhaps he remembers the white officer, encourages us to consider how Leona is a surrogate through which Rufus can achieve vengeance. Continuing, when Baldwin writes of how neither a "white God" nor "lynch mob" could stop him, we understand that Rufus has been fully transplanted to a completely different moment, a completely different space. For Rufus, Leona therefore serves as the possibility for retribution and reclamation—he can, through this sexual act, resurrect an attacked and a bruised manhood while also making the victimizer suffer.

Although literary critics appear consistent in identifying this scene as a clear indication of how Rufus's history with racial violence permeates and defines his relationship with Leona, many tend to circumscribe the layering evident within Baldwin's play with memory, symbolism, and representation. In "Another Look at *Another Country*: Reconciling Baldwin's Racial and Sexual Politics," Susan Feldman argues, "Through this relationship, Baldwin illustrates how misogynistic violence ultimately stems from male castration anxiety, from Rufus's own anxiety over his social disempowerment and the threat this disempowerment presents to his masculine identity."[20] In "James Baldwin and Sexuality," Justin Joyce and Dwight McBride state that in "linking sexuality and masculinity under the rubric of violence, Baldwin represents Rufus, it seems, as unable to completely give himself over to his desire for Leona without enacting a viciously violent fantasy, without in short, playing the role of the Black rapist ravaging the white woman."[21] In mentioning these critics, my intention is not to suggest that their critique of gender and violence is ill informed or misplaced. Undoubtedly, no one who reads this scene can argue against the violence enacted on a white and female body. My concern, however, lies in pushing the analyses a bit deeper into the intricacies of the moment, in nuancing the symbolic value of Leona's body. Joyce and McBride's poignant observation of Rufus's inability to fully relinquish himself opens the door for my reading into his encounters with Southern white racism. In addition, just as the Black saxophonist's and the white officer's individual identities are elided into greater representations of particular communities, so too is Leona's. She is, all at once, the collectivity of her identity markers: white, female, Southern, poor, and also each of these separately. Even more, she represents for Rufus, or at least triggers in him, memories of the South as white, male, anti-Black, and violent. If one problematically reduces Rufus's behavior to that of the Black rapist "ravaging the white woman," then one misses the opportunity to responsibly make sense of his misogyny as the byproduct of his confrontation with racial absurdity.

Rufus's relationship with Leona symbolizes his desire to reconcile the fraternal crisis precipitated by the incident with the white boot-camp officer. The violence and even the performance of the "Black rapist" point to the vulnerability in his manhood and his state of powerlessness. Through Leona's body and her intimate companionship, he seeks to repair the racial divide, to mend the wounded parts of his life. His racial past complicates his misogyny; it does not excuse it. This, again, showcases the power of anti-Black racism as idea versus act. When operating as an ideology, it seduces its victims into abuse through their pursuits of vengeance. Fascinatingly, however, Baldwin's choice to utilize the white female body as the tablet for the rescripting of Black and white male relations is brilliant in its subtle contextualization and its play with gender and sexuality. If the white male officer and Black male Rufus are at odds, or experiencing a breakdown in fraternity, one must consider the role or position of white female subjectivity in the exchange. Post emancipation, and most notably during the nadir of American history, white men would often use the fiction of the ravaged white woman as justification for the lynching of Black men and the Black male body. In this sense, white womanhood presented an inescapable threat for Black manhood and was always already an impending terror. To escape lynchers who were afforded safety in the "forever beyond" by corrupt systems of power, or to escape lynching in general, Black men would have to learn to reconcile their subjectivities to those of white men using the white female as a mediating body. That is, Black men would have to learn appropriate ways of playing with the most prized "possession" of white men in order to find peace. These racial politics of respectability and patriarchy inevitably inform Leona's function in Rufus's negotiation with the absurd. To be clear, she is more than woman; she represents the paradox of the absurd—a key to his happiness and reacquisition of power or meaning as well as a constant reminder of his worthlessness, invisibility, or the sign of burdened blackness.

Leona's role as a mediating subject secretes itself in both the conversation leading up to the party and the sexual encounter on the balcony. At times, she vacillates between being an individual and the representation of a regional ideology, or, as Rufus thinks, "Something touched his imagination for a moment, suggesting that Leona was a person and had her story and that all stories were trouble."[22] However, this thought is quickly dismissed, and Rufus latches on to the idea of her as white female body. In fact, his inquiry, "Didn't they warn you down home about the darkies you'd find up North?" recouples their interracial exchange with past race relations.[23] Culturally positioned as a threat to white womanhood, Rufus understands with a boot-to-mouth viscerality how his subjectivity is overwritten with the language or rhetoric of warning. He, as Black male body without manhood, is never legible in the Southern white economy, is always misread and thus unknowable. Nevertheless, I argue, the longing to be known, sitting at the core of his vulnerability, almost mockingly colors their exchanges.

Leona's engagement with Rufus and her apparent desire to learn about his world or him hold Rufus in a way that guarantee climactic conflict. From the outset of their exchanges, questions litter the conversation. When responding to his question, "You seen anything you want since you been in New York?" with a firm and exclamatory, "I want it all!" Leona reifies the racial divide between her and Rufus while also mirroring his disillusionment.[24] Coming from a different social and racialized space, Rufus knows he can never respond to the question of "want" with "it all," as such entitlements are knowingly forbidden for Black bodies. Her proclamation, then, even if replete with naïveté, moves from a position of privilege; a position Rufus can never occupy. And yet, while standing on the balcony, arguably empowered by his proximity to whiteness, he notices the *all* absurdly out of his grasp:

> At the same time he realized how far they were above the city and the lights below seemed to be calling him. He walked to the balcony's edge and looked over. Looking straight down, he seemed to be standing on a cliff in the wilderness, seeing a kingdom and a river which had not been seen before. He could make it his, every inch of the territory which stretched beneath and around him now.[25]

Baldwin plays with setting. Once again situated on a balcony, though distinct from the one beginning the novel, Rufus's position is one of visioning, even as he is the subject of multiple gazes. Different from the novel's earlier moment of disillusionment, this balcony placement figures Rufus's longing. Like Leona, he wants it all. Unlike for her, his racial subjectivity excludes such possibility. However, this is an exclusion that escapes him in the moment. Unfortunately for Leona, her body's symbolic power mediates his delusion while constructing the method by which he will express his longing. Her body, a site of reconciliation for Rufus's fraternal crisis with white men/manhood, will also serve as the site for him to acquire his longing emanating from below. Leona will become the "territory which stretched beneath and around him."

The sexual exchange between Rufus and Leona, while often reduced to critiques of violence and misogyny, ultimately points toward a battle and argument over ownership. Rufus's pursuit, and by extension his penetration, is one of reacquisition. Leona's white female body, the negotiating tool for historical white male violence and denial of the other, presents itself as the mediating site. Even without knowledge, her subjectivity affords Rufus the opportunity to reclaim parts of his self and ontology previously stolen, stripped, and lost. Readings of Leona as abused body are complicated by Baldwin's insistence on the vulnerable interplay and understanding between the two actors. As if knowing Rufus's need for Black male redemption, as if knowing his efforts to escape Black tragic manhood, "she carried him, as the sea will carry a boat: with a slow, rocking and rising and falling motion, barely suggestive of the violence of the deep."[26] Leona's carrying of Rufus punctuates how the white female body serves as a site of negotiation. Furthermore, the intimate motion of their sex undermines the violence that creeps into the description. But, to be sure, the violence is there. It, as the narration conveys, is of the deep. Deep here alludes to the historical, the buried, the archive of cultural violence done perhaps onto the Black body. For Rufus, the deep violence instigates his handling of Leona. Somewhere amid this journey, this attempt to reconcile and reclaim, "he felt himself strangling, about to explode or die."[27] Often missed within the criticism, Rufus's physical experience also reflects a violence enacted upon him. Though it is impossible to read him as the sexual victim of Leona in the situation, the moment begs for us to consider just how he might have been the "rape" victim of that which she symbolizes. His proximity to explosion or death relays how Leona's symbolic power has contributed to his flirtation with the absurd and the tragic. In considering both as receivers of violence in this encounter, *Another Country* pushes one to read this as combat, as a struggle to maintain or protect self. Leona's protection is a historic one, the assumed and always present one given her privileged subject position. Conversely, Rufus's needs to be stated, scripted, acknowledged, and it comes through in the moment where "a moan and a curse tore through him while he beat her with all the strength he had and felt the venom shoot out of him, enough for a hundred Black-white babies."[28] Complex manhood and masculinity endow Rufus, who appreciates and loathes Leona in this moment. Bifurcated identity, race, and gender permit such complicated expressions of tenderness and anger. His penis, the ultimate symbol of his Black manhood and thus one of the major foci in his historical oppression, also becomes his weaponry. The resistance to castration is pronounced through his ability to shoot his venom—the metaphoric source of his blackness. Thus, the intimate dance between Black male and white woman presents a fascinating production of violence and love. Baldwin's choreography is neither sloppy nor irresponsible; rather, in its intentionality, it reveals the intricate relationship necessary for the saving of Black manhood. The white mediating subject presents itself as both surrogate and sacrifice, an offering to the ills of a past that will not stop haunting until it is adequately and appropriately fed.

Black manhood, as the abstract object of salvation, requires the Gordian play of distinct subjectivities. Conceptions and interrogations of love—investment and visibility—must emerge from the body in need of saving. As such, Rufus's draw to the saxophonist earlier in the chapter might be read as an understanding of how his suffering self poses a particular question to the world. The saxophonic question "*Do you love me?*" is directed to Rufus's white world—for his need, his very livelihood, rests in overcoming the denouncement of his Black self. Leona's white and female body thus becomes a possible remedy for his budding psychosis and a medium he needs to fight the racially absurd. This demands of Leona a very sensitive acknowledgment, a consciousness of how racial absurdity functions within an American space, and a willingness to intentionally fight alongside Rufus. Unfortunately, whether the consequence of her own history with violence or her desire to forget the culture of the South in general, Leona prefers to not see the playing out of race; this very blindness proves detrimental to her relationship and is partially responsible for Rufus's tragedy.

Despite Leona's ability to "carry" Rufus in their intimate balcony exchange, she does not possess the power to sustain and thus to save him. The mediating subject, while critical to the journey toward salvation, can never assume the salvific endowment. Its role does not extend beyond itself, is only to usher or *carry* one to the point of engagement with the agent with the capacity to save. As such, the power of her love is limited by a circumstantial ephemerality. Evanescent in essence, white female companionship does not present itself as the balm to Rufus's fraternal crisis. His crisis, a sort of Baldwinian absurdity, is dictated by the intersection of racialized and gendered systems of power. Racism, anti-Black to be specific, is decidedly white and male for the Black male body. Rufus's struggle for investment and visibility then becomes a breakdown between him and those who represent the system of power—white men. As a white woman, Leona can help him but so much, as she is also the victim of a patriarchal system of oppression that, inadvertently, constricts her ability to reconcile. She cannot help Rufus claim the territory beneath his feet, cannot help him to make the kingdom and the river his. For that, he would need a being endowed differently, someone with access to the multiple spaces that simultaneously deny and oppress him.

Leona's inability to save Rufus goes beyond the limitations of her subject position; her unwillingness or inability to recognize the ways in which Rufus suffers and thus is struggling to live speeds up his process of unraveling. Unbeknown to Rufus, the hope embedded in his interracial heterosexual union with Leona would not be enough to fight the racial absurdity of America, especially with Leona's blindness. The black and white magnetism magnifying their attraction in private spheres would be transformed into repulsion within the free public space. The taboo nature of their relationship, when subjected to the regulating white gaze (usually male), would disrupt the peace and attempts at healing. Soon after leaving the comfort of Rufus's home, they encounter the intolerance of America and learn of the inescapability of racial absurdity. Walking into the streets of the village reminds Rufus and Leona of the racial politics of respectability, how Black bodies are neither historically allowed nor presently tolerated to intermingle intimately with white female bodies. Service without sociality dictates the extent of Black male–white female relationships. Subsequently, their desire and decision to flaunt disobedience toward social laws and mores demands reprimand. Even before the world can warn them, however, Rufus receives admonition from his closest friend.

Vivaldo, who at this point in the novel seems to be Rufus's closest possibility for discovering someone with the full capacity to save thanks to his ability to access those portals of identity that exclude Black men, also reveals the complexity of salvific manhood. When hearing of the potential of Rufus and Leona living together, he tells his friend of his disapproval. Couching his antagonism in the ways of the world—how the racialized society has not matured to the point of appreciating interracial intimacy—he also spills his own white male privilege. Responding to his Black friend's acknowledgment of the world's ignorance, he states, "Trouble is, I feel too paternal towards you, you son of a bitch."[29] Evoking the notion of paternalism here in a moment where he gently attempts to regulate Black male behavior uncomfortably approximates Black and white male relationships during and post slavery. Forever boy or *son*, Rufus is denied access to the fullness of manhood, or at least is thought to be unable to properly navigate his social reality. White and male philosophies of Black male social immaturity creep into Vivaldo's well-meaning concern while also highlighting the metaphoric space-in-between him and Rufus. Understanding the layered and problematic meanings tucked in Vivaldo's "care," Rufus retorts, "That's the trouble with all you white bastards."[30] Rufus's employment of "trouble" differs from his friend's in that it addresses, more fundamentally, the obstacle that hinders reconciliation of fraternal crises. His proclamation of trouble diagnoses a flaw in white male subjectivity. Whereas Vivaldo sees his paternalism as love, Rufus discerns it as oppression—a closed door to the possibility of acceptance, of visibility. For our unknowable Black male, his legibility depends on his "white" friend's ability to see him beyond the scope of boyhood, to trust him to the point of human maturity.

Vivaldo's "benign" paternalism and white male patriarchy become violently affirmed through a society that has no allegiance to Rufus as a Black man overstepping the boundaries of race and gender. Journeying out together, Rufus and Leona experience the challenge to their freedom to love. The absurd world "stared unsympathetically out at them from the eyes of passing people; and Rufus realized that he had not thought at all about this world and its power to hate and destroy."[31] Part of Rufus's freedom to not think of the destructive power of the world comes under the beautiful fraternity he holds with Vivaldo—his Italian friend. Rufus comes to realize the truth found within Vivaldo's paternalistic care; this world, being the product of racialized ideologies of power, has no love for that which it does not ordain. At the same time, Baldwin's protagonist expresses an awareness of white male freedom and movability. Vivaldo's white masculinity protects Rufus's interracial love with Leona from the racism of New York City. However, in Vivaldo's absence, Rufus is incessantly reminded of the powerlessness of his Black manhood and how he does not have the right to Leona—to engage intimately with whiteness, particularly white femaleness. Rufus notes, "Without Vivaldo, there was a difference in the eyes which watched them. Villagers, both bound and free, looked them over as though where they stood were an auction block or a stud farm."[32] In the absence of an endorsing or protecting white manhood, Rufus is reduced to that of just a Black body. As a disembodied subject, his person can only be seen as object, as a figure of abjection without a voice. Allusions to the auction block or stud farm further confirm the degree to which Rufus, because of this intimacy with whiteness, a perverse flirtation with freedom if you will, remains fettered to the idea of slavery. Viewed through a Foucauldian lens, the white gaze regulates Rufus's blackness, keeps him isolated from contact with the world. Slowly he begins to disintegrate from the hope of reconciliation and starts, in the spirit of paranoia, to destroy Leona and himself. In becoming a racial leper, he is inevitably consumed by the racially absurd and, in moments reminiscent of Richard Wright's Bigger Thomas, seems to play the role the world wishes for him—the mad Black man. That Vivaldo's presence engenders a "difference in the eyes" suggests the power and privilege of white and male subjectivities. His ability to protect or to cloak Rufus from the abusive gaze of society furthers cements his capacity to save. Despite the obvious problems with an endowment built upon discourses of privilege and oppression, the reality for Rufus lies in how this man occupies the very spaces necessary for salvation. Perhaps in realizing the complicated relationship between privilege and salvation, Rufus spirals into an abyss of abjection. What happens when we consider Rufus's madness as an expression of his disillusionment, as the direct consequence of this haunting and epiphanic moment of existential realization?

Rufus's newfound madness is heavily rooted in his preoccupation with having his Black manhood surveyed and regulated by a power-stripping white gaze. His relationship with Leona highlights the truth of American race relations in a way previously unknown. But it also reveals to Rufus, despite his every attempt to settle the paradox of the absurd or to overcome the crisis of manhood engendered by racial disharmony, that he is powerless in the face of the oppressive white world. Subsequently, this knowledge begets uncertainty in his epistemology of blackness; it forces a peculiar and unhealthy questioning, "What is the meaning of being a Black man in pre–Civil Rights America?" And as Camus predicts, in discussing the individual's encounter with existential truth, Rufus is consumed by the idea of living a life without meaning and without power: "There exists an obvious fact that seems utterly moral: namely, that a man is always prey to his truths. Once he has admitted them, he cannot free himself from them. One has to pay something. A man who has become conscious of the absurd is forever bound to it."[33] Unquestionably predatory in nature, Rufus's truths are the products of systems and structures of power and oppression. More specifically, Rufus is but allowed to know the constructed inferiority of his blackness and the unattainability of his manhood. Attempting to find peace, then, in a world that is built upon these truths, Rufus finds alienation, depression, madness, and tragedy predestine his fate. Furthermore, his absurdity experiences a transformation under the auspices of a gendered racialization, becomes a racial absurdity. Similar and yet unlike that of Camus, Baldwin's subject is bound to a different existential crisis. Racial absurdity emerges from the darkness of an anti-Black ethos and brings forth an experience where the Black male body, in this case, must find a way to discover meaning in a world that means to hold him at a distance as the forever captive, rejected, or abjected. And if unable to do so, the world becomes one dedicated to his ultimate and complete demise.

As Rufus finds himself chained to the racially absurd, all of his strength and manhood is summoned in an effort to resist the rejection of his Black self. His fight against the world becomes a battle with representations and re-presentations of whiteness as he violently lashes out for the preservation of his Black manhood. In the process, the love he has for Leona and her caring or *carrying* womanhood is eclipsed by the hate he holds for her whiteness. Her dismissal of the world's intolerance, the ease with which she receives their disapproving gazes, is perceived as a sort of insensitive indifference to the warring Rufus. The ensuing ambivalence leads to a questioning of her love, moves him to question the motive behind her attraction and the manner in which she views his Black manhood. Convincing himself that he was nothing more than a body for her, he acquiesces to the stereotypes of blackness—becoming the brute that "twisted his fingers in her long pale hair and used her in whatever way he felt would humiliate her most. It was not love he felt during these acts of love: drained and shaking, utterly unsatisfied, he fled from the raped white woman into the bars."[34] The transformation of love into violence urges a reconsideration of the dangerous play between an individual bound to racial absurdity and a mediating subject. Rufus and Leona's relationship can, as previously articulated, only aspire toward a proximity to healing or freedom. The mediating subject, as a selfless and at times noble sacrifice, will assume a position of abuse necessitated by untamable longings for agency by the truly oppressed. This requires the impossibility of love, as the need for and reclamation of autonomy breeds a parasitic power. According to Bryan Washington, Rufus "struggles for power and control over Leona, the southern white woman who, insofar as she represents white liberal guilt, repeatedly submits to her lover's physical and psychological abuse."[35] His struggle for power, while channeled through the relationship with Leona, has less to do with her and more to do with the world she so conveniently forgives and unconsciously represents. Baldwin is careful in suggesting that the violence enacted on her body is not enough to satiate the fury and rage consuming Rufus, for she alone is not the problem, is not the trouble. We know this because he looks for other targets and "began to pick fights with white men", hoping to reclaim some form of power and meaning.[36] Unfortunately, his hope is never actualized, his relationship with Leona reaches a point of irreparability, and even his relationship with Vivaldo begins to suffer.

Though pain captures the failed relationship between Rufus and Leona, the relationship didactically points the reader to the significance of same-gender intimacy. Additionally, it magnifies the complex fissures present within Rufus's closest intimate relationship. Tension between Rufus and Vivaldo delineates the severity of Rufus's struggle with the world and racial absurdity while also communicating the critical moment indicating his inexorable demise. Vivaldo, recognizing the dire situation between Rufus and Leona, attempts to save the latter from the abuse of the former. Reading Vivaldo's intention through the lens of absurdity, Rufus accuses his best and only friend of trying to take Leona from him, of echoing the world's proclamation that he, as a Black man, has no right to freely love. This exchange, in addition to accentuating his unhealthy psychosis, bares Rufus's bruised manhood and the depth of his vulnerability. It is here that the reader first glimpses the extent of Vivaldo's white privilege, as the same infuriating blindness in Leona manifests itself in the Italian male. He cannot separate his friend's unusual behavior from that which causes it and thus misses the true source of the problem. Nevertheless, after threats of killing him and after Vivaldo returns from sending Leona off to his place for safety, Rufus makes his issue emotionally clear:

How I hate them—all those white sons of bitches out there. They're trying to kill me, you think I don't know? They got the world on a string, man, the miserable white cock suckers, and they tying that string around my neck, they killing *me*. . . . Sometimes I listen to those boats on the river—I listen to those whistles—and I think wouldn't it be nice to get on a boat again and go someplace away from all these nowhere people, where a man could be treated like a man. . . . You got to fight with the landlord because the landlord's *white!* You got to fight with the elevator boy because the motherfucker's *white*. Any bum on the Bowery can shit all over you because maybe he can't hear, can't see, can't walk, can't fuck—but he's *white!*[37]

Here, through the voice of his struggling protagonist, Baldwin gives voice to racial absurdity. The metaphoric lynching of blackness, the denial of manhood, and a never-ending fight with white power has come to define Rufus's life, has stripped him of the power to love. Raw and honest, Rufus's pronouncement of hate alongside the desire to be "treated like a man" highlights what he is fighting against and what he is fighting for. In short, his suffering is, simply, the rejection of his Black manhood.

Perhaps through some genuine resentment or some unconscious guilt, Vivaldo refutes the illogicality consuming Rufus by suggesting that white people like Vivaldo and Leona love him. Rufus's reaction, a fierce recantation of the idea of being authentically loved, invites the reader to understand the depth of his loneliness. He dissects Leona's love and makes it plain for the blind Vivaldo, "'She loves the colored folks so *much* . . . sometimes I just can't stand it. You know all that chick knows about me? The *only* thing she knows?' He put his hand on his sex, brutally, as though he would tear it out."[38] Baldwin's intention here, despite scholarly criticism to the contrary, is not ambiguous. He seeks to show that the Black male body, ideologically, was never manumitted from slavery. Black men even in the late 1950s were constantly battling against the phenomenon of being reduced to their physical selves, of being seen only for what they could produce as laborers of the "state" or sexual beings of the "street." Put more generically, and even universally, "What becomes clear in *Another Country* is that rescuing human relationships from the sexual marketplace is not a choice available to us in a postmodern world."[39] And this compounds Rufus's struggle against whiteness. Indeed, many of his intimate relationships with white people leave him feeling like nothing more than a Black brute from slavery's mythology. We hear this in his relationship with Leona but also in a white male—Eric—the thespian of the novel who returns later on and becomes a vehicle for reconciliation, in some scholars' estimation. Eric, who also is from the South, uses his white male privilege to unintentionally fetishize the Black male bodies of Henry (the handyman and husband of the domestic who worked for his family), LeRoy (the young male with whom he enjoyed his first sexual experience), and Rufus (the man who fell victim to his use of power and prestige). As Baldwin ends the emotional scene with Vivaldo and Rufus, he reminds the reader of how Rufus was first presented in the novel—destitute, alone, and on the precipice of tragedy.

When Baldwin begins *Another Country*, he paints a very dark picture of Rufus and hurries the reader into a confrontation with the drummer's abjection. Within the first fifty pages we learn that Rufus is "one of the fallen . . . one of those who had been crushed on the day, which was every day, these towers fell"; we learn that the first character we meet, Rufus, is "entirely alone, and dying of it."[40] We learn of his strained relationship with the white world, of his inability to deal with or make sense of or survive the racial intolerance and absurdity that has led him to literal and metaphoric homelessness—where he must prostitute himself for food and warmth and shelter. In essence we learn, quite early, what makes this figure tragic and why Baldwin may be writing. But then there is a moment where we hope—just as Rufus hopes, where we see the possibility for redemption—where our spirits warm at Rufus's revolt against the racially absurd as he conjures the strength to visit, even in his debased state, his friend Vivaldo. Our fingers might even be shaking as we turn the pages, as Baldwin's authorial genius turns us from readers into spectators. We can hear Bessie Smith as Rufus hears her singing on Vivaldo's phonograph; we can feel his hurt, his pain, his plea, his dissipating light in his darkest hour, and his silent call to Vivaldo—that saxophonic question of love. What we realize through this textuality is that the friendship Rufus shares with Vivaldo is a beautiful fraternity—is unlike any other relationship in the novel. This is Baldwin's purpose—to afford something to help us breathe, and we do, in knowing that the friendship can and just might serve as refuge, that Vivaldo represents a salvific figure.

Approaching the end of the first book, Vivaldo and Rufus encounter Richard and Cass (the married white couple of the novel) and leave the reader secure in thinking all is well. We again meet Jane—Vivaldo's estranged white girlfriend from the past, the novel's symbol of the world's desire to splinter their bond. Moments later, Rufus leaves them to their dysfunctional bliss and takes the reader onto the platform of the subway where he ponders morbid thoughts of its collapse and the train "rushing under water . . . [with] the people screaming at windows and doors and turning on each other with all the accumulated fury of their blasphemed lives."[41] Remembering Rufus's struggle against racial absurdity, this is a reflection of how nihilism has consumed his being—there is no hope, no order, no reason—it has been replaced by suffering. Baldwin places Rufus under the scrutiny of the white gaze one last time to remind the reader of what has, to a certain degree, motivated his movements. The book ends with him on the George Washington Bridge, eerily reminiscent of Baldwin's deceased friend Eugene Worth. The last we hear from Rufus's character is the echo of the saxophonist, a deep questioning of the world and of God: "You bastard, you motherfucking bastard. Ain't I your baby, too? [. . .] He lifted himself by his hands on the rail, lifted himself as high as he could, and leaned far out. The wind tore at him, at his head and shoulders, while something in him screamed, Why? Why?"[42] In eighty-seven pages, Baldwin offers his protagonist to suicide—in less than nearly one fifth of the novel the reader witnesses a man's descent from the willingness to love to the unwanting of life. I argue that while Baldwin writes Rufus as the tragic figure, the real tragedy of the novel is learned in the three hundred pages that follow. Only after Rufus's suicide does Baldwin make his point, and it comes through Vivaldo's relationship with Ida (Rufus's sister) and Eric (the white lover from the past).

Baldwin uses Ida's character in order to reveal particular elements within himself, but, more importantly, to capture personality elements of his character Vivaldo. In his chapter "Baldwin's Blueprint for a New World," Stanley Macebuh argues, "Ida Scott, is, quite simply, the personification of Baldwin's rage, [and] this personified rage in conjunction with Rufus's life and suicide provides Baldwin with a useful instrument for plausibly achieving the self-confrontation of the other characters in the novel."[43] While disagreeing with a large part of his analysis, I agree with his reading of Ida. In my estimation, Ida's role, beyond complicating the narrative of midcentury interracial relationships, is to function as a mirror for Vivaldo. His relationship with her, as Rufus's sister, indicates a desire to understand Rufus's blackness in ways he did not during their friendship. The more Ida recognizes this the harder she reminds him of his inauthentic love for her brother and of his white male privilege. Responding to his question of whether or not she loves him, she states, "What I don't understand . . . is how you can talk about love when you don't want to know what's happening. And *that's* not *my* fault. How can you say you loved Rufus when there was so much about him you didn't want to know?"[44] Consistently throughout the novel and in most of their arguments, Ida reiterates the problem of not knowing or wanting to know "what's happening." For Baldwin, the state of unknowing is an exercise of privilege, a privilege often employed by a white society blind to how African Americans suffer from historical and systematic oppression. Therefore, Vivaldo examples that particular form of privilege and the willful neglect that comes with it through his relationship with Ida.

When John Hall interviewed James Baldwin in 1970, Baldwin stated the following in regard to writing Rufus's character:

I didn't think anyone had ever watched the disintegration of a Black boy from that particular point of view. Rufus was partly responsible for his doom, and in presenting him as partly responsible, I was attempting to break out of the whole sentimental image of the afflicted nigger driven that way (to suicide) by white people.[45]

From reading the novel, it is easy to see Rufus's self-destructiveness and the role the racially absurd world played in that destruction. The intimacy of Leona, the warmth of Cass's smile, the genuine generosity of Eric, and the friendship of Vivaldo, however, make it difficult to simply attribute Rufus's death to an unrelenting whiteness. Nevertheless, in one of the final moments of the novel, in an intimate exchange between Vivaldo and Eric, Baldwin expresses the true tragedy of Rufus's death.

Vivaldo and Eric, sitting alone within the darkness of the latter's apartment, converse over the intricacies of their many intersecting relationships. In his most vulnerable state during the entire novel, Vivaldo shares with Eric his thoughts surrounding Rufus and his suicide. Remembering the last night he saw Rufus, the night when Rufus mustered the will to go to his friend, he recalls,

> When he looked at me, just before he closed his eyes and turned on his side away from me, all curled up, I had the weirdest feeling that he wanted me to take him in my arms. And not for sex, though maybe sex would have happened. I had the feeling that he wanted someone to hold him, to hold him, and that, that night, it had to be a man. . . . I guess I still wonder, what would have happened if I'd taken him in my arms, if I'd held him, if I hadn't been—afraid. I was afraid that he wouldn't understand that it was—only love. Only love. But, oh, Lord, when he died, I thought that maybe I could have saved him if I'd just reached out that quarter of an inch between us on that bed, and held him.[46]

In the words of Camus, "In a sense, as in melodrama, killing yourself amounts to confessing. It is confessing that life is too much for you or that you do not understand it."[47] Rufus's suicide was indeed a confession. On one hand, it is just what Camus suggests, an acknowledgment that life is too much. Yet, on the other, Rufus's tragic demise confesses his need for love. Vivaldo, his lone friend within the novel, was endowed with the salvific manhood strong enough to save him. Rufus's suicide precipitates his friend's confession, an admission to his unwillingness to reach a quarter of an inch, to eliminate that symbolic space-in-between them. Ida's role punctuates Vivaldo's tender moment with Eric. She embodies the Baldwinian idea of radical love. For Baldwin, *Another Country* is more than fiction; it represents the flaw of the American people, their unwillingness to love beyond themselves, to risk their privilege and security, despite the possibility for misunderstanding or discomfort, for the sake of saving another. This is the real tragedy, the message undeniably woven in the multiple relationships making up the fabric of the novel. In the end, this story is not about sexuality, interracial relationships, Black musical expression, or New York City; it is about the power of love and the tragedy that is guaranteed in its absence.

4

Theatrics of Mask-ulinity
Radical Male Intimacy and Black Power in
Tell Me How Long the Train's Been Gone

There is a truth in the theater and there is a truth in life—they
meet, but they are not the same, for life, God help us, *is* the truth.
And those disguises which an artist wears are his means, not of
fleeing from the truth, but of attempting to approach it.

—JAMES BALDWIN

If any artist can be said to have approached the truth of life in the mid- to
late twentieth century, we must know him as James Baldwin. The United
States of Baldwin's imagination, that is to say, the sociocultural space he
witnessed as man and artist, was perfecting a masterful performance in its
own theater of the absurd. Moving beyond (or perhaps more closely to)
traditional ideals of Americanness, the country choreographed a series of
violent movements intended to restore and/or retain some semblance of
racial hierarchy and white supremacy. And thus, chaos, absurdity, darkness, and tragedy became the ruling tonalities of an articulated American
self in this moment. Baldwin's writing, then, served as a vehicle to get
closer to his country's ailments, to obtain, if you will, a closer seat to the
decaying body of the great republic. At its heart, Baldwin would find a
racial pathology not textualized by blackness but rather a symptom of a
fragile and waning whiteness. The darkness navigated by Black folk was
the direct product of a desperation engulfing white folk. Subsequently,
Baldwin's novel writing ought to be understood as a systematic treatment

of America's dying spirit, an intervention into what could easily have been its full undoing. And, therefore, if America needed anything by the time Baldwin published his fourth novel, it needed salvation. With a certain level of perverse poetry, the United States in the 1960s can be read as another symbol for a national fraternal crisis, where the racial problem, as gestured toward in *Another Country*, lay directly at the center. Baldwin's novel extends hope for salvation.

By the time James Baldwin's fourth novel, *Tell Me How Long the Train's Been Gone* (1968), was published, the world had witnessed a series of assassinations within the United States. For Baldwin, the murder of Medgar Evers (1963), John Fitzgerald Kennedy (1963), El-Hajj Malik El-Shabazz (1965), and Dr. Martin Luther King Jr. (1968), proved that America still had much to do in its push for racial equality and social justice. Although Dr. King's assassination occurred after Baldwin had finished writing the novel, the hostile racial moment of the 1960s surely affected the tone of the work and may account for why many critics read it as detrimentally polemic and as a product of propaganda. Additionally, while experiencing the height of the Civil Rights Movement, with its inevitable spate of assassinations, the United States of the 1960s ushered in the Black Power Movement as a critical response to what many saw as the ineffectuality of the Civil Rights Movement. Led by a mixed collective of disillusioned youth, the new movement for racial equality eschewed passive resistance as a strategy in favor of more "aggressive" forms of protest and defense. Yet, despite *Train's Been Gone* being birthed within the neo-nadir of American race relations, it has been considerably neglected within literary criticism and continues to be one of Baldwin's least studied novels. *Train's Been Gone*, in capturing the tension of the two interrelated movements, emerges, for critics at least, as in line more with Baldwin's fiery essays and less with his other novels.

The rhetoric of rage exhibited in *Train's Been Gone*, most notably through conversations between the protagonist, Leo Proudhammer, and his Black radical lover, Christopher Hall, solidified for the American public that Baldwin's intention, or maybe his unavoidable succumbing, was to shed his cloak as artistic witness and assume the role of political proselytizer. Such thoughts reveal why criticism of the novel generally leaned toward a denouncing of it as a novelistic failure. Summarizing W. J. Weatherby's extensive survey of reviews, Randall Kenan noted the unbalanced critiques in his essay "James Baldwin, 1924–1987: A Brief Biography" by stating that while "some called it a 'masterpiece'. . . others dismissed the book variously for being navel-gazing, out-of-touch with mainstream Black life, poorly written, too political at times, and a work of propaganda and for having flat characters."[1] These critics, especially Irving Howe and Mario Puzo, were quick to assess *Train's Been Gone* for its deviation from the literary styles of the novels preceding it but, more distinctly, for the change in Baldwin's authorial tone. The gentleness once used to treat issues of race and sexuality gave way to a forcefulness strongly mirroring the Black aggression of the Black Power Movement. Puzo begins his essay "His Cardboard Lovers" stating the following:

Tragedy calls out for a great artist, revolution for a true prophet. Six years ago James Baldwin predicted the black revolution that is now changing our society. His new novel, *Tell Me How Long the Train's Been Gone* is his attempt to re-create, as an artist this time, the tragic condition of the Negro in America.[2]

The distinction Puzo makes here between the "artist" and the "prophet" is meant to highlight the necessary differentiation between Baldwin as novelist and essayist. He alludes to *The Fire Next Time* in an effort to establish the similar work being done between the essay collection and *Train's Been Gone*, a novel produced years later but with the same goal of making plain the "tragic condition of the Negro in America." However, for him, the difference in genre required Baldwin to relinquish the prophetic hat he wore in writing *The Fire Next Time* to adorn himself as artist.

According to Puzo, Baldwin fails to make this transition at the expense of *Train's Been Gone*'s success, and instead it becomes "a simpleminded, one-dimensional novel with mostly cardboard characters, a polemical rather than narrative tone, weak invention, and poor selection of incident."[3] Puzo's critique of the novel, while merited in some regards, falls victim to both a gross misreading and an unrealistic idea that the novel can, in some peculiar way, operate outside the historical moment claiming its genesis.

Baldwin does not sway from his standard use of the "real" as inspiration for his fiction and does with *Train's Been Gone* what he had done with every novel that preceded it—that is, use the profoundly personal to shape the narrative he wishes to tell. And maybe the difference this time is that the personal is inextricably linked to the political ills of the day and does not solely focus on his normal themes of family, religion, and sexuality. Even still, Puzo's reading of *Train's Been Gone*, along with others like it, errs, as Lynn Orilla Scott points out, in not recognizing that "*Tell Me How Long the Train's Been Gone* is about, among other things, the problem and uses of racial anger rather than the unmediated expression of anger that these critics interpreted it to be."[4] Even more, the shortcoming of the reviews, aside from a cultural misreading of how rage and anger function within the novel, stems from how "most reviews did not make any direct reference to the sexual relationship between Leo Proudhammer and his brother Caleb or even to the later sexual relationship between Leo and Black Christopher."[5] By simply concentrating on the radically charged rhetoric of revolution and by ignoring the moving and personal relationships of the novel, reviewers missed the very heart of the narrative. Furthermore, in not acknowledging how "these relationships carry a great deal of symbolic weight and are key to any meaningful reading of the text," critics such as Puzo engage in epistemological violence.[6] I argue that an examination of male relationships in *Train's Been Gone*, in particular Leo's relationships with his brother Caleb and the "brother" of the movement, Christopher, greatly enhances our understanding of the work the novel performs. It will, quite forcefully, undermine the accusation embedded in the statement, "Novelists are born sinners and their salvation does not come so easily, and certainly the last role the artist should play is that of the prosecutor, the creator of a propaganda novel. A propaganda novel may be socially valuable . . . but it is not art."[7] In fact, when read correctly, *Train's Been Gone* will highlight Baldwin's continued wrestling with the complex nature of male intimacy and further example his radical idea of salvation.

Over the course of his first three novels, Baldwin constructed and expanded the idea of salvific manhood. Taking us from the triumphant to the tragic, Baldwin was clear to demonstrate how the potential for salvation does not automatically translate into saving or healing. Journeying through a series of fraternal crises, readers are forced to consider the manifold ways Black men become, or always already are, vulnerable subjects. Writing at once within and outside the parameters of literary traditions of urban realism, protest fiction, existentialism, modernism, and the Beat Generation, Baldwin made Black male intimacy and vulnerability his most consistent theme while weaving in other important and moving topoi. *Train's Been Gone*, while deviating from his popular styles or more readily identifiable techniques, remains committed to what I argue is a larger Baldwinian project. Like its predecessors, *Train's Been Gone* centers itself within a conversation of salvation mediated through same-gender male relationships. With a different sociopolitical landscape (we should note how the landscape always changes in Baldwin's novel), this novel launches from the cultural context shaping Baldwin's world at the time. Equal in triumph and tragedy, with added provocation, it promises the further development of the idea of salvific manhood. Salvation in *Train's Been Gone* demands different forms of offering and asks its witnesses to reconsider fundamental mores and ethics. Between its pages, Baldwin inspires a new type of negotiation, where the reader is truly asked to think through the gravity of vulnerability.

Baldwin's *Train's Been Gone* is a novel relayed from the first-person point of view. It centers on the life of Leo Proudhammer, a Harlemite turned thespian who spends his life constantly negotiating his race, his sexuality, and his career. While Baldwin offers the reader a plethora of themes—the difficulty of African Americans to carve out a space in theater, the complexity of interracial relationships, the struggle of Black manhood within a racially corrupt United States, the intricacies of family—his focus on relationships is undeniably consistent. Leo's journey to find self is mediated through his relationships with two other men within the novel: his brother Caleb and his lover Christopher. In a way, Caleb and Christopher offer a striking contrast to each other while at the same time playing similar roles in Leo's life. Through both men he comes to understand both the vulnerability and the power of his blackness alongside the slipperiness of his masculinity. Even more, he is exposed to a series of fraternal crises, forced to grapple with personal distance or the space-in-between plaguing his relationships with men, and compelled to make sense of the depth of salvific manhood required to save those around him, including himself. With *Train's Been Gone*, Baldwin dares to explore the darker interstices of salvation and hopes clarity for the reader comes in the end.

Symptoms of Leo's Crisis

The novel opens with Leo Proudhammer having a heart attack in the middle of a theatrical performance. He recounts the terror and confusion of the moment, how he fought through the disorientation to make it through the end of the play. After the curtain closes, signaling the play's finality, Leo collapses within the excitement of the applause. Somewhere between consciousness and delirium, he remembers being caught in the discomfort of fear and the nurturing hands of his white female casual lover, his castmate by the name of Barbara. Baldwin then takes the reader from Leo's lighthearted musings on death in his dressing room to the moment he awakes in the hospital. With Barbara by Leo's side, his doctor—a man with an accent that reminds him of a barber from his childhood—encourages his stillness and asks for Barbara to stay. Whether due to an increase in lucidity or the doctor's insistence on his not moving, Leo contemplates his situation in a stark contrast to the scene in the dressing room. He thinks,

> Now, for the first time, I began to be aware of my heart, the heart itself: and with this awareness, conscious terror came. I realized that I knew nothing whatever about the way we are put together; and I realized that what I did not know might be in the process of killing me. My heart—*if* it was my heart—seemed to be rising and sinking within me; seemed like a swimmer betrayed by an element in which, by an unanswerable tide, it was being carried far out, by an unanswerable pull, being carried far down.[8]

Leo's heart attack represents the crisis of his life. Placing it amid a performance, Baldwin means to show the relationship between the "stage" and his narrator's breakdown. Leo's career as an actor served as a severance from that which he kept close to his heart—his family, his love interests, and his community. Just as the stage divided actor from audience, his career separated him from those closest to him. As an actor, Leo's life was defined by performance, was marked by a constant flight into the imaginary. As he ascended into the world of performance, he inevitably enjoyed a peculiar detachment from that which claimed his love. For Baldwin, the heart attack represents the sobering realization of this detachment and affirms D. Quentin Miller's reading that "Leo's collapse is more significantly an identity crisis related to his latent feelings that he has neglected the anguish of his race in favor of artistic safety."[9] However, alongside the suffering of racial anguish, Baldwin's protagonist suffers a heart attack that symptomizes the crisis he faces within his personal life. Leo's heart, the sanctum of his love and the vessel marking his capacity for human intimacy, is attacked by the dissolution of his most meaningful personal relationships. The characters he plays consume his life, and his most engaging connections are forged between audiences that care nothing of the man he is without the makeup and without the performative costumes. Baldwin thus uses the heart attack to reclaim Leo from the world of detachment, to place him *still* so that he might be able to understand the consequences of his waning intimate friendships and intimacies. Noting the relationship between Leo's collapse and his consciousness, Scott notes, "Forcing him off the public stage, the heart attack provides Leo the respite necessary for self-reflection. He discovers that he has hidden behind the mask of his public life, becoming a stranger to himself."[10] When he expresses, "Then something hit me in the chest, tore through my chest to my backbone and almost knocked me down," Leo knows the "feeling" of a heart attack, but it is not until the hospital that he comes to know what exactly had attacked his heart.[11]

Amid thoughts of his heart's fragility and encouragements from Barbara for him to take it easy, Leo concedes to the reader his recognition of love and the chaos of his life. Admittedly, his life was somewhat selfish or, as he relays, "My life, that desperately treacherous labyrinth, seemed for a moment to be opening out behind me; a light seemed to fall where there had been no light before. I began to see myself in others."[12] Leo's recognition of self in this moment, a direct result of the paralyzing effect of his heart attack, reveals a confrontation that he has evaded up to this point. For the first time, he admits that he falls victim to the same longing that other people have, that regardless of his fame or fortune, he craves that basic element of humanity. What follows in his mind, however, captures Baldwin's wrestling with the precariousness of love and the subtle nuances of male emotion. Leo, in that Baldwinian voice of the witness, tells the reader,

> Everyone wishes to be loved, but, in the event, nearly no one can bear it. Everyone desires love but also finds it impossible to believe that he deserves it. However great the private disasters to which love may lead, love itself is strikingly and mysteriously impersonal; it is a reality which is not altered by anything one does. Therefore, one does many things, turns the key in the lock over and over again, hoping to be locked out. Once locked out, one will never again be forced to encounter in the eyes of a stranger who loves him the impenetrable truth concerning the stranger, oneself, who is loved. And yet—one would prefer, after all, not to be locked out. One would prefer, merely, that the key unlocked a less stunningly unusual door.[13]

In a passage thematically reminiscent of *Giovanni's Room*, *Train's Been Gone* defines love with that Baldwinian complexity, which will situate Leo as a character created to carry the heaviness of love, as someone ordained to go through "the stink of love." With a beautiful vulnerability, Leo conveys what the reader will learn is one of his most pressing struggles within the novel. He, like many of the other characters, wishes and desires "to be loved." But what plagues him, what shapes his journeys throughout the narrative, is the inability to *believe* himself worthy of that love. Consequently, he shies away from it, convinces himself that life can be fulfilling without it and that his heart can endure its absence. Here, again, Baldwin compounds the symbolism of the heart attack, suggesting to the reader that emotional and intimate reconciliation purposes Leo's quest. Reading the novel through this lens, the reader further uncovers the spurious critiques from reviewers like Howe and Puzo, who were quick to reduce *Train's Been Gone* to polemical fiction. We learn that while teeming with political allusion, the novel remains decidedly more personal than polemical.

Critics who cannot see the literary or novelistic merit of *Train's Been Gone* fail to see the personal narrative of Leo Proudhammer. While asserting that Baldwin deploys a political agenda within the novel, they fail to analyze the struggle of his protagonist and miss what I argue is the true import of the work. For as Leo lies in the hospital bed and ponders life, death, and love, he communicates that the novel is less about the politically and racially hostile 1950s and 1960s and more about an individual's (a Black man's, to be particular) grappling with love within that time. This is evidenced in one of his first flashbacks, where, moments after talking to Barbara and thinking about the precariousness of love, he remembers his brother Caleb, who was arrested from a tenement in which they used to live. He flashes back to childhood, unpacking his father's unwelcoming, unlikable presence and how Mr. Proudhammer came from Barbados to live among a people whom he despised. And how he would never take anything from Black people the way he took it from white people. He recounts the beauty of his mother, how certain "imperfections" made her uniquely beautiful. These thoughts, immediately following his philosophical musing on love, inform the reader that this novel, despite the reviews, centers on something much deeper than Baldwin's effort to castigate America for its racial intolerance and brutality, though that is definitely an extension of its aim. This novel, above anything else, focuses on a man's journey to make sense of how he loves and those he loves, the crises that unfold, and how he adapts or responds to those "private disasters." The descriptions of Mr. and Mrs. Proudhammer remind us of the familial aspects of *Go Tell It*— the migration narrative of the fathers, the "shortcomings" of the mothers. Again, *Train's Been Gone* shows how it continues to build upon Baldwin's previous work. Nonetheless, beyond the continuation, it magnifies the complex fraternal exchanges that Leo has with his brother Caleb and the Black radical Christopher.

Brothers by Blood and by Heart: Leo and Caleb

Probably one of the most complex relationships in all of Baldwin's fiction, the relationship between blood brothers Leo and Caleb Proudhammer exemplifies the complexity of the fraternal and the provocative profundity of the salvific. Baldwin quickly carves out the depth of Leo and Caleb's brotherly bond by having his narrator flash back to different moments in their childhood. The reader learns Caleb is the older of the two and how Leo was oftentimes the thorn in his brother's side. Nevertheless, there existed an undeniable love between the two young men, and Caleb was for Leo, as the saying goes, "the apple of his eye." One also learns how Caleb and Leo expressed different masculinities. Whereas Caleb was quite popular with both men and women, Leo was viewed as "Caleb's round-eyed, frail and useless sissy of a little brother."[14] Leo's gentle masculinity, a trace of the bisexuality we learn of later, allowed him to understand the "difficulty" of his brother's position at times when they were supposed to go to the movies. Essentially, the love Leo held for his big brother freed Caleb from his brotherly responsibilities and encouraged his own posturing of male independence. Even as a young boy, Leo understood the unspoken scripts of male and masculine performance. He knew particular behaviors were expected of him because of his maleness and, out of a love of his brother, he submitted to the gender laws. These instances of male performance were anything but stress-free for Leo. Increasingly, he became aware of his own vulnerability and his need for male intimacy. After being "dismissed" by Caleb and forced to go to the movies alone, he notes, "This was surely the most terrible moment. The moment I turned away I was committed, I was trapped, and then I had miles to walk, so it seemed to me, before I would be out of sight, before the block ended and I could turn onto the avenue. I wanted to run out of that block, but I never did."[15] Leo's torment in this moment is twofold. Symbolically, the moment's terribleness arises from the space-in-between guaranteed by these departures. Detachment from Caleb promises loneliness or ensures the state of being alone. Additionally, the threat of Harlem's urbanity and the possibility for violence contributed to Leo's pressing need to run and strong desire to maintain a certain performative masculinity. More importantly, however, this scene encapsulates Leo's struggle with being "locked out" of love. His walk from his brother, a mere block hyperbolized as a mile, signifies a departure from the fraternal. Caleb's dismissal and his acquiescence would form a habit of Leo walking away from love later on in life. Inevitably, as he shares in this moment, Leo never truly wants to walk alone, would much rather be accompanied by the person whom he loves, and the movie recollection highlights the degree to which fraternal crisis, Leo's in particular, is linked to male intimacy.

One of Leo Proudhammer's earliest crises comes during a time when he was forced to go to the movies alone. He recounts his fascination with whiteness and the "civic terror" he experienced in the New York underground. Lost within the fury of a train ride where he found himself consumed by whiteness and alone with one other Black man, Leo tells of the fright he experienced feeling no "colored people" were there to protect him. Speaking of the lone Black man on the train, Leo thinks of the abstract relationship he holds with the stranger: "He was my salvation and he stood there in the unapproachable and frightening form that salvation so often takes. At each stop, I watched him with despair."[16] While unacquainted, the older Black man on the train functioned as both a sign of comfort or protection within a hostile "white" world and a symbol for the longing for male intimacy. Baldwin crafts the man and the experience to showcase how Caleb's absence precipitates a small fraternal crisis for Leo. Additionally, Leo's silent reaction when the man asks him why he is alone and where his parents are exemplifies his need for nonromantic intimacy. He thinks, "I almost said I didn't have any because I liked his face and his voice and was half hoping to hear him say that *he* didn't have any little boy and would just take a chance on me."[17] Coupling Leo's liking of the man's face and voice with the hope of being his "little boy," Baldwin identifies Leo's—and indeed, Baldwin's own—longing for something both male and intimate. Subsequently, this longing becomes more easily traceable through his relationship with Caleb, a relationship rooted in a series of fraternal crises.

If Leo's experience on the train tells us anything, it is that our young narrator wrestles, very early in his life, with the state of being alone. It generates a panic within him, a deep sentiment around being lost, and pushes him to search for respite in the company of others. In addition, along with his terror-filled departure from Caleb as he scurries down the block, it accentuates his struggle with vulnerability. And in an effort to protect himself, he performs and postures a masculinity that is traditional in nature. However, in spite of fashioning himself in the manner of other boys, he knows that his expression of maleness, particularly when it comes to aggression, is not authentic. In fact, he would much rather be honest about his need for nurture and be able to express how he longs for the protection of his brother at times when he is alone. Again, in Caleb's absence, he must assume a tough persona, portraying himself as something more heartless than what he is. This reality, of course, causes him some mental anxiety, as he is often caught between what he shows to the world and what he feels inside. Noting his solitary expeditions and the encounters requiring a specific manhood, he explains, "[My] single-minded and terrified ruthlessness was masked by my obvious vulnerability, my paradoxical and very real helplessness, and it covered my terrible need to lie down, to breathe deep, to weep long and loud, to be held in human arms . . . to tell it all, to let it out, to be brought into the world, and, out of human affection, to be born again."[18] In sharing this, Leo offers a glimpse of his internal struggle. Although situations demand a real independence, his manhood demands human affection and gentleness. The world in which he lives, even as a young boy, pushes him to search for something to soothe his vulnerability. More and more, that something becomes his brother.

Caleb's absence was inextricably linked to Leo's state of being alone and his developing vulnerability. After several tormenting "solitary expeditions," Leo found himself an emotional wreck each time, cursing his brother for leaving him to lonely solitude. Nevertheless, these expeditions always end with reunion, with a comforting Caleb there to offer a place for his younger brother's refuge. Considering this, Leo's emotional crises tended to be fleeting, expected, and sufferable. That is, until they were coming home one evening and were stopped by white policemen. Placing the brothers together, Baldwin explores the racial disharmony haunting Harlem and the United States in general as he displays how Leo's racial consciousness was awakened. Like in the relationships between Rufus Scott and Vivaldo in *Another Country* and between Frank and Alonzo Hunt in *If Beale Street Could Talk*, white racism catalyzes a fraternal crisis within the relationship between Leo and Caleb. For critics, Caleb's antagonism and the dialogue surrounding the event reflect Baldwin's propagandistic tone in the novel. They read it as an indirect way of discussing the race problem in America within the guise of the literary. The problem with such readings is that they ignore the emotional exchange between the two brothers and thereby eclipse the complicated story Baldwin hopes to share about male intimacy.

In another flashback Leo recounts a dream in which Caleb chased him; he recounts his familial trouble and how they were evicted, his father losing his job, Caleb dropping out of school, and his mother going to work as a domestic for whites. He also notes his blooming sexuality and the uncomfortable dialogue with his peers. Most significant is how he recounts the strong bond he has with Caleb and his remembrance of that horrific day of his life when Caleb was arrested. On that day, after work he notices the store, which is a meeting place for them, is closed, and when he finally reaches home, there is a strong melancholic presence in the silence. Caleb is not there, and his mother breaks down in tears as she tells of the accusations. He learns Caleb is thought to have participated in the robbing and stabbing of a man at the store. Leo runs out of the house with a fervor, ends up at Miss Mildred's, and shares a strong moment with Caleb right before the police come to arrest him. Up to this point in the novel, all of Leo's flashbacks to the moments he spent with or without his brother have built up to this exampling of their fraternal bond. In an episode capturing more than the attachment guaranteed by blood or even fictive kinship, one witnesses the power of love and the unquestionable intimacy between Leo and his brother.

Miss Mildred's home paradoxically serves as a space of sanctum and seizure. Within the space, blackness is able to fully express itself without censure or taming. However, it also holds the potential, precisely because of this free-flowing blackness, for actualized threat. It becomes a site of verbal and physical violence when the cops arrive to arrest Caleb. When questioned as to why Caleb is being taken to the station, one of the officers responds, "'You're a very inquisitive bunch of niggers. Here's what for,' and he suddenly grabbed Caleb and smashed the pistol butt against the side of his head."[19] More than emphasizing the ugliness of racism and police brutality, the violent exchange foregrounds the love Leo holds for his brother. His fighting restraint to get free, holding on to an officer's leg, and being dragged along while Caleb is placed into the cop car highlight the different layers of Leo's reaction—a mixture of confusion, anger, and fear.

The arrest ends with Leo being kicked by an officer to the point of tasting blood, his unsuccessful attempts at getting in or stopping the cop car, and his emotional cries of "Please, Please. . . . That's my brother."[20] Eventually the cop car drives off and Leo is taken home, where he resists the comfort of his father and mother. The narrator's final words and thoughts at the end of the chapter go to show that the true violence of his brother's arrest was neither the verbal pejorative of "nigger" nor the physical abuse of Black bodies; rather, it was the violent tearing of one brother from another. When he tells his parents, "I hate you, I said, I hate you, and [buries himself] in the pillow which still held Caleb's smell," he expresses the pain of losing his brother and the profundity of their fraternal love.[21] Leo's rejection of his parents' attempt at comforting him and his profession of hate stem from a realization of their inability to protect both him and Caleb from racialized police violence. That they were unable to save, and that such inability causes the development of another type of distance and fraternal crisis, speaks to the larger question of salvation pervading the novel. If Caleb cannot be saved by his parents, then who can save him? If racial absurdity becomes the natural force forever haunting Leo's and Caleb's manhood, whence comes their help? And last, if Leo's father proves not to be the salvific figure, whose manhood shall save them?

A Peculiar Love between Brothers: Crisis and Redemptive Sexuality

Lynn Orilla Scott argues, "It is not accidental that Leo loses Caleb to the three institutions that most frequently shape the lives of young Black men, institutions which Baldwin believed continually perpetuated racism and denied Black masculinity."[22] For Scott, space plays a very important role in how one reads *Train's Been Gone* and Baldwin's understanding of how restricted or imprisoned Black masculinity is by systems of power. Explicit in *Train's Been Gone*, the effect of white racism on the Black male body surfaces in Caleb's prison experience and his subsequent self-expression once released and back home. In particular, his relationship with Martin Howell, a red-haired prison guard, generates a crisis in his masculinity, one later resolved through the love of his younger brother.

Allusions to slavery subtly decorate Caleb's narrative sharing of his imprisonment on a prison farm down South. Caleb delineates this when he recalls how the prisoners were oftentimes whipped and beat with rifles. Martin Howell represents the unrelenting overseer whose greater purpose beyond forcing labor is the humiliation and stripping of Black humanity. Howell seemed bent on reminding Black men both that they were "niggers" and of their place in both the prison–industrial complex and the larger world. As a way of sharing with Leo the painful subjugation, Caleb tells, "He'd say, You ain't worth shit, are you? And they'd say, No, Mr. Howell, we ain't worth shit. The first time I heard it, saw it, I vomited. But he made me say it, too. . . . That hurt me, hurt me more than his whip, more than his rifle butt, more than his fists. Oh. That hurt me."[23] The system of oppression operating within Caleb's prison experience highlights the racialization of carceral power. In locating the prison in the South, Baldwin directly creates a historical connection with the institution of slavery. Therefore, the treatment witnessed by the reader is meant to approximate the performances of power often staged during that peculiar institution. As such, *Train's Been Gone* reimagines racial absurdity in a new space in an effort to better locate Caleb's fraternal crisis, or the cause of his struggle and suffering in 1960s America. Howell's character functions, then, as both a surrogate for historical agents of oppression and a contemporary representation of white supremacist embodiment. Although it took Howell a while to get Caleb to submit to denigration, it was not without struggle. Their personal battle began on a day when the two men quarreled over Caleb's resistance to Howell's abuse of power. After the former proclaimed his name proudly, standing up defiantly to the latter's surprise, Howell said, "Nigger, if my balls was on your chin, where would my prick be?" and provoked Caleb to take up a pitchfork in ready defense.[24] Baldwin's choice of scripting here—his common use of the sexual to undergird expressions or attempts of extending power—reaffirms the relationship between sexuality and iterations of white supremacy. Howell's response to Caleb's assertion of agency with an allusion to placing his penis in Caleb's mouth echoes how white terror functions through the silencing of Black voice and its articulation of autonomy or being. For Baldwin, this phenomenon often showcases itself through the use of sex, particularly when Black manhood emerges as the target of the terror.

Caleb continues sharing with Leo and in doing so illuminates Baldwin's intervention into the prevailing discourse on male sexuality. Provocatively, Caleb discloses a self-awareness somewhat unique during the era in which *Train's Been Gone* was published, admitting to his brother,

> And, you know, it's funny, I realized right then and there, while I was watching him ride off, it wasn't, you know, exactly like what he'd *said*. I mean, shit, you know. I'm a big boy and I know the score. Shit. You know. If it came down on me like that, well, all right, I'd suck a cock, I know it, shit, if I loved the cat, why the fuck not, and whose business is it? Like, shit. You know. Ain't nobody's business. You know, like, man, I'd do anything in the world for you because you're my brother and because you're my baby and I love you and I believe you'd do anything in the world for me.[25]

The honesty of Caleb's confession uncovers the complexity of male sexuality in *Train's Been Gone*. To a degree, such a profession might allow one to read Caleb as a bisexual Black man or one open to the possibility for sexual exploration. His passionate questioning, "Why the fuck not, and whose business is it?" suggests, as Baldwin often claimed, that sexuality is a private affair. However, the emphasis on love also expresses the disarming power of human intimacy, especially when one is in need, and serves as Baldwin's peculiar way of showing how love, with all of its expressions, transcends provincial considerations of sexuality. Regardless of whether the conversation paints him as a man of ambiguous sexual practices or as a progressive ideologue, it exhibits his will to fight for his humanity and manhood. He makes this fight plain to Leo, declaring, "I'm a man. And a man can do anything he wants to do, but can't nobody *make* him do it. I ain't about to be raped."[26] Rape, as an idea, functions in *Train's Been Gone* similarly to how it did in other novels. Baldwin uses it as a literal and metaphoric device to highlight the violence endured by Black manhood. Said violence, a general reality for Black people facing the racial absurdity of the world, becomes isolated and personal for Caleb Proudhammer—the Black male of the novel who offers the reader a firsthand account of Black male existential mayhem. His constant battles with Howell, including sexual threats and physical abuse, culminate in a fraternal crisis—where his Black manhood inadvertently becomes separated from its ability to feel and to love.

Caleb's fraternal crisis deepens during his incarceration. Although the cause of his imprisonment and the treatment he faced as a result of racial absurdity represent a major part of the crisis, it is of the fraternal type because of the space-in-between men that it guarantees. Black men affected by the carceral are predestined for fraternal crisis often until or unless they are able to forge strong bonds with others imprisoned. Despite this, the carceral space plays a significant role in ensuring fraternal crisis, and Caleb recounts this to his younger brother: "They had a place there where they put you when they was displeased. It was a kind of cellar. We was already in jail, you understand, but they had a jail inside the jail."[27] Caleb's double imprisonment analogizes the state of Black manhood during the moment *Train's Been Gone* was produced. This dual isolation, this double alienation, repeats Camusian absurdity with a racial difference. The existentialists' twentieth-century despair is magnified by Black flesh, is rendered something completely new and different with simple traces of the original ideas. And for Baldwin's Caleb, loneliness lay at the heart of the "jail inside the jail": "Your brother was a very lonely man, because I knew wasn't nobody going to help me. Not even if they wanted to. And I thought of you, you know that—my big-eyed little brother? But I was glad you wasn't there. I was mighty glad you wasn't there."[28] Caleb's loneliness reflected the depth of his fraternal crisis and the absence of a salvific figure. As a vulnerable subject, Caleb thinks of the person he feels capable of saving him; ironically, that figure is Leo. When he expresses gladness with Leo's absence, he quietly admits knowing the extents to which Leo might go to save him. And in understanding how institutional apparatuses operate at the repressive state level, he wished not to place Leo in harm's way.

At the site of Caleb's rupture, where his manhood breaks under the pressure of what Baldwin might call a criminal power, his vulnerability is most exposed. For Leo, "his silence created a great wound in the universe," which illumines the space-in-between them, the vastness of Caleb's crisis, and the challenge of his salvation.[29] Leo's response uncovers his burgeoning salvific manhood and continues the process of eradicating the space-in-between them: "There was nothing for me to say; nothing. I held him, held what there was to hold. I held him. Because I could love, I realized I could hate."[30] What he feels in this moment, this ability to hate, is tied to feeling his brother's crisis and the coldness that comes with it—a coldness first witnessed and overcome when his brother was released from prison. But even more, Baldwin once again points to the power of male intimacy, particularly or symbolically expressed through the physical. To be held, for Baldwin, is to have one's vulnerability seen and protected. In holding his brother, Leo literally removes the distance between their bodies and symbolically erases the crises caused by distance. Unlike Vivaldo in *Another Country*, who refused to reach across the bed to hold a broken and vulnerable Rufus, Leo demonstrates a capacity to save. Leo's salvific potentiality comes as a precursor to this moment of gentle masculinity and sets up Baldwin's strategic combatting of white terror deployed through sexual and physical violence.

Leo noticed a severe change in Caleb days before the aforementioned conversation. Martin Howell and the prison, along with American society in general, directly deadened something in Caleb. Upon his return, Caleb "was thinner, much thinner, but harder and tougher. He was beautiful, with a very dangerous, cruel, and ruthless beauty. He had been home a week, but he and [Leo] found it hard to talk."[31] In this observation, one realizes that the beautiful bond between brothers has been supplanted by the elder's fraternal crisis. No longer does he know how to connect or open up, and he guards himself as if constantly under threat. Consequently, this greatly affected Leo, who noted, "There was something in Caleb lonely and sad, shrinking and hysterical. It broke my heart to watch him. He had been beaten too hard."[32] At this time, Leo had yet to learn the details of Caleb's prison struggles, but he knew, quite definitively, that his brother had been beaten physically, emotionally, and psychologically. Even so, he did not discover the depth of the hurt or pain until a night when he was awakened by Caleb's vulnerable expression of emotion. Baldwin displays the powerful state of the Black man as vulnerable subject when Leo relays, "I woke to the sound of weeping. Somebody was weeping, all alone, holding his breath, shaking the bed. I listened, extended, so to speak, in a terror unlike any terror I had known. How he wept! How he wept! And it was as though I were weeping; but it was much worse than that."[33] Baldwin's strategic and critical use of language in this scene delineates an important intervention in the discourse on Black manhood and masculinity. Importantly, Leo does not share that Caleb was crying; rather, he notes he was weeping, or that he wept. By "weeping," Baldwin intends to amplify the heaviness of Caleb's burden. He was not simply affected; he was afflicted. With Howell operating as an agent of racial absurdity and the prison as a literal site of torture and oppression, Baldwin offers Caleb not solely as someone who needs to heal from being wounded but also as an individual who is in need of saving. Leo's empathy in this moment and his occupation of terror create in him, or out of him, the Baldwinian witness, the figure whose seeing comes with the responsibility to act.

Leo first witnesses his brother's emptiness in this moment: "He put his arms around me; it was strange to feel that I was *his* big brother now. And he held me so tightly, or, rather with such an intensity, that I knew, without knowing that I knew it, how empty his arms had been."[34] The role reversal performed in Leo's assumption of the "big brother" position further highlights his new role as salvific man. As Caleb's emotion calmed, Leo's grew, as he promised, "If they thought Caleb was black, and if they thought that I was black, I would show them, yes, I would, one day, exactly what blackness was!"[35] Continuing through a cursing of God from the depths of his manhood, Leo begets a critique of God much akin to the rejection he first had of his parents. Caleb's brokenness, and Baldwin's construction of him as a "weeping" man, evoke the idea of a forsaking God. For Caleb, God, like his parents, was absent during Caleb's nadir. The salvation promised by God was withheld in Leo's mind and thus had to be offered through another vessel. Therefore, when he awoke to the physical and sexual excitement of his brother, his excitement grew, alongside his desire for God to watch:

I knew, I knew, what my brother wanted, what my brother needed, and I was not at all afraid—more than I could say for God, who took all and gave nothing: and who paid for nothing, though all His creatures paid. I held my brother very close, I kissed him and caressed him and

I felt a pain and wonder I had never felt before. My brother's heart was broken; I knew it from his touch. In all the great, vast, dirty world, he trusted the love of one person only, his brother, his brother, who was in his arms. And I thought, Yes. Yes. Yes. I'll love you, Caleb.[36]

Leo's excitement reflects both the physical stimulation he experiences and the fervor of a spiritual engagement. Situating himself, or acknowledging himself, as the salvific man, Leo extends a theological critique at the presence or narrative of a passive God. God, the original source of salvation, finds *Himself* evoked by an excited young man who begins to understand the power he has and the need demanded of him to save his brother. Thus, sexuality carries a particular function in this moment. On one hand, it symbolically represents the profound level of intimacy required for salvation—how close a person must be willing to get to another in order to save. On the other hand, the shared sexualities between brothers excavates a deeply personal or beautiful vulnerability masked by and hidden underneath prescriptive notions of masculinity and traditional regulations of the taboo. Therefore, what comes after Leo's acknowledgment of his brother's broken heart and need for love is a beautifully peculiar sexual exchange between brothers. Their exchange resists the label of "incest," as the narrative moment centers more on redemptive power and possibility.

Baldwin's crafting of male intimacy in this scene between brothers communicates the detrimental effects of spaces-in-between men while also gesturing toward the need for a certain level of proximity for salvation. When preachers survey their congregation for those in need of saving, they often ask, "Who among us needs to know God?" The biblical state of knowing almost always meant a sexual union, some type of intimacy. So then, as Baldwin writes out of this biblical tradition, for Leo to truly save his brother in this moment, for him to erase the separation that keeps his brother a victim of a cold world, he must bring him closer. This is precisely how Leo performs his salvific role. He tells us, "I stripped both of us naked. He held me and he kissed me and he murmured my name."[37] The brothers' nakedness represents a metaphysical vulnerability. Their flesh constitutes full access to knowing, enacts the erasure of distance. Similarly, Caleb's initializing acts of intimacy suggest their different positions, with Leo again acting as the agent of salvation. Baldwin confirms this through the symbolic utterance of Leo's name—as if he were "calling upon the name of God." The performative role of the body continues in this sexual moment:

> My brother had never, for me, had a body before. And, in truth, I had never had a body before. . . . I had already done this by myself and I had done it with other boys: but it had not been like this because there had been no agony in it, I had not been trying to give, I had not even been trying to take, and I had not felt myself, as I did now, to be present in the body of the other person, had not felt his breath as mine, his sighs and moans, his quivering and shaking as mine, his journey as mine.[38]

In this moment, the body emerges both textually and psychically for Leo as a symbol of something beyond itself. Like the church, the body becomes the literal vessel or site of salvation. Through it, just as people come to *know* God through church, Caleb comes to know Leo. Leo must occupy the church of Caleb's world, must experience his pain and his suffering prior to being able to deliver him. Baldwinian agony, here, then signifies a required empathy. In order to truly save, Leo must completely eliminate whatever space exists between him and Caleb; he must, again, occupy him. The theological allusion Baldwin makes grounds itself with a more direct connection to religious vernacular. As if directly reminiscent of the encouragements from the pastor who, from the position of occupying the church's pulpit, urges his congregation "to be present in the body of Christ," Leo acknowledges how for the first time he was "to be present in the body of the other person." Through Leo's occupation, and through this male-to-male intimacy, they became one, the space-in-between them was removed, and salvation commenced.

Leo offers Caleb, as he notes himself, what only he can offer—and in doing so saves him, if only temporarily, from the coldness of hate and being disconnected from the ability to feel. Indeed, the power of Leo's sexuality lies within his salvific manhood—his ability to avail himself physically, emotionally, and psychologically to a broken Caleb. Leo's character punctuates the significance of willingness and want in salvific exchanges. He examples the selflessness needed for it to take place, as he shares, "I wanted Caleb's joy. His joy was mine. When his breathing changed and his tremors began, I trembled too, too, with joy, with joy, with joy and pride, and we came together."[39] To be salvific, for Baldwin, requires some profound level of selflessness. It requires a complete disregard of how one might be seen or imagined after the fact. This is both a reflection of individual stakes in healing and a discourse on America's interracial nightmare. While not within the scope of *Salvific Manhood*, Leo's selfishness reflects that which is unseen in Baldwin's white America. The encouragement or hope is toward Leo, for he emerges to be for his brother what Elisha was for John, what Vivaldo failed to be for Rufus, and what Fonny might be in the chapter to follow—a man endowed with the unique ability to save another one through his willingness to feel, to love, and to be intimate. In her book on Baldwin's later fiction, Scott asserts, "What is new and striking in *Tell Me How Long the Train's Been Gone* is Baldwin's willingness to posit intraracial, homoerotic love as a 'solution' to the debasement of Black masculinity and thereby directly challenge the homophobic discourse of Black nationalism."[40] Scott's observation is slightly skewed, as the strategic play of the "homoerotic" is nothing new to Baldwin's work. As my earlier chapters have pointed out, homoerotic love has been a reoccurring component of Baldwin's search of the *fraternal*. Nevertheless, she is right in stating that *Train's Been Gone* uniquely challenges Black nationalist homophobia—as the relationship between Leo Proudhammer and a Black radical makes tremendously clear. Leo's relationship with Christopher Hall reflects Baldwin's desire to mediate, through his characters, social and sexual disconnections—but it also comes as a means to resolve the crisis of manhood Leo experiences with whiteness.

Stages and Struggles: Leo's Crossroads between Artist and Man

In chapter 1, aptly titled "The House Nigger," Baldwin displays the early symptoms of how Leo's racial self would be subordinated to his desire for success. For instance, the night that he meets the San-Marquands at a party, he positions himself in a gentle minstrel-like performance with his close white friend, Barbara King. With the San-Marquands being the artistic directors of The Actors' Mean Workshop, both Barbara and Leo see the party as an opportunity for an audition. Barbara, quite comfortable in her role as a "delicate and Southern" woman, exerts the privilege so neatly tucked away in her friendship with Leo. Contrastingly, Leo performs his blackness in such a fashion as to disgust himself—a disgust distinctly revealed in his internal self-questioning: "I was not—was I?—stupidly and servilely to do the world's dirty work for it and permit its tangled, blind, and merciless reaction to the fact of my color also to become my own. How could I hope for, how could I deserve, my liberation, if I became my own jailer and myself turned the key which locked the mighty doors?"[41] In questioning the performance given to Lola and Saul San-Marquand, Leo offers the reader a glimpse into a major part of his struggle with race and announces the crisis that will define his career. Following Barbara's lead, he naturally costumes himself with a "house nigger" mentality. And while simply performance, it holds and held great consequences for the young aspiring thespian. Fortunately, the moment came with consciousness and provoked Leo to evaluate his act(ions) with a serious introspection.

Amid his self-denigrating performance, Leo Proudhammer processes his "house nigger" theatrics and the ways in which race cleverly creeps into interracial exchanges. He knows the consequences of his near-minstrel actions and the disservice done to the African American community, which was amid a fight for a new form of equality. Nevertheless, he also knows the extreme pressures of ambition and the games of compromise Black men must play to gain access to the entertainment world. It is within this thinking that he is enraged and comes to the point of admitting,

I was human, too. And my race was revealed as my pain—my pain—
and my rage could have no reason, nor submit to my domination,
until my pain was assessed; until my pain became invested with a
coherence and an authority which only I, alone, could provide. And
this possibility, the possibility of creating my language out of my pain,
of using my pain to create myself, while cruelly locked in the depths of
me, like the beginning of life and the beginning of death, yet seemed,
for an instant, to be on the very tip of my tongue.[42]

The beauty of Leo's internal musing lies in his realization that his pain and race are inseparably bound. His consumptive rage requires him to process his pain, to mine the dark caverns of his racial self, and to confront the reality of blackness in America. For Baldwin, self-awareness demands this type of personal work and necessitates an acceptance where the African Americans know themselves through their unique, though often painful, experience. Leo begins the process in this scene when he plays out the melancholy of his people on the piano and through the blues. Consequently, by sharing a more authentic and vulnerable part of himself, he earns a spot in The Actors' Mean Workshop.

Train's Been Gone's narrator quickly learns the severe racial division while working for the San-Marquands and hoping for his big break. The small white town, home of the theater company on Bull Dog Road, microcosmically represents racially intolerant America and, like the larger country, does not hesitate in letting Leo know that he is the unwanted "Other." Be that as it may, Baldwin establishes Leo's racial crises through sexual relationships with white women. These women function, in part, as representations of the white world as well as the source of its pride. Like Rufus and Leona's in *Another Country*, Leo's relationships with white women symbolize a desire for acceptance and an act of deviance. By engaging in intercourse, he refuses to submit to the predominant narrative of the day, which renders interracial intimacy a violation of social law. Interestingly, his experiences with both Madeleine and Barbara showcase the rage first witnessed when he met the San-Marquands as well as a growing frustration with whiteness.

Madeleine, an older actress attempting to revive her career through The Actors' Mean Workshop, signifies old America—the America experienced by the older luminaries Leo had once shared the platform with. But like the younger Barbara, she also exemplifies a forbidden fruit for Leo. Moments before having sex, again, Leo recalls, "Before I had had time to pretend that I was still sleeping, I realized that I had a performance to give. I realized that I rather liked her, and that was certainly a relief. But, mainly, I wanted to get that white flesh in my hands again, I simply wanted to fuck her: and this was not because I liked her."[43] Mirroring Rufus's complex relationship with

Leona, Leo's desire for Madeleine is dichotomized into a genuine attraction for her as a woman and a seemingly perverse disdain for her white body. Their sexual escapade, the curious blending of desire and hatred, culminates with Leo's subsequent arrest and represents the crime Leo committed against the country by being physically intimate with a white woman. Being in white custody, Leo understands, more than before, the place of his blackness within the white world. This is further evidenced when he is released not on his own accord but through the efforts (read: white manhood) of Saul San-Marquand. Either way, the event repositions Leo within the town, renders him a "presence of incitement." Whether Madeleine is simply an object of sexual desire or a symbolic body through which Leo can release his racial frustration, their intimacy is a harbinger of the racial crisis he will experience shortly and with another white woman, Barbara, by his side.

In a very short time, Leo learns that the town will offer him neither forgiveness nor a single, exceptional punishment for being with a white woman. Still, he pushes the tolerance of the small white town and makes love to Barbara as if all will be understood. Jerry, a mutual friend of theirs and admirer of Barbara's, reacts in a way that showcases, again, the profoundly taboo nature of their interracial affair. As a white man, his subjectivity is directly challenged by Leo's audacity to love, emotionally and physically, Barbara. However, it is their walk through town, the peculiar and hostile journey through unforgiving whiteness, that punctuates Leo's racial crisis. In short, as they are forced to walk to the theater company, they are verbally attacked with racial epithets and demeaning derisions meant to convey a disapproval for interracial intimacy. As a result, Leo's idealistic hope for a peaceful entrance into the white world dissipates with the realization that despite his unique position as artist and no matter the level of his fame, he will always remain—to the small white town and its American father—a "nigger . . . a dead man" unworthy of intimacy, even from the body and heart of a "white whore." From the protagonist's painful encounters with whiteness and apparent detachment from his Black community, the reader comes to understand Leo's need for reconciliation and his "unusual" relationship with Christopher Hall, the symbol of Black Power in the novel.

Leo, Luminaries, and the Need for Protection

Christopher, the Black radical of *Train's Been Gone*, represents the new Black youth of 1960s America. His relationship with Leo captures the Baldwinian hope to reconcile the symbolic space-in-between him and the nascent Black Power Movement. Like Baldwin, Leo understands his role as "elder" to be one of great mentorship and responsibility. Similar to Eldridge Cleaver's admiration for the elder Baldwin, Christopher holds an endearment for Leo. Leo, having reached a point of fame and notoriety, understands the complications with being endeared. Speaking of the moment when he first intrigued Christopher and how the latter related to him, he outlines his growing dilemma in stating, "This enchanted him: which meant, fatally, that he then invested me with the power of enchantment. I did not want this power. It frightened me. But my fright frightened him, and it made him cruel: for to whom was he to turn, in all this world, if not to an elder brother who was Black like him?"[44] Similar to Baldwin, Leo's relationship with Black Power came with a price: there were expectations, somewhat unfair, that required an unconditional mentorship, even when the radical youth became cruel. According to Rolland Murray,

> This unlikely coupling illuminates Baldwin's experience of Black Power's masculinist discourse through its striking insistence that gay male subjectivity is compatible with radical politics. The relationship between Christopher and Leo magically resolves the very contradictions that Baldwin experienced in his own relationship with Black Power advocates.[45]

Murray's observation credibly presents how the relationship performs work outside of the textual space. As mentioned, part of Baldwin's inspiration was to rework the conflicting relationship he had with Black Power and its heteronormative ideology. However, Baldwin's strategic characterization does not flirt with magical realism; rather, it signals a longing for relief and a desire for amends.

As Baldwin published his later novels, criticism focused on the idea that his sojourns in Europe had caused a detachment from the Black community. His protagonist, Leo, suffers the same disconnect as he ascends to popularity within the theatrical world. One realizes the extent of his severance at his speaking engagement at a rally in downtown New York and in his description of the uneasiness between him and the other speakers. Addressing why what he did was not completely aligned with the other "luminaries," Leo asserts, "Our common situation, the fact of my color, had brought us together here; and here we were to speak as one. But our intensities, our apprehensions, were very different."[46] In Leo's mind, the differences and the quarrels they engendered were the direct consequence of one thing— simply, that he was an artist, for "[they] on the platform were united in [their] social indignation, united in [their] affliction, united in [their] responsibility, united in [their] necessity to change—well, if not the world, at least the condition of some people in the world: but how different were [their] visions of the world!"[47] The differences in the visions of the world played a significant role in the feelings of disconnect and estrangement felt by Leo. The luminaries with whom he shared the platform were of a different generation, the one before him, and reflected a world or historical moment Leo did not completely embrace. His position for Christopher was, thus, as linkage, the body that connected the young radical to the elders who came before him. Additionally, Leo was in a position of vulnerability, for his estrangement necessitated his need to be saved, and that call for salvation was unexpectedly answered by the youth.

After delivering his speech at the rally, Leo realizes, more than ever, the truth of his own subjectivity. The detachment from the people demands a strict separation of the public and the personal, and his importance requires, paradoxically, his distance. More importantly, he recognizes the danger of the times, his need to be protected, and how Black Christopher, of all people, has willingly accepted that responsibility. In a somewhat Odyssean moment, Leo sees himself as Christopher does and witnesses "the Leo who certainly did not belong to himself and who belonged to the people only on condition that the people were kept away from him, surrounded by the uncontrollable public madness, and in the very heart of danger. For it was the time of assassins."[48] Baldwin's inclination toward literary découpage leaks out in this textual moment. His autobiographical hand writes the psychological turmoil he faced as an artist in the racially violent 1960s and parallels his divorce from believing in the protective possibility of the Civil Rights Movement with his growing dependence on the Black Power Movement. What the reader must gather from this coupling of autobiography and fiction is how quietly, for both Baldwin and Leo, Black manhood longed for protection during a time ripe with racial absurdity. *Train's Been Gone*, while not delving into the complicated racial moment directly, foregrounds Leo's artistic struggle with whiteness, the threat it poses to his Black manhood, and how Black Christopher emerges as a symbol of salvific manhood.

Radical Black Intimacy: Leo and Christopher's Love

In the last section of the book, "Black Christopher," Leo has an unspoken connection with his friend Pete as they celebrate Leo's life and success before he leaves the hospital and goes home to rest. Gazing into Pete's eyes at the instance of toasting, Leo thinks,

> Some moments in a life, and they needn't be very long or seem very important, can make up for so much in that life; can redeem, justify, that pain, that bewilderment, with which one lives, and invest one with the courage not only to endure it, but to profit from it; some moments teach one the price of the human connection: if one can live with one's own pain, then one respects the pain of others, and so, briefly, but transcendentally, we can release each other from pain.[49]

While this scene foregrounds a quiet connection between Leo and Pete, captures the similarity of their pain and struggles in life, it anticipates the acknowledgment of love and intimacy between Leo and Christopher. Up to this moment, the reader has learned of Leo's struggles and successes, the beauty and ugliness of his life. Christopher has appeared spectrally within the novel but never with enough textual space for the reader to completely understand his significance. Although one remembers that he was once the source of Leo's protection and held a real enchantment for his older friend, one does not fully realize the power of their bond—the extent of their love. Then Baldwin writes, in a way only he can, the beauty of male intimacy to magnify how Leo's relationship with Black Christopher was more than a fictional journey to reconcile the disconnect from the Black community and the Black Power Movement. No, their intimacy speaks to what Leo recognized in the temporal space of Pete's toast—that life often teaches us "the price of the human connection" and how he and Black Christopher "[released] each other from pain."

When Leo and Christopher first met, Leo was comfortable in his multiple detachments. After suffering the metaphoric loss of his brother to prison, to the army, and then to Christianity, he was bent on guarding himself from more abandonment. Couple this with the profound distance between him and the white world, represented through his denounced and failed relationships with white women, and one sympathizes with his fear of closeness, his need to be separated from people. But even more, he was disconnected from himself and did not allow himself to love and be loved. He makes this clear in his first meeting with Christopher, telling him, "The only space which means anything to me . . . is the space between myself and other people."[50] Aside from hurting Christopher's feelings, he exhales his most personal struggle—one whose genesis lies within the fraternal crisis he experienced with his brother Caleb. Despite Leo's preference for space, there was something beckoning him through Christopher, and he identifies it after observing a freedom in Christopher lacking within himself: "When Christopher first met me, he decided that he needed me: that was that. He needed human arms to hold him, he could see very well, no matter what I said, that mine were empty, and that was that. If I was afraid of society's judgment, he was not."[51] The sound of freedom heard in Christopher's voice emanated from his willful vulnerability. Unlike Leo, he was not afraid to bare naked his needs, was not afraid to proclaim his desire to be held. Conversely, Leo's lack of freedom stemmed from his inability to admit a need to hold, to announce to the world his desire to love without contempt, to embrace someone within his grasp. Since the departure from his brother, he was never able to touch with the tenderness of his heart and craved it more and more, regardless of his fame and façade. Ironically, in a moment of confrontation strongly mirroring David's encounter with the disarming Giovanni in *Giovanni's Room*, Leo's emotional simulacrum is dismantled in Christopher's presence.

For the first time in a long while, he is compelled toward a metaphysical exploration of male intimacy.

Reflecting before a performance at which Christopher will be in attendance, Leo shares the depth of his intimate connection with the young Black radical. He confesses the messiness of his relationship with Barbara, how they were there for each other throughout difficult and happy times, while admitting that something was very different with Christopher. According to him,

> I found myself resisting, and wrestling with the fact that something had happened to me. I say something because I was reluctant indeed to use the word love—the word splashed over me like cold water, and made me catch my breath and shake myself. It certainly had not occurred to me that love would have had the effrontery to arrive in such a Black, unwieldy, and dangerous package.[52]

The love he felt for Christopher was unlike any love he had experienced in his adult life. For Black Christopher, with all his passionate critique of the white world, with his defiant disregard for regulating himself to other people's perceptions or standards, offered Leo a way back to himself. Baldwin ends the novel, much like he has ended others, with an ambiguous textuality. There are glimmers of hope and hints toward possibility, but there is no "real" reconciliation—or is there? Christopher's salvific manhood is magical in the later part of this Baldwin book and, like magic, only appears for a *spell*. The salvation lies not in the possibility of a sustained relationship but in the promise of how his presence reminded Leo of the power of feeling. Through their relationship, both received something they needed: Leo fortuned Christopher the guidance of a Black male mentor, and Christopher restored to Leo that which was lost with the latter's constant departures from his brother. And as for Baldwin, he once again offers the reader the saving power of male intimacy, suggesting that above fame and success, beyond blood and friendship, sometimes a man needs to be held—or, for Leo, needs someone to hold.

5

Concrete Jungles and the Carceral

Exploring Confinement and Imprisonment
in *If Beale Street Could Talk*

James Baldwin's famous short story "Sonny's Blues" opens with the unnamed narrator reading about his brother's incarceration after a drug bust. Baldwin's choice in introducing Sonny this way, as one imprisoned and suffering from addiction, speaks to the ways in which he hopes to frame the rest of the story. We learn the intricacies of Sonny's sufferings, his blues, and discover in the process how he has consistently been in flight from various spaces. All of these spaces hold or held the possibility of imprisonment, but the New York cultural space bore it most pressingly. New York, as an urban metropolitan space symbolizing the capacity to dream in the larger American imagination, served a different representative role for Baldwin's character. The bright lights and energy of the cityscape were lost to Sonny, who found himself trapped in the grit and grime promised for most of its Black residents. For Baldwin, and for Sonny by extension, Times Square highlighted the irony and elusiveness of New York's light. The dream located in the city mocked those dark men who were never truly afforded the chance to pursue the longings and desires of their hearts. Instead, they were relegated to spaces of lack and absence. In this way, Baldwin encourages us to reimagine the role of urbanity in the lives of Black men.

While *Another Country*'s gripping portrayal of Rufus Scott's existential crisis is perhaps Baldwin's most lucid exploration of suicide as a response to the absurdity of life, it is not unique in its treatment of the philosophical problem. As early as *Go Tell It on the Mountain*, Baldwin posited suicide as an unfortunate consequence of the racially absurd. One witnesses this with the suicide of Richard, John Grimes's biological father and a minimal presence within the novel. Richard's demise proves less impactful on the reader due to his relegation to memory and allusion. Unlike Rufus, he neither holds significant textual space nor demands attention from the reader; he serves, merely, as a line to progress a greater narrative surrounding the question and pursuit of the fraternal. John's unknowing of Richard prevents the latter's emergence as a phantom character, marginalizes him to a specter of flashback, and hinders the fruitful examination of the relationship between self-destructiveness and societal hostility. The furtive silence of *Go Tell It* becomes unrelentingly vocal in *Another Country*, with Baldwin's depiction of suicidal Black manhood inviting serious critical study. Somewhere in between the whispered character of Richard and the loudly pronounced Rufus, Baldwin creates another character in his fifth novel, *If Beale Street Could Talk*. Despite Baldwin's traceable preoccupation, literary criticism has been conspicuously quiet in its dealings with *If Beale Street Could Talk* and has, much like in its treatment of *Go Tell It*, glossed over the question of Black male suicide within the novel. While the different constructions of character between Richard and Rufus sufficiently explain why literary critics are more prone to ignore the former in their in-depth discussions of Baldwin and novelistic suicide, such rationality does not account for the neglect of the character Frank in *Beale Street*. Frank, while not the protagonist of the novel, is very much central to the story. Without him, one cannot expect to identify how Baldwin's preoccupation with loneliness is again translated within *Beale Street*.

James Baldwin's fifth novel, *If Beale Street Could Talk* (1974), is, in the words of Lynn Orilla Scott, "a heterosexual, blues love story, told in the first-person voice of nineteen-year-old Tish Rivers, a poor Black girl raised in Harlem."[1] Partially inspired by the incarceration of his friend Tony Maynard, Baldwin chronicles the lives of a young couple, Clementine "Tish" Rivers and Alonzo "Fonny" Hunt, as they struggle to love each other in an unforgiving urban space that literally and metaphorically imprisons Fonny's Black manhood. Baldwin indirectly returns to *Go Tell It* by emphasizing the centrality of family, dysfunction, and love. Writing with a language quite unlike that in his other novels, Baldwin chooses simplicity to deliver to his audience the unmistakable message of his radical philosophy of love.

Inevitably, this deviation from his normal lyrical voice, perhaps in his effort to present a believable female narrator, earned *Beale Street* a series of mixed reviews. For many critics, the storyline was too predictable, the novelistic structure fraught with literary compromises, and the narrative voice unconvincing. The literary experimentation, deemphasizing the artistic detail and nuance of his prior novels, led some people to argue "that the novel proved Baldwin was out of touch" and no longer the writer from the previous two decades.[2] At first glance and read the short novel of nearly two hundred pages is indeed a straightforward account of young Black love. However, with an understanding of Baldwin's personal struggles, particularly during this moment in his life, the novel must be examined for the subtle traces of his fixation with the "state of being alone." Even more, it must be taken as the fifth installment of a series of exhibitions on Black masculinity, male intimacy, fraternal crisis, and salvific manhood. Taking this into consideration, *Beale Street* is more than simply a "heterosexual, blues love story." Alongside the plight of young heterosexual love in a racist society, the complexity of male emotion, vulnerability, and intimacy is captured in the novel. In particular, *Beale Street* continues the Baldwinian exploration of tragic Black manhood through the figure of Frank Hunt while showcasing the potency of male intimacy through Frank's relationship with the beloved Fonny.

As if anticipating how *Beale Street* might be read as somewhat divorced from his other novels, and as if hoping to make clear the thematic tie linking them all together, clever Baldwin weaves a subtle line from *Another Country* into this novel. Paralleling the strategic epigraph from W. C. Handy used to frame part of Rufus's story, Baldwin chose to use W. C. Handy's "Beale Street Blues" as an inspiration for the title and larger framing of the fifth novel. Handy's "Beale Street Blues" situates the famed street in Memphis, Tennessee, as a cultural haven for African American musicality while also suggesting it as a site of secrecy. Beale Street holds truths about men that can promise devastation if the street did indeed talk. But even more, Beale Street is responsible for shaping popular artists, who go there to be shaped by the local musicians. In this way, "Beale Street Blues" becomes a lamentation for the unknown artists, the victims of others' parasitic artistry, and the unfortunate receivers of America's diluted promise. It is, quite honestly, a meditation on the space where men burdened by the absurdity of society go to be comforted through the selflessness of Black artists who create without ever receiving their due. A dark meditation on the role and position of Black art in America, Handy's "Beale Street Blues" is a reminder of how cold the streets can be and what might come of men caught within them.

Lynn Orilla Scott's book *James Baldwin's Later Fiction: Witness to the Journey* addresses the negligence of Baldwinian scholarship in its treatment of Baldwin's later novelistic endeavors. In her introduction, she points out how his last three novels "have been dismissed as less interesting, less complex, and less aesthetically viable than his early works."[3] She is not wrong in this assertion, and, for this reason, her essay on *Beale Street* has become one of the most quoted criticisms of the novel. Yet, despite the newfound interest, scholars have still failed to study the unique male relationships within the novel. Even Scott's essay fails to nuance the male characters of the work, with the exception of the character Fonny. In fact, the essay delays a very promising discussion of men and masculinity until the last paragraph and presents it without much textual attention. In that closing moment, Scott establishes a subject perfect for future scholarship and discourse. Despite this, critics of *Beale Street* remain so enraptured by the idea of a female narrator and the reemergence of a powerful Black family that the subtle constructions of Black manhood are still secondary. This is not a critique of the preoccupation, as Baldwin's bold deviation from narrative voice demands attention. Additionally, the dynamic between Tish and Fonny is so complex that it warrants a large amount of critical attention. However, beyond this, and lest we miss a very important working of the novel, a careful look at the male characters and their different relationships highlights how *Beale Street* continues to magnify a Baldwinian concern with male intimacy. While Fonny has received considerable study, his stepfather Frank remains a footnote within the criticism. Such neglect precludes us from witnessing a new perspective for Baldwin's philosophy of radical love, keeps us provincially looking at literary renderings of Black manhood, and ensures a blindness toward the work Baldwin does with gender. By centering male relationships, with a particular focus on Frank and Fonny, *Beale Street* explores how Black manhood is divested of power, the salvific nature of male intimacy, and the tragic consequences that arise when salvific manhood is beyond one's grasp.

If Beale Street could talk in the late 1960s and early 1970s, it would tell the story of Black men who, despite ambition and talent, could not fully escape the throes of America's racial absurdity. It would sing their blues in such a way that the listeners would be able to sympathize with a narrative of despair. Even more, it would cry of their invisibilities, how despite every effort to showcase their humanity, they remained unseen or tucked away in the shadows. Beale Street holds secrets not because it has to but because it is forced to. It reflects the paradox of sanctum and prison. If one visits Beale Street today, there will be a statue of W. C. Handy quietly tucked off the street in a park named in his honor. If there when Beale Street is alive, one will find Handy and his statue have become marginal to the rest of the street's activity. Handy, in fact, becomes one of many, his voice, his presence, his legacy swallowed by the larger chaos, the longer sound of pain, suffering, and a pursuit of healing. This is the reality of Beale Street, and thus, his "Beale Street Blues" delivers on his promise: a promise we see echoed with such beautiful tragedy in Baldwin's *If Beale Street Could Talk*.

Perhaps one of the strongest elements of *Beale Street* is Baldwin's decision to locate the narration in a young female character named Clementine, who goes by "Tish." Baldwin responsibly centers Black female vocality in ways that exalt an often marginalized subjectivity, and allows a surrogate voice for the voiceless Black male subject. Despite how machinations of power often situate Black manhood in a more favorable position than Black womanhood, the expression of vulnerability and the baring of hurt or suffering proved antithetical to American prescriptions of masculinity in the 1970s. Tish thus emerges as doubly functional throughout the novel and affords readers the opportunity to focus on the secreted selves of Black men, those selves whose voices would only have been heard in a place like Beale Street and perhaps only through the channeling brilliance of a musical instrument.

If Beale Street Could Talk's opening scene features an introduction of the narrator, Tish, and her talking with Fonny in prison. In describing the exchange, she notes "a wall of glass" between them.[4] This glass, separating

Tish from her love Fonny, signals the vast distance placed between them, not completely unlike the space-in-between found in other thematic threads from previous novels. With this being our first glimpse of Fonny, we are meant to understand the role of the carceral in shaping how we read his character. That is, we walk away from this moment understanding his narrative is largely dictated by a theme of imprisonment. Imprisonment in *Beale Street* is not simply the literal carceral enterprise. It also reflects the larger intangible confines that ultimately promise a transition from the cold concrete jungle to the cold bars of the carceral. For Tish, the vast notion of imprisonment hits her as she leaves Fonny and steps out into the very world, the corridors responsible for his incarceration:

> The Sahara is never empty; these corridors are never empty. If you cross the Sahara, and you fall, by and by vultures circle around you, smelling, sensing your death. They circle lower and lower: they wait. They know. They know exactly when the flesh is ready, when the spirit cannot fight back. The poor are always crossing the Sahara.[5]

Baldwin's use of the Sahara introduces a metaphor of desolation. Like the Sahara Desert, the world inhabited by Fonny, Tish, and Black folk by extension promises barrenness to those who must daily dare to cross. Even more, tragedy becomes an almost inevitable gift of this space, and one's flesh becomes the welcomed treat of those entities operating like vultures. Vultures in Fonny's milieu are those agents or institutions feeding off the tragic realities of African Americans rendered victims by racial absurdity. Tish cites lawyers and bondsmen, acknowledging how profitable their industries become due to the relationship between Black bodies and the prison–industrial complex. Beyond this, Tish's grave reflection also speaks to the issue of class. This is not solely racial: the conditions for Black tragic reality are often prepared by the circumstance of poverty. To be Black and poor in *Beale Street* is to be scavenged.

On her journey home, Tish ruminates on Fonny's fate and how it will affect their unborn child. In these thoughts, Baldwin crafts the New York cityscape we ought to be able to identify at this point. Responding to her question of what will become of Fonny, she thinks, "And if you ever did like the city, you don't like it anymore. If I ever get out of this, if we ever get out of this, I swear I'll never set foot in downtown New York again."[6] The picture of New York here differs from Baldwin's earlier constructions. This is not simply the cold and suffocating metropolis where dreamers come to watch their dreams die; rather, it is something within it, signified by the space of "downtown." This particular sector of New York captures a racial element, one that the reader comes to know a bit more intimately later in the novel. For now, we must accept Tish's assessment of America's great city and make sense of her proclaiming, "It must have the worst cops. If any place is worse, it's got to be so close to hell that you can smell the people frying. And come to think of it, that's exactly the smell of New York in the summertime."[7] Tish's justified vitriol situates New York as a carceral state. Fonny's fate, we are led to imagine in these opening moments, is currently being threatened by systems or structures of oppression. Identifying the cops as the worst cops of any city she can imagine, Tish foregrounds the prospect of anti-Black police brutality and injustice. And this shall be the source of Fonny's imprisonment; the only question truly remaining is why.

Fonny and Tish's relationship examples the power of love and support while also opening up the myriad fraternal connections Fonny holds with other men. These fraternal bonds, though arguably ancillary to the hetero-sexual love between the two main characters, instead function as some of the most critical exchanges within the work. Less concerned with creating a balanced counterpoint, Baldwin positions strong and despairing male relationships to usher in the power and necessity of male love and intimacy. In this way, Tish's narrative function pivots most convincingly with her in a position of witness. As a gendered outsider, she provides an objective lens with which we can better evaluate the relationships between men. Even more, she gives voice to those secreted truths that were similarly lost in a space like Beale Street. If we accept *Beale Street* as another one of Baldwin's contentions with male intimacy and vulnerability, then the various relationships between Fonny, Daniel, Frank, and Joseph contribute to yet another development for the notions of fraternal crisis and salvific manhood. Unlike any other of Baldwin's novels, though still connected to them through themes of suicide, racial absurdity, family, and denial, *Beale*

Street's attention to the metaphoric imprisonments plaguing Black men and their various expressions of manhood begs the following questions: How does the carceral render Black men vulnerable subjects, and how do they respond in efforts to combat it?

Through Tish's narration, the reader is introduced to Daniel, a close friend of Fonny's who is imprisoned on two separate occasions during the novel. Daniel is one of the earliest examples of Black male powerlessness, as his imprisonment reflects the hopeless struggles against corrupt white power structures. He makes clear that Black manhood is a plaything for white cops in New York City, and that his livelihood is at their disposal. Explaining to Fonny and Tish the realizations he arrived at while incarcerated, he notes, "They can do with you whatever they want. *Whatever they want*. And they dogs, man. I really found out, in the slammer, what Malcolm and them cats was talking about. The white man's *got* to be the devil. He sure ain't a man. Some of the things I saw, baby, I'll be dreaming about until the day I die."[8] By evoking Malcolm in this moment, Daniel alludes to a very particular racial discourse. He understands his imprisonment as more than the result of one crooked police officer and as more than an unfair system of justice. While his arrest reflects racial hegemony, his experience within the structure of the prison "enlightened" him to the nature of those who abuse their power. Equating the "white man" to the devil and proclaiming that he "ain't a man," Daniel critiques the humanity of the white men whom he encountered throughout his confinement. In his eyes, they were inhuman and inhumane, lacking the basic compassion for another's life and well-being. With tears upon his face, he tells Fonny the most unnerving part of his experience: "But you don't know—the worst thing, man, the *worst* thing—is that they can make you so fucking *scared*. Scared, man. *Scared*." As he relays the presence of fear, Daniel reveals a critical reaction when one first witnesses the racially absurd. It has a way, beyond feelings of dehumanization and the rendering of invisibility, of instilling fear or terror into the Black male body.

The homosociality shaping Fonny's relationship with an old friend, Daniel, becomes one of *Beale Street*'s first gestures toward the power of male intimacy and vulnerability. Their friendship, as narrated by Tish, reflects the fulfilling joy and incessant need Black men locate within each other and captures the significance of the fraternal. Tish testifies to this power when she admits, "I recognize Daniel by the light in Fonny's eyes. For, it is not so much that time has not improved him: I can see to what extent he has been beaten. This is not because I am perceptive, but because I am in love with Fonny."[9] In Tish's confession we learn the illuminating capacity of male-to-male intimacy. Fonny's light emanates from the strong relationship he holds with Daniel, and despite elapsed time, the potency remains. Even more, Daniel's full visibility for Tish, our female narrator, requires an intercessor, another body to magnify him completely. Coupled with Tish's admission of not being perceptive, there is also the limitation of the gaze imposed by gender. Here, Baldwin means to suggest the secret sight in fraternal relationships. Fonny and Daniel possess a shared visioning of each other; their bond is a private one in a sense. Tish's proximity to Fonny allows her the ability to register Daniel in certain ways. And more importantly, that her closeness is mediated by love further illustrates how Baldwin imagines the function of intimacy. Although it is easy to get lost in the light of Fonny's eyes, Tish's attention to Daniel's "beaten" status is just as important. It points, though quietly, to one of the fraternal crises within the novel.

Fonny's manhood and intimacy allows Daniel's "extent of [being] beaten" to become legible. Tish, whose love for him allows her to read Fonny and the extensions of him, accesses parts of Daniel's story via Fonny's body. The phenomenon of shared readability, of second-order access, deepens the complexity of male intimacy. Again, however, the idea of being beaten highlights how in the presence of absence or silence, Daniel has endured a crisis yet to be named in the book. The juxtaposition of his suffering with Fonny's light establishes a relationship between the two that goes beyond friendship. Without a heavy hand, Baldwin sets Fonny up with the potential to save. Perhaps Tish's recognition of this moves her out to the store moments later, as it also encourages the following proclamation: "Neither love nor terror makes one blind: indifference makes one blind. And I could not be indifferent to Daniel because I realized, from Fonny's face, how marvelous it was for him to have scooped up, miraculously, from the swamp waters of his past, a friend."[10] With Daniel emerging from Fonny's past, a past delineated as "swamp waters," readers are led to interpret a temporal and spatial distance now resolved. In fact, the symbolic space-in-between accounts for Daniel's "[being] beaten," which Tish is able to read on him and represents the space of crisis Daniel has occupied. The rarity of fraternal connection, the unusual reality of Black men escaping adolescence in New York, and the joy of two men united on the other side of that reality situate Fonny and Daniel as actors in Baldwin's constructions of fraternal crisis and salvific manhood.

The fraternal crisis underneath the joy in Fonny and Daniel's reunion highlights the role of the carceral in Black male suffering. Inevitably, Daniel's victimization stems from the initial moments of racial absurdity. Master narratives surrounding Black men, which render them always already criminal and deviant, make Daniel an easy target for law enforcement. The carceral state then extends beyond the prison proper and reflects all those technologies of power contributing to the disproportional amount of Black bodies in the system. And thus, there is no surprise when the reader learns of Daniel's imprisonment and the details surrounding his arrest. More disheartening, however, is how these technologies prey upon Black male vulnerability. Space plays a significant role in this enterprise. The concrete jungle—that unique space produced at the intersection of urbanity, poverty, and existential angst—presents itself as a site of gathering for a racially motivated and biased system. Those who inhabit such a space, in particular young Black men, become both target and sport for various agents of the law, from police officers to legal prosecutors. Thus, it is important to understand Daniel's imprisonment as a rather elaborate production, where his spatial reality offers him as a scapegoat for whatever psychic transgressions need to be committed for racial and class hierarchies to persist. Or rather, as Michelle Alexander suggests in *The New Jim Crow: Mass Incarceration in the Age of Colorblindness*, "Confined to ghetto areas and lacking political power, the black poor are convenient targets."[11] Read through Alexander, who makes connections between the prison–industrial complex and a racial caste system, Daniel's arrest reflects the presence and operation of technologies of power largely fueled by racism. Additionally, in admitting that Black men, as inheritors of a history of racial oppression, are predisposed to fear, we better recognize how white supremacist structures exploit that fear in their clever manipulations. Daniel states as much in noting, "I was alone, baby, wasn't nobody, and so I entered the guilty plea. . . . I let them fuck over me because I was scared and dumb and I'm sorry now."[12] Out of fear, and within a state of ignorance about how the law works, Daniel receives two years' imprisonment. In proclaiming a state of being alone and a sentiment of nobodiness, he also magnifies the lesser known variables playing out in systems of racial absurdity. For victims like Daniel, the system relies on disconnection and feeds off the spaces-in-between men, knowing how loneliness couples well with fear. More specifically, the system exploits the lay citizen's lack of familiarity with its various legal nuances. Daniel, pressured into a plea deal through fear and misrepresentation, could see no alternative given how the system is built. We might understand Daniel's limitations in visiting Alexander's acknowledgment: "Immunizing prosecutors from claims of racial bias and failing to impose any meaningful check on the exercise of their discretion in charging, plea bargaining, transferring cases, and sentencing has created an environment in which conscious and unconscious biases are allowed to flourish."[13] And without question, his ontological view—the feeling of being nobody—cements Daniel's cooperation with an impending and forceful apparatus.

An existing relationship between the concrete jungle and the carceral state frames Daniel's fraternal crisis. Feelings of aloneness and nobodiness create both detachment and alienation, expressions of angst that are precipitated by distances from other men. Daniel's arrest positions him as a vulnerable subject within the New York cityscape. As an inhabitant of the concrete jungle, his fate is often promised. Using the convenient cover-up of "the war on drugs," agents of the state are able to mask their pursuit of Daniel and use his possession of marijuana as a means to render him prey. And while such seizure can include larger groups of people, state agents often pounce when the target is alone, unprotected by the possibility of sousveillance and free from the indicting presence of a witness. Affirming this phenomenon, Daniel reveals, "But this night I was by myself, about to go on in, and they stopped the car and yelled at me and pushed me into the hallway and searched me. *You* know how they do it."[14] The threat of carceral terror looms ever present in the space where the Black male body meets darkness. More than an abstract notion, the nighttime in Black urbanity constitutes a policed geography. New York's skyline, then, for Black men, shrinks as the promise of dreams and aspirations, while morphing into a direct reflection of technologies of power meant to keep Black bodies tamed and contained. Realizing how the system moves directly upon the Black body, or how that body seems to invite a certain amount of surveillance, Daniel shows no surprise in his proclamation, "[And] do they *love* to pat your ass."[15] For Baldwin, carceral terror must also be viewed through a sexual deployment of power. The contention of how police officers, who are engaged in an eclipsed form of racial profiling, "love" to pat Black men's asses suggests a certain violation of the body. Not only is the Black man oppressed through the literal arrest, he is also the victim of corporeal intrusion. Daniel's emotional candor is but the evidence of how powerless he felt within white custody and how those in power, like the dogs he named them, parasitically fed off his fear. His paradox in the absurd world is captured in how while he "longs to be free to confront his life; [he] is terrified at the same time of what that life may bring, is terrified of freedom; and is struggling in a trap."[16] His fear to "confront his life" and, at moments, "to get past something, something unnamable" reflects both a racial and gendered violence; one in which the Black male body is often a neglected subject.[17] In other words, *Beale Street* "is devoted to a project of resistance that bears 'witness' to the dehumanization of the African American body" in ways that feature Black male corporeality alongside traditional analyses of Black female oppression.[18] Baldwin offers a new critique of Black male oppression that extends the discussion beyond simple racial considerations and asks us to consider how else Black men are vulnerable subjects and how they are in need of saving.

In relaying Daniel's turmoil, the crisis from the "swamp waters of [the] past," *Beale Street* constructs the homosocial relationship between Fonny and Daniel as a potentially salvific one. Fonny's male friendship, his masculinity, and his unquestionable compassion endow him with the ability to help Daniel through distress. As Tish notes, "Fonny, who is younger, struggles now to be older, in order to help his friend toward his deliverance."[19] Baldwin's decision to script Daniel's end as "deliverance," coupled with the line that follows—"*Didn't my Lord deliver Daniel? And why not every man?*"—coordinates the Fonny–Daniel relationship in clear ways. By pointing toward deliverance, *Beale Street* invites in a biblical theology where salvation centers itself. While it has always been clear that Daniel was in need of healing, perhaps less clear was Fonny's salvific role. Through Tish's perception, which we might read as a kind of deified narrative voice through its discerning capacity, we learn how Daniel's deliverance ought to come through Fonny. Our earliest substantiations come through expressions of intimacy preceding the confession of suffering: "Sometimes, when Daniel spoke, he cried—sometimes, Fonny held him."[20] Daniel and Fonny's proximity curate a space where we can identify Daniel as a vulnerable subject and Fonny as a salvific man. In this way, their proximity reflects a fraternal intimacy that prefigures salvation. By holding Daniel, Fonny erases the space-in-between men and makes room for the possibility of healing. The Black vulnerable subject, Daniel, magnifies salvation as the aim, for he "brought it out, or forced it out, or tore it out of himself as though it were torn, twisted, chilling metal, bringing with it his flesh and his blood—he tore it out of himself like a man trying to be cured."[21] As both articulation of vulnerability and petition for help, Daniel's baring of self demonstrates the recurring theme of the power of male intimacy within Baldwin's novels and solidifies Fonny as *Beale Street*'s salvific man.

Literal imprisonment and metaphoric confinement plague the character Daniel. His embodiment of the carceral and his inability to escape the blues of the concrete jungle signal his body as a site of terror. When Fonny, Tish, and Daniel find themselves singing Billie Holiday—"When he takes me in his arms / The world is bright, all right"—we witness Holiday as surrogate: "Poor Billie . . . they beat the living crap out of *her* too."[22] At once, Baldwin draws a relationship between the lady of the blues and a distant genealogical son, while also allowing Holiday to stand in for Daniel. Specifically, Daniel, like the blues woman who gives vocality to his struggle, understands how being held or embraced makes the world brighter. Fonny's arms symbolically provide for the "all right" in Daniel's world. If one of Baldwin's aims in *Beale Street* was to show the extent to which the Black man is victimized by carceral systems built out of racial absurdity, then what prison promised for Daniel played out most acutely on his body: "On the night that Fonny was arrested, Daniel was at the house. He was a little drunk. He was crying. He was talking, again, about his time in prison. He had seen nine men rape one boy: and *he* had been raped. He would never, never again be the Daniel he had been."[23] Daniel's rape signifies both a violation of humanity and the forever tortured physicality of Black manhood. As a text, his body engenders historical narratives of racial terror, scripts of how white supremacy garnered power through sexual violence, and the inescapability of psychic–corporeal memory. In stating how he would never be who he once was, Tish captures the permanently altered state of Daniel's racial and gendered ontology. His humanity, penetrated and punctured, is not fully recoverable. But Baldwin is careful not to suggest this as the necessary end for his life, as redemptive possibility and salvation lie in wait. This Baldwin affirms through the salvific manhood of Fonny—"Fonny held him, held him up just before he fell."[24]

Baldwin shows the link between race and male powerlessness or vulnerability in placing Daniel's confession of rape moments before Fonny's arrest. The goal here is to draw a parallel in the reader's mind to how Fonny is meant to suffer the same fate as his vulnerable friend, to gesture toward the forever looming possibility of rape and violence. Although Fonny is never physically raped while incarcerated, his manhood is symbolically violated in incidents leading up to his imprisonment and is policed by the same white hegemonic powers. Most notably, this is seen within his interactions with and thoughts on Officer Bell, a white policeman notorious for his violence toward the Black body. In the retrospective moment where Tish recounts how she was harassed by a "small, young, greasy Italian punk," Fonny's manhood dances the line between romantic hero and potential martyr. After beating the white boy in defense of his fiancée, Fonny has a very telling encounter with Officer Bell when the latter rushes over under the guise of civic duty. Tish's fear, understanding the racial politics of the time and reading Bell for his unmistakable allegiance to the protection of whiteness, is that the officer will attempt to kill Fonny for the beating of his racial brethren. Therefore, in an attempt to save the man she loves, she places herself in the symbolic space-in-between the two men, thinking,

But he could not kill Fonny if I could keep my body between Fonny and this cop; and with all my strength, with all my love, my prayers, and armed with the knowledge that Fonny was not, after all, going to knock *me* to the ground, I held the back of my head against Fonny's chest, held both his wrists between my two hands, and looked up into the face of this cop.[25]

Tish emerges as a powerful figure of sacrifice in this moment. By using love to restrain Fonny and womanhood to halt Officer Bell, she summons the uniqueness of her subjectivity to prevent more racial violence. It is important to note, however, that her womanhood is not enough, in and of itself, to tame the corruption boiling in the blood of Bell. Her blackness, the peculiar marker of burden within the American racial narrative, dilutes the power of womanhood granted by the same system of white male patriarchy. As such, her body alone does not guarantee Fonny's safety; this requires something carrying greater value to the white racist mind. Inevitably, this something comes through the white female subjectivity of the market owner. For as she speaks up, in defense of both Tish and Fonny, her whiteness, coupled with her female vocality, curves the pressing rage in Officer Bell's heart. And only in that moment is Fonny's manhood protected. Nevertheless, this protection will not be for long, and this is indicated in the officer's remark, "Well . . . be seeing you around."[26]

Fonny and Tish's conversation immediately following the racially charged event magnifies Black male powerlessness in the novel. Tish's actions, while noble, indirectly reflect her beloved's crisis in manhood. In her essay "The Eye as Weapon in *If Beale Street Could Talk*," Trudier Harris points out that Tish's "awareness of what white cops do to Black men forces Tish to take control; she realizes she must emasculate Fonny in this instance in order to save him."[27] It is this very act of "emasculation" that places Fonny in an awkward position within his relationship. On one hand, he knows that he owes his life to Tish, admitting to her, "Hadn't been for you, my brains might be being spattered all over that precinct basement by now."[28] However, on the other hand, he understands the loss of agency experienced in that moment. Being unable to speak for himself and being saved by the vocality of women precipitates a crisis in the very manhood that was saved. This leads him to the gentle admonishing of Tish, where he tells her, "Don't ever try to protect me again. Don't do that."[29] He follows the demand with tears and tries to get Tish to understand his position, which she does. In his mind, the stakes of silence are severe due to the inextricable link between his voice and his manhood. Ironically, such a slippery relationship between manhood and voice renders Tish's speech complicit in the stripping of power. And here lies the difficulty of Black heterosexual relationships in a world defined by absurdity. The power to save, exhibited by Tish, oftentimes conflicts with the need to survive, desired by Fonny. Fonny understands this well and communicates the quandary to the naïve Tish: "They got us in a trick bag, baby. It's hard, but I just want for you to bear in mind that they can make us lose each other by putting me in the shit—or, they can try to make us lose each other by making *you* try to protect me from it."[30] For Fonny, access to vocality equates to an access to power, a power desperately needed within the racially absurd. When his voice is denied, so is his manhood, the only thing he has to truly offer his beloved. Inevitably, a unique dialectical relationship between Black male power and oppression surfaces and ensures, to a degree, Fonny's coming imprisonment.

Moments after Daniel tells of his rape with tears in his eyes, Fonny is arrested on the accusation of raping a Puerto Rican woman known as Mrs. Rogers. Baldwin's intention is to show the complex nature of rape, how it presents itself in multiple forms and claims for itself multiple victims. The saturation of rape rhetoric in the novel aids in ushering the reader into an understanding of how Fonny, too, is symbolically raped by society in general and Officer Bell in particular. Focusing on Officer Bell's eyes, Tish relays how Bell is not just a racist but also a rapist. She notes how violated she feels under his stares; "[Bell's] eyes swept over Fonny's Black body with the unanswerable cruelty of lust, as though he had lit the blowtorch and had it aimed at Fonny's sex. When their paths crossed, and I was there, Fonny looked straight at Bell, Bell looked straight ahead. *I'm going to fuck you, boy,* Bell's eyes said."[31] The imagery in this scene evokes the perverse relationship between white power and Black male sexuality. Building off the narrative of white preoccupation with Black male virility, Baldwin identifies Fonny's "sex" as the target of Bell's racism. However, Bell's Foucauldian gaze is not predominantly fixated on Fonny's penis because of Black male physicality; rather, it holds concern over what the Black male penis represents symbolically. Bell's focus on Fonny's Black body and lustful intention to "fuck" him stem from his racist desire to destroy Fonny's manhood. His longing to rape Fonny reveals a pursuit of power, grounded in racism, that will appropriate the "superiority" of his white masculinity. Reading the Bell–Fonny exchanges through a metaphor of rape, one again understands why Fonny was so adamant about Tish not protecting him at the market. His Black male vocality becomes the means by which he resists the raping of his Black male body, the only way he can truly protect his fragile subjectivity in the racially absurd. Unfortunately, as Harris points out, when "Fonny maintains his resistance [. . .] and as long as Fonny will not submit, Bell uses the system to 'fuck' him."[32] Thus, the arrest of Fonny on charges of rape represents Officer Bell's revenge against the missed opportunity for beating his Black body outside the market. In that exchange, thanks to Tish and the Italian woman, Fonny escaped being *fucked* directly by Bell and white racism. Conversely, his escape engendered Bell's silence, gelded Bell of his white power and, by extension, his parasitic manhood. Subsequently, it also became the goad for Bell's determination to "see" Fonny again, to not rest until Fonny was suffering in prison.

The true signs of Fonny's powerlessness come while he is in prison. He is not only separated from the outside world but also removed from the only family that has loved him, the Rivers family and his stepfather Frank. His imprisonment exacerbates his feeling of loneliness and enhances his battle against the racially absurd. Early on, he struggles to make sense of his confinement, and the struggle elicits an emotional response that he cannot restrain. More than being the victim of Officer Bell's racism, more than being the sacrifice of a hegemonic system invested in scapegoating, he cannot endure the pain of being alone. The reader witnesses this when Baldwin paints the picture of incarceration, where Fonny, attempting to grasp his situation, "wonders what the whole world, his world, is doing without him, why he has been left alone here, perhaps to die. The sky is the color of the steel; the heavy tears drip down Fonny's face, causing the stubble on his face to itch. He cannot muster his defenses because he can give himself no reason for being here."[33] The inability to reason or to identify merit in his victimhood uncovers a greater sense of powerlessness. Fonny's tears are a testament to loneliness, but they are also profoundly reflective of the psychic futility that consumes him. Although the reader, and even Fonny, knows that the latter's imprisonment is the "direct result of a pathological white racism," the illogicality of racial absurdity offers him nothing to curb the existential need for meaning.[34] In isolation, Fonny realizes what has placed him there, but he does not know why. Therefore, he suffers additionally from the inability to fully understand himself as Bell's chosen scapegoat while simultaneously being held in a Tantalusian state of receding love. Yet, despite the forced separation from his world and loved ones, he finds a way to deal with the states of powerlessness and loneliness. And while he suffers the ordeal within the walls of the prison, his father, too, suffers outside.

Written in contrast to the character Joseph, Frank wrestles with an undying questioning of manhood throughout the novel. Like Daniel and Fonny, he suffers from feelings of powerlessness and loneliness. However, unlike them, he does not find the necessary coping mechanisms and falls victim to the pressures of racial absurdity in ways no other character does within the story. His lack of power surfaces through a series of relationships and events, most notably through his relationship with his wife, Mrs. Hunt, and the imprisonment of his stepson Fonny. Through Frank's character, Baldwin captures the oftentimes hopeless meandering of Black men, who must negotiate a constantly attacked or devalued manhood within a world rooted in inescapable absurdity. Even more, through the relationship between Frank and Fonny, Baldwin revisits the themes of fraternal crisis, the symbolic space-in-between, and salvific manhood. Where Fonny was able to hold Daniel up "before he fell," such presence was not possible with Frank. In turn, we ask, What becomes of the Black vulnerable subject denied intimacy with one endowed with the capacity to save? How does the imprisonment of Fonny also incarcerate his salvific manhood?

In a chapter entitled "But the Body Was Real: Sex, Love, and the Character of Revelatory Experience," Clarence Hardy argues, "Even as *Beale Street* demonstrates how central Baldwin's claim about love is for his artistic and moral vision, it also shows just how deeply his religious heritage has shaped his deepest notions of the body and love."[35] Hardy's essay explores how Baldwin's depiction of sex and sexuality are infused with religious rhetoric in an effort to communicate "the connections between sexual release and religious ecstasy."[36] Nevertheless, the coupling of religiosity and sexual intercourse also announces how many of the characters within the novel come to understand different parts of their subjective beings. This is best witnessed in the male characters of Fonny and Frank, who both enjoy religious sexual experiences. But of the two, it is Frank's experience with Mrs. Hunt that reveals the complexity of his manhood and his unique struggle with power in the novel.

Mrs. Hunt emerges as the symbol of Black Christianity within the novel and as Baldwin's critique of the religious enterprise. Her sanctity and devotion are coupled with a disdain for her imprisoned son and a neglect of her depressed husband. After she probes Frank about giving his life to the Lord, the following sexual experience highlights how her religiosity becomes a site of powerlessness for Frank. As a critic of religion, he does not live up to Mrs. Hunt's ideal of Black manhood and lives with the truth that he is not enough to bring her "sexual ecstasy." Consequently, when they make love, he assumes the persona of Mrs. Hunt's Lord and shares with the reader the painful wound of his manhood. Like that between Rufus and Leona in *Another Country*, sex between the Hunts takes on a violent scene and dramatizes Frank's pursuit and need for power. For instance, in one of Fonny's recollections, he recalls the perverse sexual exchange between his parents. Through the voice of Frank, the reader witnesses the evocation of Jesus:

Where you want your blessing? Where do it hurt? Where you want the Lord's hands to touch you? here? here? or here? Where you want this tongue? Where you want the Lord to enter you, you dirty, dumb Black bitch? you bitch. You bitch. You bitch. And he'd slap her, hard, loud. And she'd say, Oh, Lord, help me to bear my burden. And he'd say, Here it is, baby, you going to bear it all right, I know it. You got a friend in Jesus, and I'm going to tell you when he comes. . . . And, in the morning, was just like nothing never happened. She was just like she had been. She still belonged to Jesus.[37]

The Hunts' sexual exchange can be read in a number of ways. It reflects, in a sense, a twisted form of role-play, one in which Frank's virility is enhanced by the personage he assumes. It also delineates the inextricable link between religion and sexuality as it uncovers the ostensibly erotic nature of Christian mythology and doctrine. And as one reads, it is clear that Mrs. Hunt receives extensive pleasure from Frank's performance of Jesus. However, this scene tells a different story for the vulnerable Frank. The fact that he has to perform as another man, despite it being a divine being, suggests a lack within his own manhood. Frank's masculinity proves insufficient for the pleasing of his wife. He is quite aware of this reality and, in reaction to the indirect challenging of his manhood, uses the experience to assert or pursue his fleeting sense of power. The violent rhetoric (constantly referring to Mrs. Hunt as "bitch") and physicality (slapping her) display his desperate attempt to reclaim or redeem a fallen manhood. Unbeknown to Mrs. Hunt, their sexual intercourse is not role-play for Frank; he is fighting a battle against the loss of himself. Nevertheless, regardless of his efforts, at the end of his petition for redemption Mrs. Hunt remains unscathed: she still can only see him for his limited self and remains under the possession of another man—namely, Jesus. Ultimately, while critics may disagree with how one ought to read this religious and sexual moment, it is a telltale sign that Frank continuously grapples with a powerless and bruised manhood, one that is further assaulted through the arrest of Fonny.

The power Frank lacked within his marriage to Mrs. Hunt, within his household, and within the world, he found within the fraternal bond he shared with his son Fonny. Fonny, for him, was the unique reflection of his manhood and that necessary affirmation denied him by the world. When Bell's racism separated him from his beloved son, it placed him in a hastened spiral where the little power he claimed through the love shared with Fonny dissipated with each passing day. Baldwin reveals Frank's unraveling through various conversations, with the earliest being his reaction during an exchange between the Hunt and Rivers families. Responding to Mrs. Hunt's blind faith, he replies,

I don't know . . . how God expects a man to act when his son is in trouble. *Your* God crucified *His* son and was probably glad to get rid of him, but I ain't like that. I ain't hardly going out in the street and kiss the first white cop I see. But I'll be a *very* loving motherfucker the day my son walks out of that hellhole, free. I'll be a *loving* motherfucker when I hold my son's head between my hands again, and look into his eyes. Oh! I'll be *full* of love, *that* day![38]

While speaking from a place of controlled anger, Frank showcases, like Fonny, an inability to make sense of his son's imprisonment. He lacks the calm granted by Mrs. Hunt's religiosity and cannot muster the strength to love. Understanding Baldwin's radical philosophy of love, one must take Frank's incapability as a sign of dwindling power. Indeed, a significant part of his manhood and the heart of his humanity lies within his capacity to love, even while dwelling in a racially absurd world. Bell's actions and hegemonic society's injustice toward people of color systematically strip Frank of that human element, or at least they try to do so. Although Baldwin may wish for an alternative, particularly for Black men, his realism forces him to write a character like Frank, a character whose very core is affected by racial oppression. This scene thus serves as a harbinger of a greater turmoil, where Frank's descent into hopelessness is marked by a more gradual loss of power.

Periodically throughout the novel, Frank displays a profound vulnerability to Fonny's racially motivated confinement. For instance, he endures a somewhat painful conversation with Joseph after the Rivers family learns that Mrs. Rogers has fled to Puerto Rico and subsequently postponed the trial. Baldwin notes that "the effect of all this on Frank is cataclysmic, is absolutely disastrous," and foreshadows Frank's uncontrollable reaction to another example of his powerlessness.[39] In fact, Frank casually alludes to his ineffectuality by telling his friend, "It's over. They got him. They ain't going to let him go till they get ready. And they ain't ready yet. And ain't nothing we can do about it."[40] Frank's response highlights the depth of his despondency and aids in capturing the perception of futility claiming him as Fonny's father. The proclamation of it being "over" and the suggestion of how nothing can be done reveal his existential resignation. Interestingly, the pessimism taking hold of Frank is completely lost in Joseph, the symbol of Black male strength and resilience. This is evident in how Frank displaces his frustration onto his daughters, bellowing at them, "You two dizzy off-white cunts, get the fuck out of my face, you hear? *Get the fuck out of my face.*"[41] His evocation of whiteness reflects a connection between his mounting powerlessness and the racially absurd, which goes beyond a simple viewing of Fonny's incarceration as the source of his despair. It identifies a greater struggle with Black male agency somewhat compounded by his son's fight against structural corruption. Therefore, when Frank releases his emotion and "Tears drop onto the table, trickling down from the palms with which he has covered his face," Joseph and the reader understand the severity of his pain and how helpless he feels in the world, especially in the current situation.[42] Frank's semiblasphemous personification of Jesus with Mrs. Rivers, his castigation of whiteness through the projection of anger onto his daughters, and his irrepressible release of emotion with his friend Joseph all symptomatize his loss of power and the defeat he suffers at the hand of racial absurdity. More important, they also capture how fraternal crisis surfaces within the novel as well as the different ways male characters respond to the absence of male intimacy and the need for salvific manhood.

Although Frank's feelings of powerlessness stem from his inability to do anything about his son's arrest, his fraternal crisis is rooted in something a bit deeper. A major part of Frank's unraveling has to do with the distance he experiences because of the incarceration. While the corruption and attack of the Black male body contributes to his despair, it is the absence of Fonny's presence that really affects him. His fraternal crisis emerges from the lapse in male intimacy, in being cut off from the most significant person of his life. Returning to one of his favorite literary themes, Baldwin writes the Frank–Fonny father–son relationship as one defined by an inseparable bond and beautiful fraternity. At different times throughout the novel, the reader witnesses the strength of this bond and just how critical it is for Frank's salvation. We learn, through the voice of Fonny, of how Frank's ability to endure an unfulfilling marriage comes because of the father–son relationship. Additionally, Baldwin transcends the question of blood and biology by making the fact that Fonny is Frank's stepson inconsequential to the nature of their relationship. Instead, he focuses on the power of love, noting, "Mr.

Hunt, Frank, didn't try to claim him but he loved him—loves him."[43] Here, Baldwin uses love as a means to rework the father–son bond and to enhance the notion of fictive kinship. Love becomes as strong of a bond as blood and, in the instance of this narrative, becomes crucial for understanding Frank. For instance, after explaining the perverse violence between his parents, Fonny tells Tish, "Hadn't been for me, I believe the cat would have split the scene. I'll always love my Daddy because he didn't leave me."[44] Baldwin unveils the ways in which Fonny's manhood and the love within it anchor his father. And from a Camusian perspective, Fonny emerges as Frank's most important reason for being, for staying, and for living.

In his biography *James Baldwin: Artist on Fire*, W. J. Weatherby relays Baldwin's description of *Beale Street* as about "the price we have to pay and the ways in which we help each other to survive."[45] At the heart of *Beale Street* rests the theme of survival, with the most conspicuous evidence being the role family plays in the process. However, the greatest example of the narrative of survivability lies within Fonny's relationship with Frank, a relationship that leaves the reader somewhat wondering who holds the power to save. Given Fonny's imprisonment and the family's move to free and rescue him from the grips of racial absurdity, he appears as the target of salvation. Recalling Fonny's proclamation that Frank stayed for him, and remembering the moment in the novel when Tish visits her fiancée's basement apartment and notices, "There were Fonny's pencil sketches pinned on the wall, and a photograph of Frank," one wonders if Frank does not possess the salvific manhood in his relationship with his son.[46] And if we extend Harris's idea of Baldwin's "new religion," which uncovers the inextricable relationship between sexuality and religious expression, then we might read Frank's photo as some type of religious expression. If not religious, the photograph at least testifies to the substantial position Frank holds in Fonny's life and alludes to the power Frank maintains within their relationship. This is the same power that will be systematically stripped from him when Fonny gets arrested. Considering these things alongside the inherent power dynamic within traditional father–son relationships, it is quite feasible that Frank is the salvific man within the situation. After all, Fonny is caged while everyone else is seemingly free. Nevertheless, as one continues to read the novel, one learns that Frank is in a more vulnerable position than anyone else within the novel.

As Baldwin might have intended, the paternal power within father–son relationships is subverted with the introduction of radical love. Whereas the reader expects Frank to be savior and Fonny to be the saved, *Beale Street* presents a different story. Frank's salvific role consistently flirts with performance (remember his sexual experience with Mrs. Hunt) and is, at best, ephemeral. In contrast, Fonny's salvific manhood is symbolically written within the text. His craft, that of sculpture, is a direct allusion to God as creator, and he wrestles with the wood or material in an eerie parallel to biblical creation stories. His struggle with loneliness reflects the detachment a god might feel in being separated from the world he created, for Fonny's world was indeed that of his own design. His familial love with the Rivers family, his romantic love with Tish, his brotherly love with Daniel, and his male love with Frank were all maintained because of his nature and intent. Yet, despite community, he was built to endure, or rather withstand, isolation and loneliness. The same cannot be said for the others. The difference is that Tish still has her family and her family has her, Mrs. Hunt has her daughters and her daughters have her, Daniel has his mother, but poor Frank has no one. Fonny was all that he had in the world to keep him afloat, was the one body that could hold him when he was not strong enough to hold himself. Thus, when Officer Bell succeeds in arresting Fonny and separating him from all that he loved, Bell did more damage to the father than he could have ever done to the son. Fonny's reaction to the trial's postponement is best revealed through Tish's thoughts: "Something quite strange, altogether wonderful, happens in him. It is not that he gives up hope, but that he ceases clinging to it."[47] In a sense, Fonny overcomes the chaos of racial absurdity by acknowledging its evasive dance with truth and meaning. Any attempt at rationalization, at understanding the nature of a hostile or mad world, would have guaranteed his insanity. When he lets go of or "ceases clinging" to hope, he frees himself. Unfortunately, such peace does not find Frank. The news, a reminder of the incessancy of absurdity, is too much to bear. And he chooses a different alternative to cope with the unrelenting world.

Scholars remain unresolved on the exact reading of the last paragraph of *If Beale Street Could Talk*. In trying to make sense of the final moments of the novel, Scott points out how "critics such as Pratt and Hakutani, who read the last paragraph as evidence that Fonny is released from jail, find the novel too optimistic, while those critics such as Harris, who believe the novel ends with Fonny still in jail, or such as Gibson, who describe the ending as ambiguous, perceive the tone to be more nuanced."[48] What remains clear across the criticism, undoubtedly, is the idea of ambiguity. Also clear is Frank's tragic end: he "had been found . . . way, way, way up the river, in the woods, sitting in his car, with the doors locked, and the motor running."[49] His suicide, while never explained by Baldwin in depth, lacks the ambiguity that punctuates the final words of the novel. His tragedy is but the result of being unable to access the one person he loved and who loved him back. Fonny's imprisonment did more than strip Frank of his son; it took away his savior—his salvific man. Like Rufus Scott's, his suicide was an understandable defiance to Camus's critique of suicide as an evasion of the absurd; it was, instead, a confrontation with it and an admission that he could not endure it without Fonny. Camus's almost idealist reading of Sisyphus at the end of his essay is captured in the way he speaks of consciousness, in how "the lucidity that was to constitute his torture at the same time crowns his victory."[50] For Frank, there is no respite, no descent toward "the lair of the gods." Sisyphus's joy comes from the relationship he holds with his rock: it reminds him that "he is superior to his fate."[51] Fonny represents Frank's Sisyphean rock, and his incarceration strips all the hope, all the motivation, and all the will Frank has to live. Such is human intimacy for Baldwin: it is the rock that reminds one that despite the absurdity of life, despite its seeming meaninglessness, one is able to endure, to breathe, and to live.

Conclusion
Somewhere in That Wreckage

In Karen Thorsen's acclaimed documentary on James Baldwin, *James Baldwin: The Price of the Ticket*, there is a moment near the end—right before Baldwin speaks eerily about the New Jerusalem, right before the viewer hears him singing Mahalia Jackson's rendition of "Precious Lord"—when his brother, David Baldwin, invites the viewer into a profoundly emotional space. David relays to the viewer, who at this point has become more witness than spectator, some of Baldwin's last words before his death: "I pray I've done my work so, that when I've gone from here, in all the turmoil, through the wreckage and rumble, when someone finds themselves digging through the ruins . . . I pray that somewhere in that wreckage they'll find me. Somewhere in that wreckage they can use something that I left behind. And if I've done that, then I've accomplished something in life."[1] There is something in these words of Baldwin's, something in this offering from his brother highlighting the need for us to read and reread his work, to rethink his life.

Perhaps the most striking element in the experience captured by the documentary is the baring of male vulnerability. For James Baldwin, this vulnerability emerges from the prayer cloaking his work. This prayer, which is more supplication than petition, is a wish to be found, a hope that someone will stumble across his beautiful nakedness in their wrestling with his work. If we look closely, we find just that, a beauty and a nakedness slightly hidden within the guises of fiction and the blindness of cultural (mis-) readings. Even more, we witness his fragility, how soft his manhood and masculinity are to the touch of the reader's gaze, his fear and excitement to dance freely and openly with his reader. Beyond this, Baldwin also tells us there is a lesson in his vulnerability, a didactic treat for those willing to read the textuality scripted upon his personhood. And it is this textuality that hovers above the reader, that haunts and lingers under constructions of character and plot and setting and theme and trope. Of course, Baldwin's hope, or more accurately his prayer, is for us to look beyond the perfectly placed furniture into the crevices of the corner; he is praying for us to see how the shadow we often miss is the very being he desires for us to see, to witness—it is there where we find him.

David Baldwin's vulnerability is also tucked within this moment. Aside from its visual and audial rendering, where we hear the break in his voice and see the tears in his eyes, the reader is made privy to it through David's gentle handling of his brother's last words, through the ways in which he delicately holds Jimmy's memory. His willingness to share Baldwin with such transparency captures a willingness to love and a call to protect. It also speaks to the privilege of knowing Baldwin in the most intimate of ways, of being connected to an author who is now more symbol than man, more myth than memory. That David's vulnerability becomes witnessable through the sharing of his brother's words is also telling. At its core sits the realization of how discovery demands selflessness and how it begs for an investment in the search for the other. His desire to go "somewhere in that wreckage," to encourage those viewers to also go on a search for his brother, engenders the very vulnerability lying at the heart of all of Baldwin's novels. Conceivably, this is the response to the "state of being alone" that paradoxically debilitated Baldwin as man and fueled him as writer. David Baldwin's utterance and James Baldwin's evocation capture the search for the fraternal in a nonliterary pursuit. David's "utteral" conjuring of his brother, the nature of their blood kinship, and how that kinship moves through abstract, spiritual, or literary realms makes that moment so significant to the memory of Jimmy Baldwin. More specifically, it relates to the symbolic "digging through the ruins," the willingness to bask, however painfully, "somewhere in the wreckage," and the seemingly ineffable desire to discover a man and to witness all of his beauty, all of his nakedness. Interestingly, the documentary capturing of their fraternal bond beckons to the coupling of Baldwin's autobiography and his fiction, where we can detect traces of his personal life within the constructed lives of his characters.

Between David Baldwin and Eugene Worth, Baldwin found male intimacy in a way that saved him almost daily from the horrors of racial absurdity and his own struggles with notions of intimacy and love. David and Eugene stood as counterpossibilities to the tension Baldwin often faced with other male artists and activists of the time. This is most clearly represented by his relationship to young Black men rising during the Black Power Movement. In 1963, the year that witnessed the assassinations of Medgar Evers and JFK, Baldwin's powerful essay collection *The Fire Next Time* was published. He was also featured on the cover of *Time* magazine and in a story entitled "Nation: The Root of the Negro Problem." Having already established himself as a racially conscious man, and having been deemed by *Time* magazine as the spokesman of Black America or Black people in America, Baldwin became a witness to the struggle of African Americans in this country in a way that other Black writers did not. The cultural moment of the 1960s, with the height of the Civil Rights Movement and the birth of the Black Power Movement, has shaped how we understand James Baldwin as a political figure and as a creative writer. That particular era saw a redefinition of identity politics with a prioritization of Black racial consciousness. Viewed within this light, it is easy to understand why Baldwin is exalted as an essayist and neglected as a novelist—at least in Black radical discourse. Black communities' relationship with heteronormative sexuality in the 1960s allowed no room for the types of discussions exampled by Baldwin's fiction. Thus, if they were to accept Baldwin as a writer and a representative of his race—they must only consider his contributions, thought to be witnessed only in his essays, as a fierce critic of American injustice. Because of this, Baldwin's relationship with the Black Power Movement and many of its leaders appeared strained at best. While he was respected by figures like Huey P. Newton and Bobby Seale, the larger "movement" understood Baldwin's personal self as incompatible with movement politics. The prime embodiment of this disconnect was personified by Eldridge Cleaver and his scathing critique of Baldwin.

In his noteworthy *Soul on Ice* (1968), the Black Panther turned philosophical prisoner began his satirically titled essay "Notes of a Native Son" by stating the following:

> After reading a couple of James Baldwin's books, I began experiencing that continuous delight one feels upon discovering a fascinating, brilliant talent on the scene, a talent capable of penetrating so profoundly into one's own little world that one knows oneself to have been unalterably changed and *liberated*, liberated from the frustrating grasp of whatever devils happen to possess one. Being a Negro, I have found this to be a rare and infrequent experience, for few of my Black brothers and sisters here in America have achieved the power, which James Baldwin calls his revenge, which outlasts kingdoms: the power of doing whatever cats like Baldwin do when combining the alphabet with the volatile elements of his soul.[2]

Echoing popular perceptions of the day, Cleaver's remarks reveal an indisputable reverence for a man he hardly knew but deeply admired. His ability to relate to Baldwin's expression of "rage" or frustration and the admission of how in reading Baldwin he obtained some form of liberation suggest a somewhat ineffable level of appreciation. In Baldwin, Cleaver found the narrative of Black existential struggle, the strong voice of indignation, and an unequivocal commitment to the plight of Black people. Baldwin rendered legible the Black man as vulnerable subject. In a sense, Baldwin might even have stood as the face of Black Power ideological dissent, representing a new-age Socrates dedicated to unveiling the hypocrisy of American morality and social practice. For quite some time, Cleaver "loved" Baldwin; as he stated, "I, as I imagine many others did and still do, lusted for anything that Baldwin had written. It would have been a gas for me to sit on a pillow beneath the womb of Baldwin's typewriter and catch each newborn page as it entered this world of ours."[3] Yet, despite his esteemed view of Baldwin, which itself bordered on the erotic, something changed in Cleaver, and he mentions that it happened, unsettlingly, when he read *Another Country*. In Cleaver's estimation, Rufus Scott, the protagonist of Baldwin's controversial novel, was nothing more than "a pathetic wretch who indulged in the white man's pastime of committing suicide, who let a white bisexual homosexual fuck him in his ass, and who took a Southern Jezebel for his woman, with all that these tortured relationships imply, was the epitome of a Black eunuch who has completely submitted to the white man."[4] Additionally, he argued that as a character written by Baldwin, Scott reflected the author's racial self-hatred and his enslavement to the debilitating ideology of white America. While Cleaver's is an extreme example of how we understand or view Baldwin, there is something very telling in the former's work. More precisely, Cleaver symbolizes the systematic repackaging of Black manhood and masculinity during the era of Black Power and how such representational ideological intolerance pushed Baldwin further into the margins. Although many historians would be correct in arguing that in spite of Cleaver's heterosexist critique Baldwin remained connected to the fight for Civil Rights, no one can deny the personal turmoil it caused the established face of Black America.

Even though Baldwin never directly responded to Eldridge Cleaver and the eviscerating commentary, he was deeply affected. In an interview, he noted,

My real difficulty with Cleaver, sadly, was visited on me by the kids who were following him, while he was calling me a faggot and the rest of it. . . . I had to try to undo the damage I considered he was doing. I was handicapped with *Soul on Ice*, because what I might have said in those years about Eldridge would have been taken as an answer to his attack on me. So I never answered it.[5]

As he discloses his hurt in this response, he also shares the most difficult part of the entire ordeal. The derisive pronouncements surrounding sexuality alone did not bother Baldwin, as he was, perhaps, accustomed to that kind of intolerance. But the effects of those comments on his relationships with other members of the new Black radical movement were almost unbearable. Cleaver's heteronormative and rigid eloquence sought to metaphorically castrate Baldwin. Even if the former was regarded as psychologically "ill" or malevolently misguided, the latter was made to endure a very real divorce from a new population of Black men. Cleaver's reading of Baldwin precipitated a series of fraternal crises; some Baldwin would be able to overcome, but many he would not. Baldwin in the age of Black Power came to play out the very characters we have tracked over the course of *Salvific Manhood*. Fraternal crisis, symbolic space-in-between, and salvific manhood coalesce to tell the story of Baldwin himself, and his last novel is best read as a key to unlocking the project of mythologizing him.

If *Salvific Manhood* were a different project—or if it had the textual space to pursue a different subtext within Baldwin's novels—it would highlight the deeply personal nature of each novel. From *Go Tell It on the Mountain* to *Just Above My Head*, Baldwin left traces of himself and his story in the narratives of the characters we have come to love. He was there on the threshing floor with John; he was tucked within the shadows of Giovanni's room; he was there on the bridge with Rufus, or on the stage with Leo; and he felt the cold steel of New York's streets and prison bars with Fonny. "He is the man. He was there. He suffered." Despite this, what we remember about Baldwin outside of his faithful students is the Baldwin Cleaver idolized, whom *Time* magazine stamped as the voice of Black America. The other Baldwin—the vulnerable, the personal, and the intimate one—remains in the shadows. The question for us is, How will we remember Baldwin in an age that witnessed the first Black President, the birth of the Black Lives Matter movement, and the continued assault on the Black body? If not careful, because Baldwin's political voice fits so perfectly in its addressal of today's ills, we run the risk of reproducing the same mythology born after his death and at the turn of the century. If not careful, we will do to him what he refused to do to Malcolm X for Columbia Pictures. That is, we will reshape who he is to fit into the imaginings of a disingenuous public imaginary. We will misremember him. And thus, the last reading *Salvific Manhood* advances is a treatment of his last novel as a reveal of how we might remember and mythologize Jimmy Baldwin most responsibly.

I anticipate some readers might wonder about my choice to fold a critical reading of *Just Above My Head* into the conclusion for this book. I admit, Baldwin's last novel definitely deserves its own space of analysis. I agree that, as his longest novel, it presents so many ripe moments in need of deconstruction and mining, so surely it merits a greater thematic treatment.

However, I also believe *Just Above My Head* divulges something more to us in the way I wish to present it. When Baldwin says, "I pray that somewhere in that wreckage they'll find me," we ought to recognize how his last novel constitutes quite a bit of that "wreckage and rumble." Indeed, the novel's breadth and ambitious narratives require a figurative "diggin' through the ruins." Somewhere, if we are truly lucky, we find even more of Baldwin. The late author confirms this for us in an interview:

> So in a sense the novel is a kind of return to my own beginnings, which are not only mine, and a way of using that beginning to start again. In my own mind I come full circle from *Go Tell It on the Mountain* to *Just Above My Head*, which is a question of a quarter of a century, really. And something else begins now. I don't know where I go from here yet.[6]

If Baldwin's full circle means anything, it confirms how each of his novels is connected not just with one another but also with Baldwin himself. *Just Above My Head* ought to be examined with the same attention as all of Baldwin's novels, but for *Salvific Manhood* it represents the completion of a novelistic journey. The novel, while standing independently of the others, also serves as their conclusion. And so, it is within this Baldwinian novelistic coda that we learn other ways of remembering Baldwin. After all, literature for Baldwin was a means to salvation and carried a certain salvific potentiality of its own. We witness this truth many times in his final novel.

Nearly twenty-six years after publishing his first novel, *Go Tell It on the Mountain*, James Baldwin publishes his last, *Just Above My Head* (1979). The novel centers on the life of Arthur Montana, a famed gospel singer whose death, like Rufus Scott's in *Another Country*, coalesces the personal stories of those he loved. His brother Hall, the narrator Baldwin chooses to punctuate his own novelistic journey, tells Arthur's life. To put it simply, the novel is about the price of human love—its triumph and failure, its beauty and ugliness, its prison and freedom. When one reads it, it is not drastically different from the novels that precede it. In fact, it is the culmination of them, an odic pastiche that pieces together the five other novels with an agonized textuality. The agony, of course, stems from how

Just Above My Head continues to highlight Baldwin's search for the fraternal, how it carries his preoccupation with loneliness over 584 pages. But it also reminds the reader that each novel never really ended, shows that their publications were merely literary pauses necessary for new transitions. While different, this last novel returns us to every novel that Baldwin wrote. It forces us to remember *Go Tell It on the Mountain*, where young John experiences a fraternal crisis with his father Gabriel and is led to search for male intimacy in the figure of Elisha—where Elisha is endowed with Baldwin's first sculpting of salvific manhood and will undergo a series of transformations throughout the rest of the novel. We remember *Giovanni's Room*, where David and Giovanni's love is destroyed by David's inability to let go of American innocence and puritan morality—where Baldwin teaches the consequences that emerge when men are not strong enough to love themselves. *Just Above My Head* also recalls *Another Country* and *If Beale Street Could Talk*, where the suicides of Rufus Scott and Frank Hunt come through solitary confrontations with the racially absurd while revealing the power of male love (physical and emotional) to save. And last, it echoes *Tell Me How Long the Train's Been Gone*, where the brotherly loves of Leo and Caleb Proudhammer (in blood) as well as Leo and Christopher Hall (in spirit) are prescribed as necessary to overcome a racially and socially hostile world. To a certain degree, *Just Above My Head* symbolizes Baldwin's quest, as man and as author, for intimacy. Each page is saturated with emotion and captures, in the spirit of all the words that came before, Baldwin's radical philosophy of love.

Again, like Baldwin's previous novels, *Just Above My Head* foregrounds relationships between men and the power of male intimacy. However, it features at least four prominent male relationships—more than in any other of his novels—with a myriad of different outcomes. Baldwin thus creates an emotionally taxing experience for his reader, who is forced to anticipate and endure the ebb and flow of human tragedy and triumph. The relationships the protagonist Arthur holds with Crunch, Jimmy, and Hall conclude an epic journey through Baldwin's novel, marking a fitting end to Baldwin's creative and at times personal novelization of male intimacy. Even more, these male relationships solidify the various ways in which

Baldwin implicates himself as a character in his own fiction and how he was, to the last page of his last novel, in search of the fraternal.

In book 3 of the novel, Hall recounts Arthur's first trip South with his gospel quartet, "The Trumpets of Zion." He notes that for the first time in his young manhood, his brother needs more than what the family alone can offer him. Within the basement of a church, Arthur becomes aware of his sexuality and of a longing much deeper than it. In this moment, his family and his past horrifying sexual experience do not matter; "Yet a need is growing in him, a tormenting need, with no name, no object. He is beginning to be lonely—we, who love him, are not enough."[7] Sister Dorothy Green cannot satisfy this growing need either, and while her presence elicits a sexual reaction from him, he knows "that he is not for her." He thinks of Jason Logan (Crunch) in this moment, wondering where the eldest member of the group and his close friend is. After Baldwin details a somewhat terrifying sexual exchange between Arthur and Dorothy, he sets the reader up for one of the deepest representations of male intimacy within the novel. Crunch has finally arrived in Nashville and, while talking with him, "Arthur realizes, for the first time, consciously, that Crunch listens to him, responds to him, takes him seriously."[8] One wonders if it is Arthur's realization or the natural tenderness in him that provokes a space of vulnerability, for Crunch opens himself up and voices his struggle to love the mother he knows to be a "whore." As he shares his longing for her to allow his love, he weeps; he shares with Arthur a vulnerability society has taught him, along with every other Black boy, for that matter, to hide. Something else happens in this vulnerable space, something started in *Tell Me How Long the Train's Been Gone.*

Similar to the profound emotional exchange between Leo Proudhammer and his brother Caleb following the latter's release from prison, Arthur and Crunch consummate their fraternal bond within a space of male emotion. As Arthur comforts Crunch and they cry together, they learn something about themselves and each other. In an instance, they discover "how much each cares about the other" and owe the space of vulnerability to it.[9] Physical intimacy follows the emotional catharsis: the two men make love and bask in the awkwardness that comes when young men step into their sexuality and the previously "straight" dance in the homoerotic. This newfound intimacy does not come without attachment, as both men share themselves and bare themselves—naked. For Arthur, he learns the fragility of Crunch's manhood: "He wanted to take Crunch in his arms and protect him—from the dawn and the road and the cars and trees outside."[10] Arthur's desire to protect is somewhat prophetic as, amid their escape into each other and their sojourn in the South, Crunch announces that he, like Arthur's brother, was going to be shipped off to the Korean War. The news proves to be the first fraternal crisis between the two young men: the intimacy they just discovered, the love that they were cultivating, would inevitably be interrupted by America's need to make "the world safe for democracy again" and its need for "some niggers for the latrine detail."[11] Crunch's pending departure catalyzes the men's consummation of their fraternal bond and preemptively reconciles, for a moment, the symbolic space-in-between that would be caused by the war.

Physical male intimacy between Arthur and Crunch, while definitely a challenge to heteronormativity and heterosexism, plays a powerfully symbolic role in *Just Above My Head*. On the one hand, it amplifies the difficulty of same-sex relationships in the 1950s, but on the other, it speaks to the curative potential of male closeness. Thus, when vulnerability gives way to stimulation and the two men find themselves naked in each other's arms, the threat of the space that would unavoidably grow between them dissipates. Given Arthur's youth, Crunch assumes the "burden" of moving the "train" alone: "He held him closer, falling in love, his prick stiffening, his need rising, his hope rising; the train began to move, Arthur held him closer, and Crunch moved closer, becoming more naked, praying that Arthur would receive his nakedness."[12] Both men's bodies work together in this intimate moment to reconcile the budding space to come. Crunch's desire, a reflection of his loneliness and need for male intimacy, is answered, is received, and eventually the men move each other to orgasm. The height of Arthur and Crunch's intimacy symbolizes the demand of love, the need for both parties to surrender in the face of adversity, of judgment, and of fear. Baldwin writes this surrender through the physical act of consummation, where "Crunch lay on his belly for Arthur and pulled Arthur into him, and Arthur lay on his belly for Crunch, and Crunch entered Arthur—it was incredible that it hurt so much, and yet, hurt so little, that so profound an anguish, thrusting so hard, so deep, accomplished such a transformation."[13] What may be mistaken as sexual intercourse between two men must be read, indeed, for its *transformative* effect. Their sexual exchange was metaphysical; it represented the surrendering of manhood, and each man relinquished his to the other. Arthur's love with Crunch, the emotional and the physical, introduces the reader to the salvific power of male intimacy—Crunch was saved through Arthur's heart and body; Arthur saved through Crunch's.

The freedom of that night does not last for long; life has a way of intervening. Eventually, Crunch goes off to war and, upon his return, presents Arthur with fraternal crises resistant to reconciliation. In a sense, the war remade Crunch's manhood, hardened him and placed him farther from the space of vulnerability. Additionally, perhaps because of this remaking, Crunch extends his male intimacy to Julia instead of Arthur. Such a repositioning is hard to read, especially given how Julia suffered a crisis of womanhood in being raped by her father. Crunch, sensing her need for redemption, places his salvific manhood within her world, leaving Arthur alone and without. Interestingly, it is neither Julia nor the war that finalizes the fraternal crisis between Arthur and Crunch; it is something much deeper and something that Arthur, even with his salvific nature, cannot overcome—fear. There exists no question that the two men love each other, no question that Arthur means more to Crunch than anyone else in the world; but the balance of what they mean to each other haunts Crunch. "If he had felt a certain panic, bewilderment, at the realization that he had fallen in love with a male, this panic was as nothing compared to his private apprehension that he was more in love with Arthur than Arthur was with him."[14] Baldwin means to suggest here that fraternal crises are oftentimes the byproduct of fear, where one male in the relationship fears the possibility of losing the other. Inevitably, this is what ends Arthur's love with his first male love and what pushes him to the point of guarding his heart for the rest of his life. For Hall, "Crunch did not know how to deal with Arthur, or how to deal with the implications in his life as a man of having a male love. It would have been simpler if he had simply managed to stop loving him."[15] And he tries, albeit unsuccessfully, but the effort alone is enough to push Arthur back into a search, a search for the male intimacy unable to be found in his brother or his father. It will be found again, however, in Julia's younger brother—Jimmy.

Arthur's failed relationship with Crunch is somewhat redeemed through the character Jimmy, the often neglected brother of a child evangelist. Though Baldwin offers the reader insight into the life and struggles of Jimmy the character, and thus his need for Arthur's salvific manhood, one does not see the blooming of their fraternity until late in the novel. It comes as Hall reminisces on Arthur's sojourn in Europe and how he realizes that his younger brother is basking in a state of loneliness. In an effort to make sense of his brother's crisis, the absence of intimacy that surely haunts him, Hall suggests, "He wishes that I were there, but he needs someone else more than he needs me, he needs a friend. He needs someone to be with, needs someone to be with him."[16] Hall's discernment in this reflection is Baldwin's intervention in the discourse of human relations, particularly around the question of intimacy. For both men, the written and the writer, familial and platonic love cannot attenuate the need for romantic love. Arthur needs, as diagnosed by his older and prescient brother, "someone to be with," and that someone willingly fills the prescription when the Montanas end up South after Arthur's return from across the great pond.

According to Hall, the distance once separating Arthur from Jimmy could possibly be the result of his relationship with Julia and Arthur's relationship with Crunch. In the absence of the latter relationship and with the transformation of the former, Arthur's path to Jimmy is now clear. For Hall, this is inevitable, and had it not been for the nebulosity of other bonds "Arthur might have realized that his reaction to Jimmy, what Jimmy caused him to feel, was not very far from what is called love at first sight: and what is not far from love at first sight probably *is* love at first sight."[17] Hall reads the situation correctly, and Baldwin, quite purposeful in allowing a certain amount of time and distance between the two new love interests, illuminates the complexity of human love, especially as it involves two Black men. Both Arthur and Jimmy need time to grow, to love, to lose love, and to fear so that they might know the important sacredness of their fraternal bond. Arthur, while older and ostensibly more experienced in matters of the heart, "had to pull himself to a place where he could say to Paul, his father, and to Hall, his brother, and to all the world, and to *his* Maker, *Take me as I am!*"[18] This is the proud proclamatory place that David of *Giovanni's Room* never reached, at least not in his textual life, and it connotes one of the struggles of salvific men—the dilemma of loving oneself enough to proclaim it to the world so that someone else can be saved. Conversely, Jimmy needs to get beyond thinking that his life was "nothing more than a series of ruptures."[19] Together through the words of Baldwin and the narration of Hall, one learns that Arthur and Jimmy become exactly what the other needs and that their fraternal love moves them beyond reconciling the crises of the past into constructing new things for the future.

Although committed to showcasing the beauty of male intimacy and same-sex love, Baldwin is careful not to romanticize or idealize Arthur and Jimmy's union. Like all relationships, theirs comes with quarrels, frustrations, and moments of disconnect. *Just Above My Head* never intends to be a romance novel and is perhaps more tragic than anything else. Baldwin's pen seems tilted toward such darkness, seems bent on exposing what the world was either too cowardly or too apathetic to see. Nevertheless, even within this darkness, Baldwin paints an amazing picture of same-sex love and male intimacy. Through Arthur and Jimmy, he unveils the hope embedded in fraternal pursuits and intimates the possibility of redemption. Considering this, one understands Hall's reading of Jimmy and his presence in Arthur's life, comes to believe him when he states,

I mean that Jimmy's presence in Arthur's life, Jimmy's love, altered Arthur's estimate of himself, gave him a joy and a freedom he had never known before, invested him with a kind of incandescent wonder, and he carried this light on stage with him, he moved his body differently since he knew that he was loved, loved, and, therefore, knew himself to be both bound and free, and this miracle, the unending wonder of this unending new day, filled his voice with multitudes, summoned from catacombs unnameable, whosoever will.[20]

What Hall captures in his reading is the power of possibility that resides in fraternal love. Jimmy's role, above the emotional and physical, was of a spiritual nature; he served as Arthur's source of salvation as Arthur had done for so many others in the novel, including Jimmy. Even more, Jimmy revealed Arthur to himself, reflected the beautiful manhood that he witnessed and allowed for him to believe. The tragedy comes in time, however. Baldwin, even while exalting such a powerfully fraternal moment, understands that the heart's serendipity is regulated by time. And unfortunately, he leaves the reader thinking, along with the narrator, that despite this miracle of fraternal love, Arthur "simply, finally, saw it coming, saw that he couldn't avoid it, had been running toward it too long, had been alone too long, didn't trust, really, any other condition. Jimmy came too late."[21] This sobering realization connotes the heart of Arthur's fraternal crisis. Not that the breakdown of human intimacy is too great to conquer, as his relationship with Jimmy testifies against the notion; rather, that when one has dwelled without the fraternal for so long, when one has been plagued by the absurd state of Black male loneliness, even the greatest love one has felt fails in the effort of reconciliation. The possibility Jimmy symbolizes offers hope to that which Baldwin argues haunts the human heart, but as we learn, possibility alone is not enough. In the end, when the Trumpets of Zion have called a man home, all we have left in this search, this journey to reconcile, to know, and to love is memory. And it is the memory of Arthur that shapes his relationship with his brother Hall for the reader; that relationship captures the spirit of the fraternal most poignantly in Baldwin's last novel.

Just Above My Head ends as it begins, with Hall attempting to make sense of his brother's life through a series of memories. He talks to the reader in the way Ralph Ellison's protagonist does at the end of *Invisible Man*, in the way W. E. B. Du Bois does at the end of *The Souls of Black Folk*: with a very palpable resolve. It is as if by narrating this story, like Ellison's unnamed and Du Bois's spectral selves, Hall learns something, reaches a destination he has been seeking. In talking to the reader, he notes,

> You have sensed my fatigue and my panic, certainly, if you have followed me until now, and you can guess how terrified I am to be

approaching the end of my story. It was not meant to be my story, though it is far more my story than I would have thought, or might have wished. I have wondered, more than once why I started it, but—I know why. It is a love song to my brother. It is an attempt to face both love and death.[22]

As the narrator, Hall uncovers his own quest and how he, like the other men of the novel, has been searching for some form of reconciliation. His narration, his story, is a way of him making sense of Arthur's death, surely. But it is also a way for him to understand his life. As he recalls that tragic moment when "something hits [Arthur], lightly, in the chest, and between the shoulder blades," when he notes that his brother "wants to get away from here, suddenly, away from these people, these eyes, this death. For, it *is* death, the human need to which one can find no way of responding, the need incapable of recognizing itself," he magnifies Arthur's most significant struggle.[23] He understands why Arthur's heart ruptures and why he tumbles to his death in the London stairwell, understands it as the demand the world can make upon a person. Arthur's demise stems from his inability to recognize self in a world that wanted him to be its everything else; he had no space, no time, no connection with the one person meant to love him like no one other—himself. Within that confusion, as Hall points out, lies Arthur's fear:

All Arthur wanted was for the people who *made* the music, from God knows who, to Satchmo, Mr. Jelly-Lord, Bessie, Mahalia, Miles, Ray, Trane, his *daddy*, and *you*, too, mother-fucker, *you*! It was only when he got scared about what *they might think of what he'd done to their song—our* song—that he really started to be uptight about our love.[24]

Arthur's crisis, as well as his untimely tragedy, comes from the fear of judgment, the fear of not living a life or singing a song as the world expected. He was driven to a point of sacrifice, and his death symbolizes how we, as a people and a world, push the most selfless among us to be our saviors. For this reason and others, Baldwin's Arthur represents one of the strongest symbols of salvific manhood.

So then, what does one make of *Just Above My Head* as a novel? It is, as Hall confesses, "a long song for [his] brother." The narrative is not about Arthur, though he is the central character; the novel, instead, is about Hall Montana and the search to find his brother—the beauty and the ugliness, the good and the bad. But as critical readers we must dig deeper, for there is something very telling in Hall's first words at the beginning of the last chapter. There are moments, quite apparent if one has indeed "followed," where the voice of Hall is lost to the voice of Baldwin. This is not just Hall's story; it is also Baldwin's. It is not a coincidence that the gospel singer's name is Arthur; it is not a coincidence that his love, or the possibility of love, comes through a character named Jimmy. As an author, Baldwin did not intend for this to be, but it became; he has wondered about why he started it, but, alas, he knows. In fact, in an interview he admits, "That book is not directly autobiographical at all, but it is autobiographical on a much deeper level."[25] And this is the strength of *Just Above My Head*: it is the end of something for Baldwin—he has finally told his story, come to understand himself, to recognize himself through his novels. Literary critics will question and historians will deny, but one who reads him closely will know. Baldwin tucked himself into the pages of his novel, hoping that like the good brother Hall, someone would seek him out, sift through the mess and ambiguity and find him standing there, alone, singing a song about himself.

Hall's resolve comes through the responsible remembrance of his brother. The symbolic space-in-between them, captured and represented by Arthur's death, is reconciled through fraternal memory—the way one loves another when he has left this earthly place. Baldwin's labor, through flashback and memory, is to highlight Hall's realization:

> I wonder, more and more, about what we call memory. The burden—the role—of memory is to clarify the event, to make it useful, even, to make it bearable. But memory is, also, what the imagination makes, or has made, of the event, and, the more dreadful the event, the more likely it is that the memory will distort, or efface it. It is, thus, perfectly possible— indeed, it is common—to act on the genuine results of the event, at the same time that the memory manufactures quite another one, an event

totally unrelated to the visible and uncontrollable effects in one's life. This may be why we appear to learn absolutely nothing from experience, or may, in other words, account for our incoherence: memory does not require that we reconstitute the event, but that we justify it.[26]

I quote these last words at length for a variety of reasons. Most important of these comes from my belief of how we remember James Arthur Baldwin. Like most of our prominent African American figures, his life is prone to mythology. This is not, all in all, a bad thing, as the preservation of greatness comes with such an act. My struggle, however, is magnified by Hall's words, for like him, I understand that mythmaking sometimes gives way to manufacturing and in that act one runs the risk of distorting the subject being mythologized. We call this memorialization, never realizing the disservice we have done in selectively trying to preserve. We move, sometimes selfishly, knowing that "the song does not belong to the singer" or how "the sermon does not belong to the preacher."[27] This is to say, the lives of our artists do not belong to them, and sometimes we keep these artists from themselves. This was Baldwin's fate, and if we are not careful, we run the risk of missing his last prophetic message—to at least remember his song as he sang it.

This book is, if anything, a project of salvation. It hopes to add to the literary, public, and private memories we hold of James Baldwin. By examining all of his novels, from *Go Tell It on the Mountain* to *Just Above My Head*, it seeks to remember the Baldwin that scholarship too often forgets or distorts, the Baldwin preoccupied with this "state of being alone," the Baldwin who understood the absence of male intimacy as the presence of a vulnerable subject. Baldwin was, undeniably, a great essayist. His writings on the race question in America and his critique of social relations are arguably unmatched by any of his era. However, there is something equally valuable in his novels, a personal nakedness absent from his nonfiction and rich with, though guised, vulnerable narrative. To this end, this project encourages us to revisit the work of James Baldwin and calls for responsible mythologizing, for we must be careful, in our resinging, to preserve the voice that originally sang the song. I am convinced that when Baldwin is writing, he is singing to us: as lovers, *Just Above My Head*; as critics, "Take Me As I Am!"

NOTES

Introduction

1. Cynthia Bannon's *The Brothers of Romulus: Fraternal* Pietas *in Roman Law, Literature, and Society* centers the discussion of the fraternal through an analysis of its centrality in Roman law and culture. Fruitful to *Salvific Manhood*, Bannon's exploration highlights how very early on the notion of fraternity influenced social structuring throughout the Roman Empire. Specifically, her work traces the myriad ways in which what she labels "fraternal pietas" became a model for other types of relationships. My reimagining of the fraternal parallels some of this thinking in its push to move beyond blood and legality, to elevate the fraternal into the space of the symbolic. Her work also provides a somewhat useful etymological tracing of *frater* and fraternal.
2. Baldwin, "Sonny's Blues," 103.
3. Baldwin, "Sonny's Blues," 103.
4. Baldwin, "Sonny's Blues," 104.
5. Baldwin, "Sonny's Blues," 115.
6. Baldwin, "Sonny's Blues," 118.
7. Baldwin, "Sonny's Blues," 132.
8. Baldwin, "Sonny's Blues," 138.
9. Baldwin, "Sonny's Blues," 139.
10. Baldwin, "Sonny's Blues," 140.
11. McBride, "'How Much Time,'" 1–12.

1. Wrestling for Salvation

1. Hardy, *James Baldwin's God*, ix–x, x.
2. Fabre, "Fathers and Sons," 123.

3. Macebuh, *James Baldwin*, 53.

4. Hardy, *James Baldwin's God*, 22.

5. Washington, "Wrestling with 'The Love,'" 91.

6. LeSeur, *Ten Is the Age*, 18.

7. Pratt, *James Baldwin*, 51.

8. MacInnes, "Dark Angel," 121.

9. Baldwin, *Go Tell It*, 12.

10. Baldwin, *Go Tell It*, 12–13.

11. Baldwin, *Go Tell It*, 13.

12. Baldwin, *Go Tell It*, 15.

13. Baldwin, *Go Tell It*, 19.

14. Baldwin, *Go Tell It*, 22.

15. Du Bois, *Souls of Black Folk*, 45.

16. Baldwin, *Go Tell It*, 23.

17. Baldwin, *Go Tell It*, 23.

18. Baldwin, *Go Tell It*, 28.

19. Baldwin, *Go Tell It*, 30.

20. Baldwin, *Go Tell It*, 32.

21. Baldwin, *Go Tell It*, 32.

22. Baldwin, *Go Tell It*, 33.

23. Baldwin, *Go Tell It*, 34.

24. Rosenblatt, "Out of Control," 86.

25. Baldwin, *Go Tell It*, 38.

26. Baldwin, *Go Tell It*, 42.

27. Baldwin, *Go Tell It*, 42.

28. Baldwin, *Go Tell It*, 43.

29. Hardy, *James Baldwin's God*, 32.

30. Fabre, "Fathers and Sons," 122.

31. Rosenblatt, "Out of Control," 87.

32. MacInnes, "Dark Angel," 124.

33. MacInnes, "Dark Angel," 124.

34. Porter, *Stealing the Fire*, 68.

35. Baldwin, *Go Tell It*, 77.

36. Baldwin, *Go Tell It*, 81.

37. Baldwin, *Go Tell It*, 107.

38. Baldwin, *Go Tell It*, 107.

39. Baldwin, *Go Tell It*, 109.

40. Baldwin, *Go Tell It*, 109.

41. Baldwin, *Go Tell It*, 120.

42. Fabre, "Fathers and Sons," 123.

43. O'Neale, "Fathers, Gods, and Religion," 140.

44. O'Neale, "Fathers, Gods, and Religion," 140.

45. Byerman, "Secular Word, Sacred Flesh," 190.

46. Byerman, "Secular Word, Sacred Flesh," 190.

47. Pratt, *James Baldwin*, 54.

48. Pratt, *James Baldwin*, 54.

49. Baldwin, *Go Tell It*, 145.

50. Baldwin, *Go Tell It*, 159.

51. Baldwin, *Go Tell It*, 124.

52. Baldwin, *Go Tell It*, 160.

53. Baldwin, *Go Tell It*, 161.

54. Baldwin, *Go Tell It*, 166.

55. Baldwin, *Go Tell It*, 172.

56. Rosenblatt, "Out of Control," 87.

57. Baldwin, *Go Tell It*, 53.

58. Washington, "Wrestling," 85.

59. Pratt, *James Baldwin*, 57.

60. Crawford, "Reclamation of the Homoerotic."

61. Crawford, "Reclamation of the Homoerotic," 75.

62. Baldwin, *Go Tell It*, 55.

63. Baldwin, *Go Tell It*, 55.

64. Baldwin, *Go Tell It*, 55.

65. 1 Sam. 18:4 (KJV).

66. Crawford, "Reclamation of the Homoerotic," 76.

67. Byerman, "Secular Word, Sacred Flesh," 189.

68. Byerman, "Secular Word, Sacred Flesh," 189.

69. Henderson, "Refiguring the Flesh," 153.

70. Hardy, *James Baldwin's God*, 103.

71. Hardy, *James Baldwin's God*, 103.

72. Allen, "Religious Symbolism and Psychic Reality," 173.

73. Henderson, "Refiguring the Flesh," 152.

74. Henderson, "Refiguring the Flesh," 151.

75. Baldwin, *Go Tell It*, 228.

76. Baldwin, *Go Tell It*, 228.

77. Baldwin, *Go Tell It*, 153.

78. Baldwin, *Go Tell It*, 229.

79. Baldwin, *Go Tell It*, 230.

80. Baldwin, *Go Tell It*, 230.

81. Fabre, "Fathers and Sons," 127.

82. Baldwin, *Go Tell It*, 231.

83. Baldwin, *Go Tell It*, 238.

84. Baldwin, *Go Tell It*, 238.

85. Baldwin, *Go Tell It*, 241.

86. 1 Sam. 21:42 (KJV).

87. Baldwin, *Go Tell It*, 244.

88. Baldwin, *Go Tell It*, 245.

89. Baldwin, *Go Tell It*, 262.

90. Baldwin, *Go Tell It*, 262–63.

91. 1 Sam. 21:41 (KJV).

92. Sylvander, *James Baldwin*, 43.

2. Flight, Freedom, and Abjection

1. Field, *Historical Guide to James Baldwin*, 4.

2. Thorsen, *James Baldwin: The Price*.

3. Weatherby, *James Baldwin: Artist*, 118.

4. Fiedler, "A Homosexual Dilemma," 146–47.

5. Ross, "White Fantasies of Desire," 16.

6. McBride, "Straight Black Studies," 68.

7. McBride, "'How Much Time,'" 6.

8. Leeming, *James Baldwin: A Biography*, 74–75.

9. Thorsen, *James Baldwin: The Price*.

10. Ross, "White Fantasies," 25.

11. Johnson-Roullier, *Reading on the Edge*, 143.

12. Henderson, "James Baldwin's *Giovanni's Room*," 298.

13. Macebuh, *James Baldwin*, 166.

14. Bone, "James Baldwin," 28.

15. Bone, "James Baldwin," 38.

16. Welsh, "James Baldwin," 76.

17. Drowne, "Irrevocable Condition," 73.

18. Drowne, "Irrevocable Condition," 74.

19. Drowne, "Irrevocable Condition," 74–75.

20. Porter, *Stealing the Fire*, 140.

21. Porter, *Stealing the Fire*, 140–41.

22. Bone, "James Baldwin," 38.

23. Johnson-Roullier, *Reading on the Edge*, 138.

24. Campbell, *Exiled in Paris*, 118.

25. Campbell, *Exiled in Paris*, 119.

26. Baldwin, *Giovanni's Room*, 8.

27. Baldwin, *Giovanni's Room*, 8.

28. Baldwin, *Giovanni's Room*, 9.

29. Kristeva, *Powers of Horror*, 1

30. Baldwin, *Giovanni's Room*, 9.

31. Baldwin, *Giovanni's Room*, 9.

32. Kristeva, *Powers of Horror*, 1.

33. Baldwin, *Giovanni's Room*, 10.

34. Baldwin, *Giovanni's Room*, 10.

35. Baldwin, *Giovanni's Room*, 10.

36. Baldwin, *Giovanni's Room*, 23.

37. Baldwin, *Giovanni's Room*, 23.

38. Baldwin, *Giovanni's Room*, 26.

39. Baldwin, *Giovanni's Room*, 26.

40. Baldwin, *Giovanni's Room*, 27.

41. Baldwin, *Giovanni's Room*, 28.

42. Mitchell, "Femininity, Abjection," 267.

43. Baldwin, *Giovanni's Room*, 29.

44. Baldwin, *Giovanni's Room*, 29.

45. Baldwin, *Giovanni's Room*, 22.

46. Reid-Pharr, *Black Gay Man*, 131.

47. Baldwin, *Giovanni's Room*, 34.

48. Porter, *Stealing the Fire*, 138.

49. Baldwin, *Giovanni's Room*, 35.

50. Baldwin, *Giovanni's Room*, 38.

51. Baldwin, *Giovanni's Room*, 39.

52. Baldwin, *Giovanni's Room*, 41.

53. Baldwin, *Giovanni's Room*, 41.

54. Baldwin, *Giovanni's Room*, 139.

55. Baldwin, *Giovanni's Room*, 139.

56. Baldwin, *Giovanni's Room*, 61.

57. Reid-Pharr, *Black Gay Man*, 129.

58. Baldwin, *Giovanni's Room*, 62.

59. Macebuh, *James Baldwin*, 76.

60. Drowne, "Irrevocable Condition," 78.

61. Baldwin, *Giovanni's Room*, 64.

62. Baldwin, *Giovanni's Room*, 64.

63. Baldwin, *Giovanni's Room*, 75.

64. Baldwin, *Giovanni's Room*, 75.

65. Baldwin, *Giovanni's Room*, 78.

66. Baldwin, *Giovanni's Room*, 83.

67. Baldwin, *Giovanni's Room*, 84.

68. Baldwin, *Giovanni's Room*, 87.

69. Baldwin, *Giovanni's Room*, 87.

70. Baldwin, *Giovanni's Room*, 88.

71. Baldwin, *Giovanni's Room*, 114.

72. Baldwin, *Giovanni's Room*, 141.

73. Baldwin, *Giovanni's Room*, 142.

74. Baldwin, *Giovanni's Room*, 168.

3. Alone in the Absurd

1. Camus, *Myth of Sisyphus*, v.

2. Camus, *Myth of Sisyphus*, v.

3. Leeming, *James Baldwin: A Biography*, 200.

4. Baldwin, *Another Country*, 1.

5. Baldwin, *Another Country*, 1.

6. Baldwin, *Another Country*, 2.

7. Baldwin, *Another Country*, 3.

8. Baldwin, *Another Country*, 3.

9. Baldwin, *Another Country*, 3.

10. Baldwin, *Another Country*, 3.

11. Baldwin, *Another Country*, 3.

12. Baldwin, *Another Country*, 8.

13. Baldwin, *Another Country*, 9.

14. Omry, "Baldwin's Bop," 27.

15. Camus, *Myth of Sisyphus*, 6.

16. Baldwin, *Another Country*, 9.

17. Baldwin, *Another Country*, 12–13.

18. Camus, *Myth of Sisyphus*, 10.

19. Baldwin, *Another Country*, 22.

20. Susan Feldman, "Another Look," 93.

21. Joyce and McBride, "James Baldwin and Sexuality," 132.

22. Baldwin, *Another Country*, 13.

23. Baldwin, *Another Country*, 13.

24. Baldwin, *Another Country*, 19–20.

25. Baldwin, *Another Country*, 20.

26. Baldwin, *Another Country*, 21.

27. Baldwin, *Another Country*, 22.

28. Baldwin, *Another Country*, 22.

29. Baldwin, *Another Country*, 27.

30. Baldwin, *Another Country*, 27.

31. Baldwin, *Another Country*, 27.

32. Baldwin, *Another Country*, 29.

33. Camus, *Myth of Sisyphus*, 31.

34. Baldwin, *Another Country*, 53.

35. Washington, *Politics of Exile*, 132.

36. Baldwin, *Another Country*, 53.

37. Baldwin, *Another Country*, 67.

38. Baldwin, *Another Country*, 68.

39. Washington, *Politics of Exile*, 132.

40. Baldwin, *Another Country*, 4.

41. Baldwin, *Another Country*, 85.

42. Baldwin, *Another Country*, 87.

43. Macebuh, *James Baldwin*, 87.

44. Baldwin, *Another Country*, 324–25.

45. Standley and Pratt, *Conversations with James Baldwin*, 104.

46. Baldwin, *Another Country*, 343.

47. Camus, *Myth of Sisyphus*, 5.

4. Theatrics of Mask-ulinity

1. Kenan, "James Baldwin, 1924–1987," 52.

2. Puzo, "Cardboard Lovers," 155.

3. Puzo, "Cardboard Lovers," 155.

4. Scott, *James Baldwin's Later Fiction*, 21.

5. Scott, *James Baldwin's Later Fiction*, 22.

6. Scott, *James Baldwin's Later Fiction*, 22.

7. Puzo, "Cardboard Lovers," 155.

8. Baldwin, *Train's Been Gone*, 7.

9. Miller, "Playing a Mean Guitar," 134.

10. Scott, "Challenging the American Conscience," 169.

11. Baldwin, *Train's Been Gone*, 4.

12. Baldwin, *Train's Been Gone*, 8.

13. Baldwin, *Train's Been Gone*, 9.

14. Baldwin, *Train's Been Gone*, 29.

15. Baldwin, *Train's Been Gone*, 30.

16. Baldwin, *Train's Been Gone*, 35.

17. Baldwin, *Train's Been Gone*, 36.

18. Baldwin, *Train's Been Gone*, 41.

19. Baldwin, *Train's Been Gone*, 125.

20. Baldwin, *Train's Been Gone*, 126.

21. Baldwin, *Train's Been Gone*, 126.

22. Scott, *James Baldwin's Later Fiction*, 57.

23. Baldwin, *Train's Been Gone*, 232.

24. Baldwin, *Train's Been Gone*, 233.

25. Baldwin, *Train's Been Gone*, 233.

26. Baldwin, *Train's Been Gone*, 234.

27. Baldwin, *Train's Been Gone*, 234.

28. Baldwin, *Train's Been Gone*, 235.

29. Baldwin, *Train's Been Gone*, 239.

30. Baldwin, *Train's Been Gone*, 239.

31. Baldwin, *Train's Been Gone*, 202.

32. Baldwin, *Train's Been Gone*, 204–5.

33. Baldwin, *Train's Been Gone*, 209.

34. Baldwin, *Train's Been Gone*, 209.

35. Baldwin, *Train's Been Gone*, 210.

36. Baldwin, *Train's Been Gone*, 211.

37. Baldwin, *Train's Been Gone*, 211.

38. Baldwin, *Train's Been Gone*, 211.

39. Baldwin, *Train's Been Gone*, 211.

40. Scott, *James Baldwin's Later Fiction*, 59.

41. Baldwin, *Train's Been Gone*, 98.

42. Baldwin, *Train's Been Gone*, 99.

43. Baldwin, *Train's Been Gone*, 246.

44. Baldwin, *Train's Been Gone*, 107.

45. Murray, *Our Living Manhood*, 37.

46. Baldwin, *Train's Been Gone*, 109.

47. Baldwin, *Train's Been Gone*, 109.

48. Baldwin, *Train's Been Gone*, 113–14.

49. Baldwin, *Train's Been Gone*, 313.

50. Baldwin, *Train's Been Gone*, 448.

51. Baldwin, *Train's Been Gone*, 442.

52. Baldwin, *Train's Been Gone*, 452.

5. Concrete Jungles

1. Scott, *James Baldwin's Later Fiction*, 62.

2. Weatherby, *James Baldwin*, 318.

3. Scott, *James Baldwin's Later Fiction*, xiii.

4. Baldwin, *Beale Street*, 4.

5. Baldwin, *Beale Street*, 6–7.

6. Baldwin, *Beale Street*, 9.

7. Baldwin, *Beale Street*, 9.

8. Baldwin, *Beale Street*, 103.

9. Baldwin, *Beale Street*, 99.

10. Baldwin, *Beale Street*, 99.

11. Alexander, *New Jim Crow*, 124.

12. Baldwin, *Beale Street*, 102.

13. Alexander, *New Jim Crow*, 117.

14. Baldwin, *Beale Street*, 107.

15. Baldwin, *Beale Street*, 107.

16. Baldwin, *Beale Street*, 106.

17. Baldwin, *Beale Street*, 109.

18. Phillips, "Revising Revision," 72.

19. Baldwin, *Beale Street*, 106.

20. Baldwin, *Beale Street*, 106.

21. Baldwin, *Beale Street*, 106.

22. Baldwin, *Beale Street*, 104.

23. Baldwin, *Beale Street*, 174.

24. Baldwin, *Beale Street*, 174.

25. Baldwin, *Beale Street*, 137.

26. Baldwin, *Beale Street*, 139.
27. Harris, "Eye as Weapon," 208.
28. Baldwin, *Beale Street*, 141.
29. Baldwin, *Beale Street*, 140.
30. Baldwin, *Beale Street*, 142.
31. Baldwin, *Beale Street*, 172.
32. Harris, "Eye as Weapon," 210.
33. Baldwin, *Beale Street*, 179.
34. Scott, *James Baldwin's Later Fiction*, 109.
35. Hardy, *James Baldwin's God*, 65.
36. Hardy, *James Baldwin's God*, 65.
37. Baldwin, *Beale Street*, 17.
38. Baldwin, *Beale Street*, 65.
39. Baldwin, *Beale Street*, 186.
40. Baldwin, *Beale Street*, 188.
41. Baldwin, *Beale Street*, 190.
42. Baldwin, *Beale Street*, 190.
43. Baldwin, *Beale Street*, 15.
44. Baldwin, *Beale Street*, 17.
45. Weatherby, *James Baldwin*, 317.
46. Baldwin, *Beale Street*, 61.
47. Baldwin, *Beale Street*, 191.
48. Scott, *James Baldwin's Later Fiction*, 87.
49. Baldwin, *Beale Street*, 197.
50. Camus, *Myth of Sisyphus*, 121.
51. Camus, *Myth of Sisyphus*, 121.

Conclusion
1. Thorsen, *James Baldwin: The Price*.
2. Cleaver, *Soul on Ice*, 97.
3. Cleaver, *Soul on Ice*, 97.
4. Cleaver, *Soul on Ice*, 97.
5. Standley and Pratt, *Conversations with James Baldwin*, 252.
6. Standley and Pratt, *Conversations with James Baldwin*, 191.
7. Baldwin, *Just Above My Head*, 181.
8. Baldwin, *Just Above My Head*, 189.
9. Baldwin, *Just Above My Head*, 191.

10. Baldwin, *Just Above My Head*, 193.
11. Baldwin, *Just Above My Head*, 203.
12. Baldwin, *Just Above My Head*, 208.
13. Baldwin, *Just Above My Head*, 216.
14. Baldwin, *Just Above My Head*, 218.
15. Baldwin, *Just Above My Head*, 346.
16. Baldwin, *Just Above My Head*, 459.
17. Baldwin, *Just Above My Head*, 466.
18. Baldwin, *Just Above My Head*, 472.
19. Baldwin, *Just Above My Head*, 471.
20. Baldwin, *Just Above My Head*, 561.
21. Baldwin, *Just Above My Head*, 569.
22. Baldwin, *Just Above My Head*, 517.
23. Baldwin, *Just Above My Head*, 581.
24. Baldwin, *Just Above My Head*, 577.
25. Standley and Pratt, *Conversations with James Baldwin*, 278.
26. Baldwin, *Just Above My Head*, 554.
27. Baldwin, *Just Above My Head*, 576–77.

BIBLIOGRAPHY

Alexander, Michelle. *The New Jim Crow: Mass Incarceration in the Age of Colorblindness*. New York: New Press, 2010.

Allen, Shirley. "Religious Symbolism and Psychic Reality in Baldwin's *Go Tell It on the Mountain*." In Standley and Burt, 166–88.

Baldwin, James. *Another Country*. New York: Random House, 1962.

——. *Giovanni's Room*. New York: Random House, 2000.

——. *Go Tell It on the Mountain*. New York: Dell, 1985.

——. *If Beale Street Could Talk*. New York: Random House, 1974.

——. *Just Above My Head*. New York: Random House, 1979.

——. "Sonny's Blues." In *Going to Meet the Man*, 101–41. New York: Random House, 1948.

——. *Tell Me How Long the Train's Been Gone*. London: Michael Joseph, 1968.

Bannon, Cynthia J. *The Brothers of Romulus: Fraternal Pietas in Roman Law, Literature, and Society*. Princeton NJ: Princeton University Press, 1997.

Bone, Robert. "James Baldwin." In *James Baldwin: A Collection of Critical Essays*, edited by Keneth Kinnamon, 28–51. Upper Saddle River NJ: Prentice-Hall, 1974.

Byerman, Keith. "Secular Word, Sacred Flesh: Preachers in the Fiction of Baldwin and Morrison." In King and Scott, 187–204.

Campbell, James. *Exiled in Paris: Richard Wright, James Baldwin, Samuel Beckett, and Others on the Left Bank*. New York: Simon & Schuster, 1995.

——. *Talking at the Gates: A Life of James Baldwin*. New York: Penguin, 1991.

Camus, Albert. *The Myth of Sisyphus and Other Essays*. New York: Random House, 1955.

Clark, Keith. *Black Manhood in James Baldwin, Ernest J. Gaines, and August Wilson*. Urbana: University of Illinois Press, 2002.

Cleaver, Eldridge. *Soul on Ice*. New York: Dell, 1968.

Crawford, Margo. "The Reclamation of the Homoerotic as Spiritual in *Go Tell It on the Mountain*." In *James Baldwin's Go Tell it on the Mountain: Historical and Critical Essays*, edited by Carol Henderson, 75–86. New York: Peter Lang, 2006.

Drowne, Kathleen. "'An Irrevocable Condition': Constructions of Home and the Writing of Place in *Giovanni's Room*." In *Re-viewing James Baldwin: Things Not Seen*, edited by D. Quentin Miller, 72–87. Philadelphia: Temple University Press, 2000.

Du Bois, W. E. B. *The Souls of Black Folk*. New York: Penguin, 1995.

Fabre, Michael. "Fathers and Sons in James Baldwin's *Go Tell It on the Mountain*." In *James Baldwin: A Collection of Critical Essays*, edited by Keneth Kinnamon, 120–38. Upper Saddle River NJ: Prentice-Hall, 1974.

Feldman, Susan. "Another Look at *Another Country*: Reconciling Baldwin's Racial and Sexual Politics." In *Re-viewing James Baldwin: Things Not Seen*, edited by D. Quentin Miller, 88–104. Philadelphia: Temple University Press, 2000.

Fiedler, Leslie. "A Homosexual Dilemma." In Standley and Burt, 146–49.

Field, Douglas. *A Historical Guide to James Baldwin*. Oxford: Oxford University Press, 2009.

Hardy, Clarence E. *James Baldwin's God: Sex, Hope, and Crisis in Black Holiness Culture*. Knoxville: University of Tennessee Press, 2003.

Harris, Trudier. "The Eye as Weapon in *If Beale Street Could Talk*." In Standley and Burt, 204–16.

Henderson, Carol. "Refiguring the Flesh: The Word, the Body, and the Rituals of Being in *Beloved* and *Go Tell it on the Mountain*." In King and Scott, 149–65.

Henderson, Mae. "James Baldwin's *Giovanni's Room*: Expatriation, 'Racial Drag,' and Homosexual Panic." In *Black Queer Studies: A Critical Anthology*, edited by E. Patrick Johnson and Mae Henderson, 298–322. Durham NC: Duke University Press, 2005.

Johnson-Roullier, Cyraina. *Reading on the Edge: Exiles, Modernities, and Cultural Transformation in Proust, Joyce, and Baldwin*. Albany: State University of New York Press, 2000.

Joyce, Justin, and Dwight McBride. "James Baldwin and Sexuality: *Lieux de Mémoire* and a Usable Past." In Field, 111–40.

Kenan, Randall. "James Baldwin, 1924–1987: A Brief Biography." In Field, 21–60.

King, Lovalerie, and Lynn Orilla Scott. *James Baldwin and Toni Morrison: Comparative Critical and Theoretical Essays*. New York: Palgrave Macmillan, 2006.

Klein, Marcus. "A Question of Identity." In *James Baldwin*, edited by Harold Bloom, 17–36. New York: Chelsea House, 1986.

Kristeva, Julia. *Powers of Horror: An Essay on Abjection*. New York: Columbia University Press, 1982.

Leeming, David. *James Baldwin: A Biography*. New York: Alfred A. Knopf, 1994.

LeSeur, Geta. *Ten Is the Age of Darkness: The Black Bildungsroman*. Columbia: University of Missouri Press, 1995.

Lynch, Michael. "A Glimpse of the Hidden God: Dialectical Visions in Baldwin's *Go Tell It on the Mountain*." In *New Essays on Go Tell It on the Mountain*, edited by Trudier Harris, 29–58. Cambridge: Cambridge University Press, 1996.

Macebuh, Stanley. *James Baldwin: A Critical Study*. New York: Third Press, 1973.

MacInnes, Colin. "Dark Angel: The Writings of James Baldwin." In *Five Black Writers: Essays on Wright, Ellison, Baldwin, Hughes, and LeRoi Jones*, edited by Donald B. Gibson, 119–42. New York: New York University Press, 1970.

McBride, Dwight. "Straight Black Studies: On African American Studies, James Baldwin, and Black Queer Studies." In *Black Queer Studies: A Critical Anthology*, edited by E. Patrick Johnson and Mae Henderson, 68–89. Durham: Duke University Press, 2005.

———. "'How Much Time Do You Want for Your Progress?': New Approaches to James Baldwin." In *James Baldwin Now*, edited by Dwight McBride, 1–12. New York: New York University Press, 1999.

Miller, D. Quentin. "Playing a Mean Guitar: The Legacy of Staggerlee in Baldwin and Morrison." In King and Scott, 121–48.

Mitchell, Keith. "Femininity, Abjection, and (Black) Masculinity in James Baldwin's *Giovanni's Room* and Toni Morrison's *Beloved*." In King and Scott, 261–86.

Murray, Rolland. *Our Living Manhood: Literature, Black Power, and Masculine Ideology*. Philadelphia: University of Pennsylvania Press, 2007.

Omry, Keren. "Baldwin's Bop 'N' Morrison's Mood: Bebop and Race in James Baldwin's *Another Country* and Toni Morrison's *Jazz*. In King and Scott, 11–35.

O'Neale, Sondra. "Fathers, Gods, and Religion: Perceptions of Christianity and Ethnic Faith in James Baldwin." In Standley and Burt, 125–44.

Phillips, Michelle. "Revising Revision: Methodologies of Love, Desire, and Resistance in *Beloved* and *If Beale Street Could Talk*." In King and Scott, 63–81.

Porter, Horace A. *Stealing the Fire: The Art and Protest of James Baldwin*. Middletown CT: Wesleyan University Press, 1989.

———. "The South in *Go Tell It on the Mountain*: Baldwin's Personal Confrontation." In *New Essays on Go Tell it on the Mountain*, edited by Trudier Harris, 59–76. Cambridge: Cambridge University Press, 1996.

Pratt, Louis H. *James Baldwin*. Boston: Twayne, 1978.

Puzo, Mario. "His Cardboard Lovers." In Standley and Burt, 155–58.

Reid-Pharr, Robert. *Black Gay Man: Essays.* New York: New York University Press, 2001.

Rosenblatt, Roger. "Out of Control: *Go Tell it on the Mountain* and *Another Country.*" In *James Baldwin*, edited by Harold Bloom, 77–96. New York: Chelsea House, 1986.

Ross, Marlon. "White Fantasies of Desire: Baldwin and the Racial Identities of Sexuality." In *James Baldwin Now*, edited by Dwight McBride, 13–55. New York: New York University Press, 1999.

Scott, Lynn Orilla. "Challenging the American Conscience, Re-imagining American Identity: James Baldwin and the Civil Rights Movement." In Field, 141–76.

———. *James Baldwin's Later Fiction: Witness to the Journey.* East Lansing: Michigan State University Press, 2002.

Standley, Fred L., and Louis Pratt. *Conversations with James Baldwin.* Jackson: University Press of Mississippi, 1989.

Standley, Fred L., and Nancy V. Burt, eds. *Critical Essays on James Baldwin.* Boston: G. K. Hall, 1988.

Sylvander, Carolyn Wedin. *James Baldwin.* New York: Ungar, 1980.

Thorsen, Karen, dir. *James Baldwin: The Price of the Ticket.* Nobody Knows Productions, 1989.

Washington, Bryan. *The Politics of Exile: Ideology in Henry James, F. Scott Fitzgerald, and James Baldwin.* Boston: Northeastern University Press, 1995.

———. "Wrestling with 'The Love That Dare Not Speak Its Name': John, Elisha, and the 'Master.'" In *New Essays on "Go Tell It on the Mountain,"* edited by Trudier Harris, 77–96. Cambridge: Cambridge University Press, 1996.

Weatherby, W. J. *James Baldwin: Artist on Fire.* New York: Donald I. Fine, 1989.

Welsch, Gabriel. "James Baldwin: Nothing Less Courageous." In *James Baldwin*, edited by Harold Bloom. Bloom's BioCritiques. Philadelphia: Chelsea House, 2006.

Zaborowska, Magdalena. *James Baldwin's Turkish Decade: Erotics of Exile.* Durham NC: Duke University Press, 2009.

INDEX

abjection: and *Another Country*, 105, 108, 120–22, 125; and *Giovanni's Room*, 17, 76, 80–81, 82, 83, 93

absurdity, racial, 7, 8, 9, 11, 131, 158, 164–66, 189, 200; and *Another Country*, 17, 100–101, 110–12, 114–27, 161; and *Go Tell It on the Mountain*, 33, 161–62; and *If Beale Street Could Talk*, 18, 167–68, 170, 171–73, 176–78, 181–85, 194; and *Tell Me How Long the Train's Been Gone*, 144–47, 149. *See also* race, issues of; racism

Alexander, Michelle, 170–71

Allen, Shirley, 52

The Amen Corner, 13

Another Country, 12, 14, 17, 100, 101–29, 142, 163, 190–91, 192, 193; abjection in, 105, 108, 120–22, 125; crisis in, 100, 102, 109–10, 112, 114, 116, 118, 120, 122; and intimacy, 101–2, 105, 108–10, 119, 123, 126, 128; and issues of race, 110–25, 127–29, 132, 161; and issues of sexuality, 108, 112–17, 119, 122–25, 128–29, 179, 191; and loneliness, 107–10, 121, 124–25; and

love, 102, 107–10, 117–18, 120, 122–23, 124, 126–29, 148; and manhood, 100–102, 104–11, 113–24, 128, 162; and racial absurdity, 17, 100–101, 110–12, 114–27, 161; and racism, 111–16, 118, 120, 124; and rape, 113–14, 116–17, 122; and salvation, 100–102, 117–19, 121, 126, 128–29, 148; and the space-in-between, 112, 120, 128; and suicide, 17, 101–2, 106, 126–28, 161–62, 185, 191, 194; violence in, 104–5, 108, 110–14, 116–18, 120, 122–24

Baldwin, David, 16, 187–89

Baldwin, James, 127, 131, 187–93, 203; and autobiography, 16, 20–22, 24, 34, 41–42, 45, 47–48, 50, 55, 59, 61, 64–70, 72–74, 101, 156–58, 162–63, 189, 194–95, 202; and bisexuality, 13–14, 191; in "God Is Love" photo, 2; and homosexuality, 6, 13–14, 16, 47–48, 156; and loneliness, 15–16, 59, 62, 68, 70, 188, 203; as a "race man," 13, 14, 189–92; and religion, 2–6, 13, 41–42, 50, 61; and salvation, 2–4, 6–8, 9–11, 15–18, 193

—Works: *The Amen Corner*, 13; *Another
Country*, 12, 14, 17, 100, 101–29, 132,
142, 148, 161–62, 163, 179, 185, 190–91,
192, 193, 194; *The Fire Next Time*, 12,
14, 133, 189; *Giovanni's Room*, 13–14,
17, 61–97, 100, 102, 138, 159, 192, 194,
199; *Go Tell It on the Mountain*, 7,
13, 15–17, 19–59, 61, 62, 63, 66, 68,
69, 72, 94, 102, 161–62, 192, 193, 194,
203; *If Beale Street Could Talk*, 18,
142, 162–85, 192, 194; *Just Above My
Head*, 15, 18, 192–203; *Nobody Knows
My Name: More Notes of a Native
Son*, 12, 14; *Notes of a Native Son*,
12, 13; "Sonny's Blues," 6–11, 161; *Tell
Me How Long the Train's Been Gone*,
17–18, 132–60, 192, 194, 195
Bannon, Cynthia, 5, 205n1
"Beale Street Blues," 163–65
bisexuality: and *Giovanni's Room*, 74,
82–83, 92, 94–95; and James Baldwin, 13–14, 191; in *Tell Me How Long
the Train's Been Gone*, 140, 146. *See
also* queerness; sexuality, issues of
Black Arts Movement, 14
Black Nationalism, 17
Black Power Movement, 14, 17, 132–33,
155, 156, 158–59, 189–92
Bone, Robert, 68–69
Byerman, Keith, 50–51

Campbell, James, 73
Camus, Albert, 17, 99, 100–102, 106, 110,
121–22, 128, 147, 183, 185
Carr, Lucien, 64
Christianity. *See* religion

Civil Rights Movement, 13, 14, 132, 158,
189, 191
Cleaver, Eldridge, 156, 189–92
Cole, William, 62–63, 64
confinement. *See* imprisonment
Crawford, Margo, 47
crisis: in *Another Country*, 100, 102,
109–10, 112, 114, 116, 118, 120, 122; in
Giovanni's Room, 61, 65, 66, 69–70,
75–97; in *Go Tell It on the Mountain*, 22–23, 24–28, 30, 32–44, 49, 51,
56–57, 59, 194; of identity, 22–23, 38,
42, 49, 109–10, 122, 137; in *If Beale
Street Could Talk*, 163, 167, 169–71,
175, 178, 182; in *Just Above My Head*,
196–200; and manhood, 26, 49, 69,
78–79, 81, 88, 100, 106, 109, 114, 116,
121, 152, 163, 167, 170, 175–76, 197;
religious, 4, 38–43, 51; in *Tell Me
How Long the Train's Been Gone*, 137,
139, 141–42, 144, 147–48, 155, 159. *See
also* fraternal crisis

découpage, literary, 67–68, 72, 157
Drowne, Kathleen, 70–71, 90
Du Bois, W. E. B., 200

Ellison, Ralph, 101, 200
Evers, Medgar, 132, 189

Fabre, Michael, 21, 40, 56
Feldman, Susan, 113
Fiedler, Leslie, 63
Field, Douglas, 62
The Fire Next Time, 12, 14, 133, 189
Fisk Jubilee Singers, 19

fraternal crisis, 6, 8–10, 16–18, 132, 135, 192; in *Another Country*, 100, 102, 112, 114, 116, 118; in *Giovanni's Room*, 66, 69–70, 75–97; in *Go Tell It on the Mountain*, 24, 27–28, 32–38, 41–42, 44, 49, 56–57, 59, 194; in *If Beale Street Could Talk*, 163, 167, 169–71, 178, 182; in *Just Above My Head*, 196–200; in *Tell Me How Long the Train's Been Gone*, 141–42, 144, 147–48, 155, 159

fraternal intimacy, 5–9, 18, 68, 126, 128, 189; in *Another Country*, 101–2, 109, 123; in *Giovanni's Room*, 61–62, 70, 72, 74–78, 81, 84, 90–92, 94; in *Go Tell It on the Mountain*, 15, 39, 44–54, 57–59; in *If Beale Street Could Talk*, 163–65, 167–69, 173–74, 178, 182; in *Just Above My Head*, 15, 194–200; in *Tell Me How Long the Train's Been Gone*, 134–36, 140–41, 143, 146, 150–52, 158–60

fraternal love. *See* love: fraternal

George Washington Bridge, 99, 126, 192

Giovanni's Room, 13–14, 17, 61–97, 100, 102, 138, 159, 192, 199; and abjection, 17, 76, 80–81, 82, 83, 93; and bisexuality, 74, 82–83, 92, 94–95; and crisis, 61, 65, 66, 69–70, 75–97; and homosexuality, 62–78, 80–89, 91–92, 95–97; and intimacy, 61–62, 70, 72, 74–78, 81, 84, 87–88, 90–92, 94; and issues of race, 61, 63–68, 72; and issues of sexuality, 61–78, 80–89, 91–92, 94–97; and loneliness, 62, 70, 77–78; and love, 17, 61–63, 64, 73, 74, 78–80, 84, 90, 91–97, 194; and man-

hood, 17, 61, 66, 68–70, 76–91, 93–97, 102; and masculinity, 69, 78–84, 86, 88–89; and salvation, 17, 61, 65, 66, 68, 69–70, 84–85, 87, 89, 93–94, 97; and same-sex desire, 61–64, 75–78, 80–84, 89, 91–92, 95–97; and the space-in-between, 61, 66, 74, 76, 88, 90, 92, 93–94

"Go Tell It on the Mountain," 19, 31

Go Tell It on the Mountain, 7, 13, 16–17, 19–59, 61, 62, 63, 66, 68, 69, 72, 94, 192, 193, 203; and crisis, 22–23, 24–28, 30, 32–44, 49, 51, 56–57, 59, 194; and homoeroticism, 22, 26, 46–50, 58; and homosexuality, 22, 26, 46–50, 53, 58–59; intimacy in, 15, 19, 22, 27–28, 38–39, 44–59, 194; and issues of race, 31, 33, 36–37, 39, 41, 43–44, 50, 161–62; issues of sexuality in, 22, 25–26, 46–50, 53, 58–59; and kinship, 21, 23, 28, 32–37, 40, 44–45, 47; loneliness in, 15–16, 34–35, 37–38, 52, 57, 59; love in, 16–17, 23–24, 27–28, 31, 32–34, 37–38, 40–42, 44–49, 52, 56–58; and manhood, 17, 19, 20, 22–24, 16–28, 34–35, 38–39, 44–45, 48–54, 57–59, 194; and masculinity, 26, 38–39, 47–50; and racial absurdity, 33, 161–62; and racism, 50; religion in, 13, 16–17, 20–31, 33–43, 45–47, 49–59, 69, 102; salvation in, 15, 17, 19–20, 27–28, 34, 38–39, 44–45, 49–50, 52–57, 59, 194; and the space-in-between, 24, 27, 33, 40, 42, 44, 47, 49, 52, 57, 59; and suicide, 161–62; and violence, 28, 30, 32–33, 36–37, 50, 54–55

Hall, John, 127
Handy, W. C., 103–4, 163–64, 165
Happersberger, Lucien, 64
Hardy, Clarence, 20–21, 22, 34, 51–52, 178–79
Harlem, 7, 13, 70, 72, 135, 140, 142, 162
Harris, Trudier, 175, 177, 183, 185
Henderson, Carol, 52–54
Henderson, Mae, 66–67
Holiday, Billie, 173
Holland, Sharon Patricia, 15
homoeroticism, 16; in *Go Tell It on the Mountain*, 22, 26, 46–50, 58; in *Just Above My Head*, 196, 199; in *Tell Me How Long the Train's Been Gone*, 152. See also homosexuality; same-sex desire
homosexuality: in *Another Country*, 128, 191; in *Giovanni's Room*, 62–78, 80–89, 91–92, 95–97; in *Go Tell It on the Mountain*, 22, 26, 46–50, 53, 58–59; and James Baldwin, 6, 13–14, 16, 47–48, 156; in *Just Above My Head*, 195–97; in *Tell Me How Long the Train's Been Gone*, 134, 146, 149–52. See also homoeroticism; queerness; sexuality, issues of
Howe, Irving, 133, 138

If Beale Street Could Talk, 18, 142, 162–85, 192; and crisis, 163, 167, 169–71, 175, 178, 182; imprisonment in, 18, 162, 165–68, 170–71, 173–74, 176–79, 181–85, 192; and intimacy, 163–65, 167–70, 173–74, 178, 182, 185; and issues of race, 163–68, 170–84; and issues of sexuality, 172, 174, 176–77,

179–80, 183–84; and kinship, 182–83; and loneliness, 162, 171, 177–78, 184; and love, 162–64, 166–67, 169, 175, 178, 180–84, 194; and manhood, 162–65, 167–70, 174–84; and masculinity, 163–65, 172, 175–84; and racial absurdity, 18, 167–68, 170, 171–73, 176–78, 181–85, 194; and racism, 163, 167–68, 170–78, 180–84; and rape, 174, 176–77; and religion, 179–84; salvation in, 18, 163, 165, 168, 169–70, 172–74, 178, 182–85, 194; and the space-in-between, 166, 170–71, 173–75, 178; and suicide, 162, 168, 185, 194; and violence, 172–77, 179–80, 183
imprisonment: in *If Beale Street Could Talk*, 18, 162, 165–68, 170–71, 173–74, 176–79, 181–85, 192; in "Sonny's Blues," 7, 161; in *Tell Me How Long the Train's Been Gone*, 144, 145, 147–49, 153, 158, 159, 195. See also loneliness
incarceration. See imprisonment
intimacy, 64, 188–89, 203; in *Another Country*, 101–2, 105, 108–10, 119, 123, 126, 128; in *Giovanni's Room*, 61–62, 70, 72, 74–78, 81, 84, 87–88, 90–92, 94; in *Go Tell It on the Mountain*, 15, 19, 22, 27–28, 38–39, 44–59, 194; in *If Beale Street Could Talk*, 163–65, 167–70, 173–74, 178, 182, 185; in *Just Above My Head*, 15, 194–200; and manhood, 38, 50, 76, 105, 163, 169; and religion, 3–4, 6, 45–47, 50–53, 57–58; and salvation, 3, 19, 27, 39, 49–50, 52, 57, 87, 101, 134–36, 150–52, 160, 165, 169–70, 173–74, 178, 182, 185, 195–

homosexuality; salvation: queering of; sexuality, issues of

race, issues of, 13, 14, 108, 131–33, 189–92; in *Another Country*, 110–25, 127–29, 132, 161; in *Giovanni's Room*, 61, 63–68, 72; and *Go Tell It on the Mountain*, 31, 33, 36–37, 39, 41, 43–44, 50, 161–62; in *If Beale Street Could Talk*, 163–68, 170–84; and queerness, 15, 48, 61, 63–68, 156; in *Tell Me How Long the Train's Been Gone*, 17, 133–35, 137, 139, 141, 142–49, 152–55, 194. *See also* absurdity, racial; racism

racial drag, 66–67, 72

racism, 13, 131, 191; in *Another Country*, 111–16, 118, 120, 124; in *Go Tell It on the Mountain*, 50; in *If Beale Street Could Talk*, 163, 167–68, 170–78, 180–84; in *Tell Me How Long the Train's Been Gone*, 17, 139, 142–45, 148, 154–55. *See also* absurdity, racial

rape: in *Another Country*, 113–14, 116–17, 122; in *If Beale Street Could Talk*, 174, 176–77; in *Just Above My Head*, 197; in *Tell Me How Long the Train's Been Gone*, 146

Reid-Pharr, Robert, 86, 89

religion: and Black tradition, 1–6, 13, 19, 20, 22, 35–37, 40–41, 45, 59, 102, 179; and crisis, 4, 38–43, 51; in *Go Tell It on the Mountain*, 13, 16–17, 20–31, 33–43, 45–47, 49–59, 69, 102; in *If Beale Street Could Talk*, 179–84; and intimacy, 3–4, 6, 45–47, 50–53, 57–58; and James Baldwin, 2–6, 13, 41–42, 50, 61; and love, 2–3, 8, 17, 23–24, 40–

41, 46; and salvation, 2–4, 6, 16–17, 38–39, 52–53, 55, 57, 149–51; in "Sonny's Blues," 6, 8; in *Tell Me How Long the Train's Been Gone*, 149–51, 159

Rosenblatt, Roger, 31, 46

Ross, Marlon, 15, 64–65

salvation, 132, 134–35, 192, 203; and *Another Country*, 100–102, 117–19, 121, 126, 128–29, 148; in *Giovanni's Room*, 17, 61, 65, 66, 68, 69–70, 84–85, 87, 89, 93–94, 97; in *Go Tell It on the Mountain*, 15, 17, 19–20, 27–28, 34, 38–39, 44–45, 49–50, 52–57, 59, 194; in *If Beale Street Could Talk*, 18, 163, 165, 168, 169–70, 172–74, 178, 182–85, 194; and intimacy, 3, 19, 27, 39, 49–50, 52, 57, 87, 101, 134–36, 150–52, 160, 165, 169–70, 173–74, 178, 182, 185, 195–200; and James Baldwin, 2–4, 6–8, 9–11, 15–18, 193; in *Just Above My Head*, 15, 197–201; and love, 2–3, 8, 17, 28, 45, 57, 93, 118, 128–29, 150, 152, 194, 198–99; and manhood, 3, 6, 7, 10, 11, 16, 17, 27, 39, 49, 50, 52, 57, 59, 61, 66, 68, 69–70, 87, 94, 97, 100, 102, 117–18, 119, 128, 134–36, 143, 148, 151, 158, 160, 163, 165, 167, 170, 174, 176, 178, 182–84, 192, 194, 197–98, 201; and masculinity, 3, 20, 38–39, 148, 152; queering of, 4, 6, 9, 20, 58, 69; and religion, 2–4, 6, 16–17, 38–39, 52–53, 55, 57, 149–51; in "Sonny's Blues," 6–8, 9–11; in *Tell Me How Long the Train's Been Gone*, 17, 132, 134–36, 141, 144, 147–52, 157–58, 160

147–52, 157–58, 160; and the space-in-between, 135–36, 140, 147–48, 150–51; and violence, 140, 143–49

Thorsen, Karen, 187

Time, 14, 189, 192

violence, 131, 158; in *Another Country*, 104–5, 108, 110–14, 116–18, 120, 122–24; in *Giovanni's Room*, 76; in *Go Tell It on the Mountain*, 28, 30, 32–33, 36–37, 50, 54–55; in *If Beale Street Could Talk*, 172–77, 179–80, 183; in

Just Above My Head, 197; in *Tell Me How Long the Train's Been Gone*, 140, 143–49

Washington, Bryan, 46, 123

Weatherby, W. J., 133, 183

Welsch, Gabriel, 69

Whitman, Walt, 64, 65

Work, John Wesley, Jr., 19

Worth, Eugene, 99–100, 101, 102, 103, 106, 189

Wright, Richard, 12, 13, 101, 121

IN THE EXPANDING FRONTIERS SERIES

Undesirable Practices: Women,
Children, and the Politics of the Body
in Northern Ghana, 1930–1972
by Jessica Cammaert

Intersectionality: Origins,
Contestations, Horizons
by Anna Carastathis

Abuses of the Erotic:
Militarizing Sexuality in the
Post–Cold War United States
by Josh Cerretti

Queering Kansas City Jazz: Gender,
Performance, and the History of a Scene
by Amber R. Clifford-Napoleone

Postcolonial Hauntologies: African
Women's Discourses of the Female Body
by Ayo A. Coly

Terrorizing Gender: Transgender
Visibility and the Surveillance
Practices of the U.S. Security State
by Mia Fischer

Romance with Voluptuousness:
Caribbean Women and Thick
Bodies in the United States
by Kamille Gentles-Peart

Salvific Manhood: James Baldwin's
Novelization of Male Intimacy
by Ernest L. Gibson III

Nepantla Squared: Transgender Mestiz@
Histories in Times of Global Shift
by Linda Heidenreich

Transmovimientos: Latinx Queer
Migrations, Bodies, and Spaces
edited by Ellie D. Hernández, Eddy
Francisco Alvarez Jr., and Magda García

Wrapped in the Flag of Israel: Mizraḥi
Single Mothers and Bureaucratic Torture
by Smadar Lavie

Queer Embodiment:
Monstrosity, Medical Violence,
and Intersex Experience
by Hilary Malatino

Staging Family: Domestic Deceptions
of Mid-Nineteenth-Century
American Actresses
by Nan Mullenneaux

Hybrid Anxieties: Queering the French-
Algerian War and Its Postcolonial Legacies
by C. L. Quinan

Place and Postcolonial Ecofeminism:
Pakistani Women's Literary and
Cinematic Fictions
by Shazia Rahman

Gothic Queer Culture:
Marginalized Communities and
the Ghosts of Insidious Trauma
by Laura Westengard

To order or obtain more information on these or other University of Nebraska Press
titles, visit nebraskapress.unl.edu.

CPSIA information can be obtained
at www.ICGtesting.com
Printed in the USA
LVHW041622160921
697980LV00006B/1057